Kauai

100 Years in Postcards

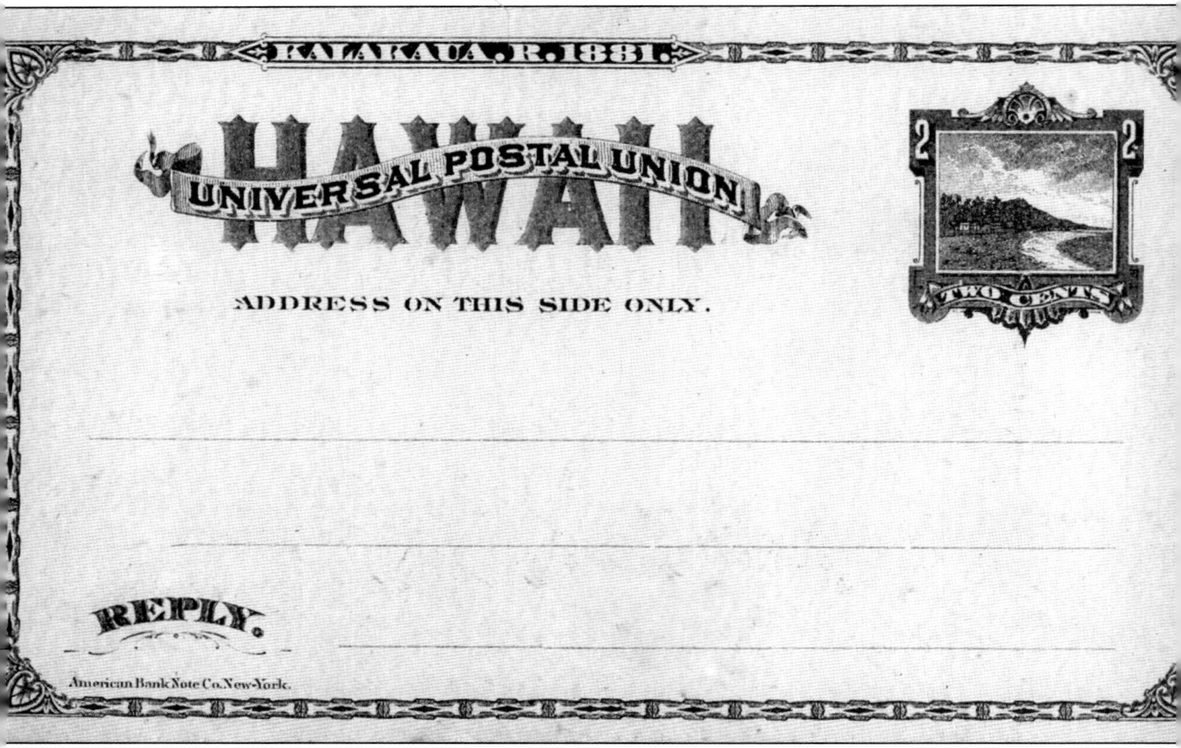

This Hawaiian two-cent postcard from King Kalakaua's reign coincides with the around-the-world trip he took in 1881. He was the first Hawaiian king to make such a tour. Kalakaua traveled to Japan, Siam, China, Burma, India, Egypt, Italy, Belgium, Germany, France, Spain, Portugal, Great Britain, and the United States and met heads of state as well as Pope Leo XII. (1.)

ON THE COVER: An aerial view of the newly completed Nawiliwili Harbor shows the completed breakwater, the entrance to Huleia Stream, and Haupu Ridge. In 1935, what would become a golf course was covered in sugarcane. (0, A.)

POSTCARD HISTORY SERIES

Kauai

100 Years in Postcards

Stormy Cozad

ARCADIA
PUBLISHING

ISBN 978-0-7385-7493-6

Published by Arcadia Publishing
Charleston, South Carolina

Printed in the United States of America

Library of Congress Control Number: 2010941637

For all general information contact Arcadia Publishing at:
Telephone 843-853-2070
Fax 843-853-0044
E-mail sales@arcadiapublishing.com
For customer service and orders:
Toll-Free 1-888-313-2665

Visit us on the Internet at www.arcadiapublishing.com

To my mother, Annette Cozad, and cousin Martha Coleman, who gave me a love of history and an understanding as to why we should record it for later generations; and to my grandchildren Claire, Andrew, Koen, Quinn, Zander, and Azure, who represent the future

Contents

ACKNOWLEDGMENTS

I want to acknowledge the many people who believed in this project and helped me locate the Kauaians who would know the information I was looking for. It was often a friend of a friend of a friend. With so many venues that no longer in exist, it was a treasure hunt for the best information. I wasn't fully successful chasing waterfalls, but maybe a reader will identify them.

Thanks go the following: Carol Hamamura, Kazuo Senda, David Scott, Randy Wichman, Reginald Gage, Chris Faye, Aletha Kaohi, Edward Punua, Victor Punua Sr., Julie Souza, Tom Tannery, Kathrine Mata, Larry Rivera, Rusty Hutchinson, Gary Bolster, Carol Kanehe, Phil Fudge, Stephanie P. Ano, Paul Curtis, the Lihue Library staff, Stacie Victorino, Ed Terui, Chipper Wichman, Sherry Walker, Renee Takahashi, Pat Nitta, Amy Sunada, Carolyn Nii, Dorothy Cataluna, Mel Ventura, Robert J. Siemers, Owen Ota, Pam Jardin, BJ Nace, Evelyn Masaki, Fujiko Nonaka, Agnes Keaolani Marti-kini, Haunani Kaiminaauao, Cynthia Powell, Greg Kamm, Takashi Fujita, Katie Cassel, John Plews, Chuck Blay, Stella Burgess, and Barbara Richter. I couldn't have done it without you!

Most importantly, I must thank my husband, Gaetano Vasta, who scanned every postcard—and many more than the 214 that made it into the book.

Introduction

John P. Charlton of Philadelphia patented the commercial postcard in 1861. Originally, only the Post Office Department was allowed to print postcards, and it held that monopoly until 1898 when the US Congress passed the Private Mailing Card Act. Some of the first cards were seen as advertising at the Chicago's World Fair in 1893. However, King Kalakaua of the Kingdom of Hawaii had postcards from 1881. For being in an isolated spot in the middle of the Pacific, his monarchy was by no means backward. The king was very up on the latest trends of his day.

At first, postcard senders were allowed to write only on the front of the card as the back was reserved for the address. By 1908, a US population of about 88,000,000 people had sent 677 million penny postcards.

Some deltiologists, or people who collect postcards, have divided old cards into six groups. The earliest postcards are divided into the following eras: Private Mailing Card, 1898–1901; Undivided Back, 1901–1907; and Divided Back, 1907–1915. The Divided Back period is often referred to as the golden age of postcards, perhaps because Eastman Kodak entered the marketplace with an affordable camera and printed black-and-white photographs with postcard backs as well as the fact that postcards could be found worldwide by this time. The end of this era came as World War I began and the telephone took over as the favored form of communication. The White Border period was from 1915 to 1930, and postcard racks were seen near every tourist attraction. Next came the Linen card era from 1930 to around 1945 to 1950. The Modern/Photochrome era dates from 1939 until the present. The Union Oil Company began selling cards at its service stations, and with each advanced technique in color, the quality of the postcard has increased. With the introduction of the Internet and e-cards, the greeting card has lost some ground, but the postcard still remains very popular.

This book is based on my collection of vintage postcards of Kauai spanning 100 years as well as a few from the Senda family's collection. W.J. Senda did not open his photography studio until July 1, 1913, and most of the earliest postcards I found of Kauai were his. We did not have the population or the amount of visitors that Honolulu attracted, and thus did not generate the same need for postcards of our many attractions.

The few Kauai postcards came from Honolulu and were printed in Germany. The reader should remember that for travelers to visit Kauai required an additional, often rough ride on a sailing vessel or steamer with no upscale hotel to host them. Until the 1950s, most visitors who came for pleasure stayed with residents in their homes. Business travelers stayed in business hotels near the docks by coastal towns. Kauai's golden era of postcards began with the building of several destination resorts: the Coco Palms, the Hanalei Plantation, and the Kauai Surf. It also coincided with the first increases in postcard postage, to 2¢ on January 1, 1952 and to 3¢ on August 1, 1958.

What is fascinating to note is the amount of change that can occur over each decade. The fact Kauai has had three hurricanes means that tourist attractions that had been a must-see often became a "can't see any more" because they were gone. Therefore, postcards from the 1980s and 1990s have been included because of the changes that occurred after Hurricane Iwa (pronounced "Eva") on November 24, 1982, and Hurricane Iniki (pronounced "E-Nee-Key") on September 11, 1992. Even though Iwa was not a direct hit, it caused $664 million in damage, made one-eighth of all Kauai homes uninhabitable, and destroyed many hotel and restaurant properties in the Poipu area. Hurricane Iniki was a direct hit and caused considerably more damage to the entire island. Property loss was around $2.6 billion. On August 6, 1959, Hurricane Dot had primarily affected the north shore of Kauai.

Publishers and Photographers

All images contained herein—except for three from Carol Hamamura's collection of W.J. Senda's postcards, three from David Scott, and one from Reg Gage—are from the author's private collection of rare Hawaiian and Kauai postcards. A few of the images are one-of-a-kind real-photo cards, but most are printed cards for purchase. Those published by companies or business enterprises, with registered trademarks, or with indications of a copyright are credited by number at the end of each caption.

The following numbers are used to reference publishers:

0 Unknown publisher
1 American Bank Note Company, New York, New York
2 Island Curio Store, Honolulu
3 Island Curio Co., Honolulu, T.H.
4 Island Curio Co., Jas. Steiner, Honolulu
5 H.F. Hill, Honolulu
6 Hawaii and South Seas Curio Co., Honolulu
7 Honolulu Paper Co., Ltd., Honolulu T.H.
8 Colour Picture Publishers, Inc., Boston
9 Island Curio Co., Honolulu, Hawaiian Islands
10 Hawaiian Views, Dist. by Max Basker & Sons, Honolulu
11 Continental Card of Hawaii, Mike Roberts, Honolulu
12 Hawaiian Resources Co. Ltd., Honolulu
13 Exhibit Supply Co., Chicago
14 World Wide Distributors Ltd., Honolulu
15 Hawaiian Service, Inc., Honolulu
16 Kauai Eye, Koloa
17 Ponoi Craft by WW Distributors, Ltd., Honolulu
18 McGrew Color Graphics, Kansas City, Missouri
19 Irving Rosen Color Productions, Honolulu
20 Mel Ong Brown, Kauai, Hawaii
21 Alan-Randel Co., Studio City, California
22 WW Distributors Ltd., Honolulu
23 Continental Card, Honolulu
24 I Sight Studios, Kauai, Hawaii
25 Camera Hawaii, Honolulu
26 Hawaiian Service Inc.
27 Mike Roberts Color Productions, Berkeley, California
28 Tongg Publishing Co., Honolulu
29 The Lihue Store, Lihue, Kauai, Hawaii
30 Island Heritage, Honolulu
31 Ray Helbig's Hawaiian Service, Honolulu
32 Christian's, Honolulu
33 Kauai Business Services, Lihue, Hawaii
34 Pacific Film Corporation, Honolulu
35 Hawaiian Service, Louise and George Armitage, Honolulu
36 Lum & Feher, Ltd., Honolulu
37 Maui Pacific Traders, a division of The Islander Group, Mililani, Hawaii
38 Hawaiian Resources, Waialua, Hawaii
39 O.S.P. Publishing, Inc., Monterey Park, California
40 A Continental Card by Hawaiian Service, Inc., Honolulu
41 World Productions Corporation, Honolulu
42 Lesco, Ltd., Honolulu
43 Raphael Tuck & Sons, London, England
44 Visual Impact, Honolulu

When known, photographers are credited with a corresponding letter as follows:

A William Junokichi Senda
B Douglas Peebles
C Keith Karasic
D Mary Ceria Williams
E Bert Phillips
F Frank J. Wilken
G Larry Witt
H Dane B. Warner
I Ray Jerome Baker
J Ed Cooper
K B. Abraham
L Ray Jerome Baker
M R. Wenkam
N Werner Stoy
P Carl Shaneff
Q Bud Thuener
R Mac Miller
S Don Ceppi
T Richard Gates
U Peter French
V Veronica Carmona
W Loye Guthrie
X Paul Oliver
Y Ray Atkeson
Z John Jones
ZZ Ric Noyle

One

The Hawaiian Mystique

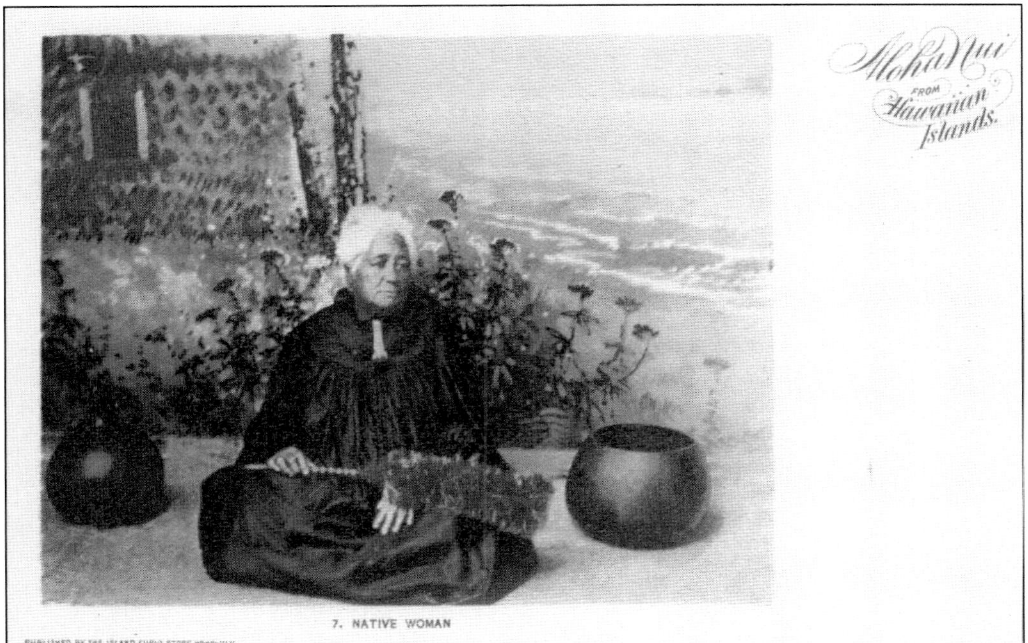

From the 1900s, Hawaiians were on postcards in native garb. This lady is not a lowly native but one of high standing, for she is wearing a *lei niho palaoa* denoting high rank. It is often carved from a whale tooth and is hung on as many as 700 strands of woven hair. Today, these are mostly seen in museums. (2.)

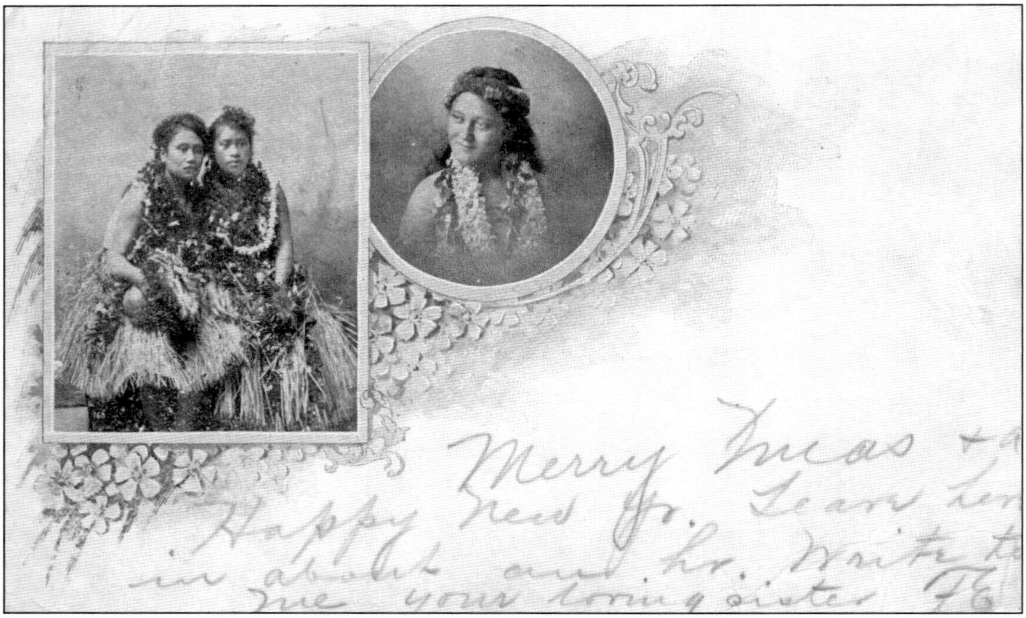

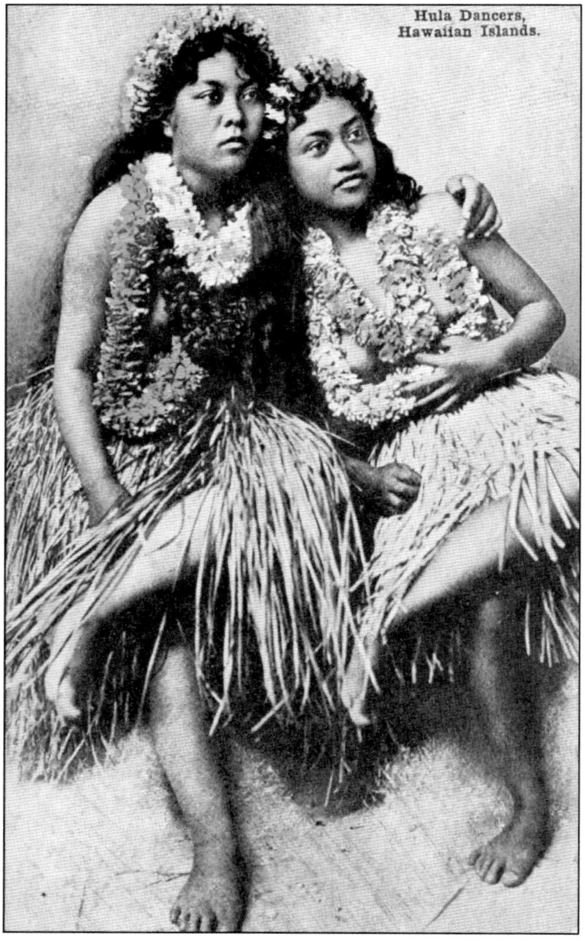

This card posted in 1901 was just one of the ways Americans became acquainted with Hawaii, a relatively new territory of the United States. Much of what Americans knew about Hawaii was learned from these small glimpses into a culture that seemed exotic and foreign. (0.)

In the early 1900s, Hawaii seemed too remote a destination for most travelers, American or otherwise. Less than several thousand brave, rich adventurers graced Hawaiian shores. However, beautiful, graceful dancers with swaying hips, grass skirts, and fragrant leis beguiled these adventurers. The Hawaiian mystique was forming. (3.)

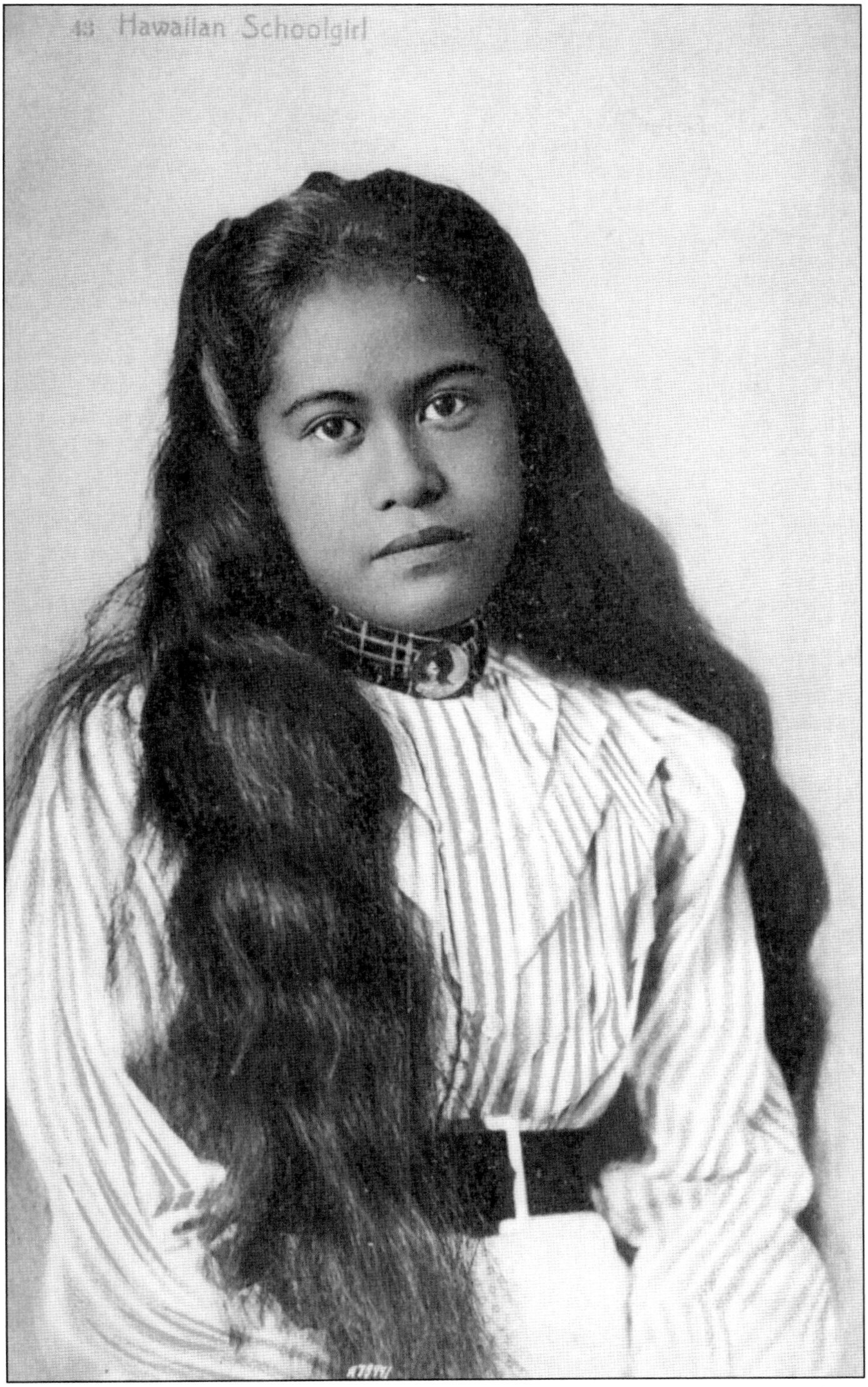

It seems odd to choose a schoolgirl as subject matter for a postcard. Perhaps, besides creating a romantic mystique around Hawaii, the publisher also wished to convey the fact that Hawaii educated its people as well. In fact, after only two generations from the establishment of a written language in 1826 by missionaries, Hawaii had the highest literacy rate of any country in the world. (4.)

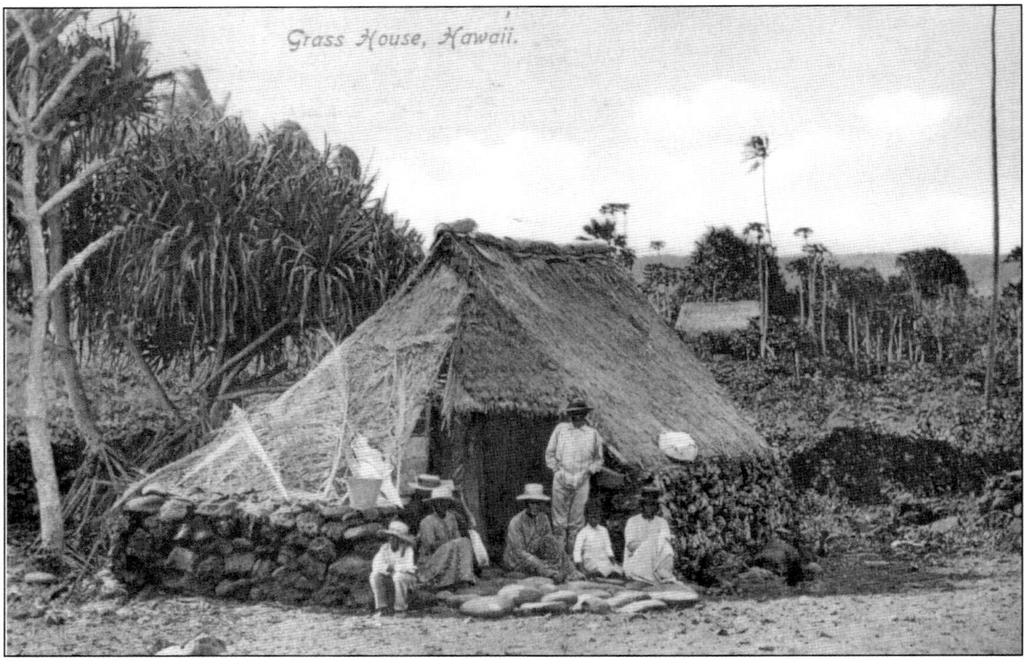

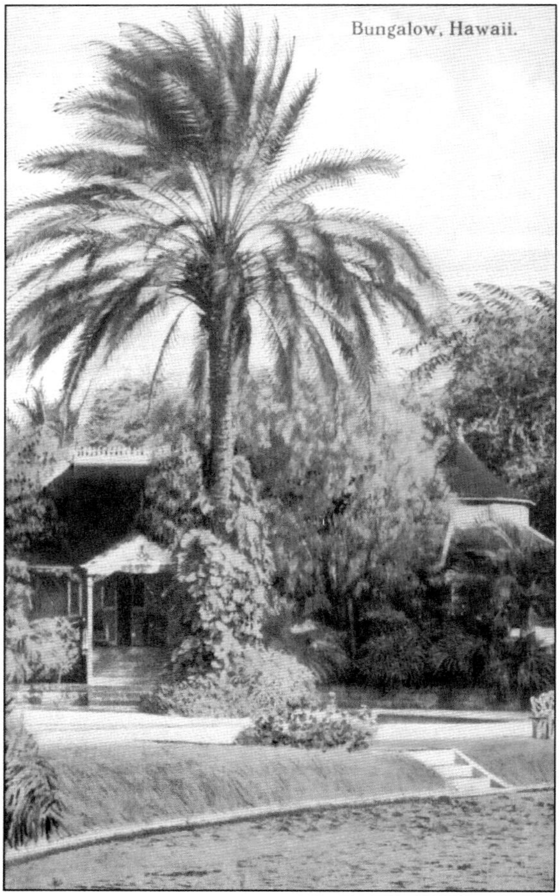

The myth that everyone in Hawaii lives in a *hale pili*, grass hut, is actually one of the most enduring; up to this day, some visitors are disappointed that locals no longer live in them. The odd fact is that by the time postcards were frequently being mailed around 1898, grass houses were already on the decline. This card was sent in 1908. (5.)

Written on the reverse side of this card is "Hawaiian homes are built with the view of thorough enjoyment of outdoor life. There are broad lanais or verandas covered with *punees* or couches and swung over the pillars are hammocks in which the dwellers swing in soft dreamy sleep lulled with the sound of the ukulele or native guitar." All this adds to the Hawaiian mystique. (6.)

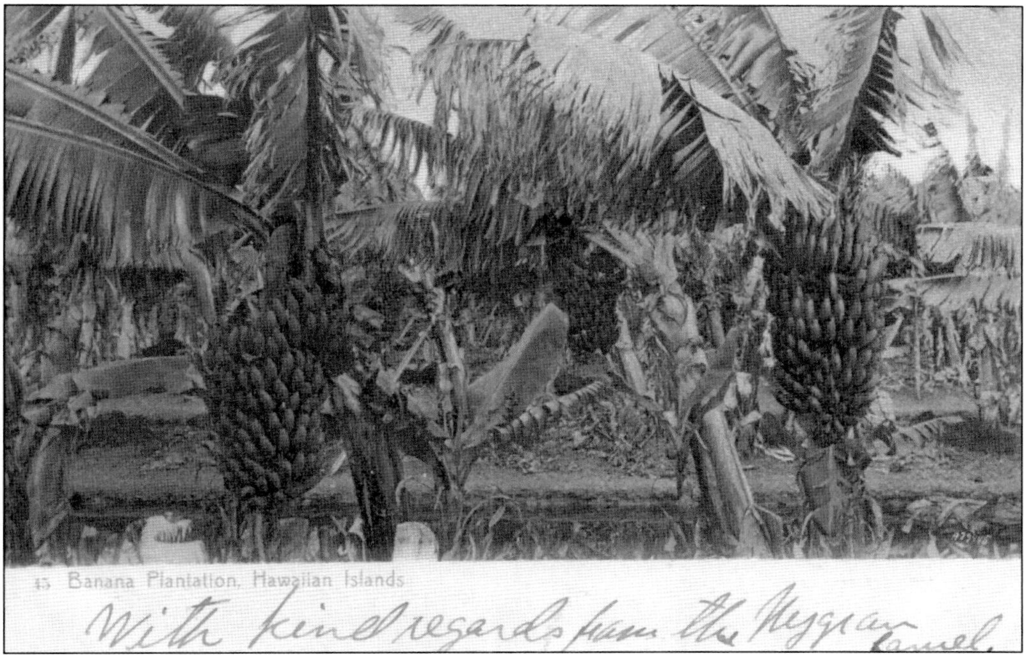

Voyagers who settled the Hawaiian Islands centuries ago brought bananas. The ancient Hawaiians, however, never had plantations. Bananas are an exotic fruit grown in warm, tropical climates and were new to visitors from northern climates, such as the writer of this 1909 postcard. (4.)

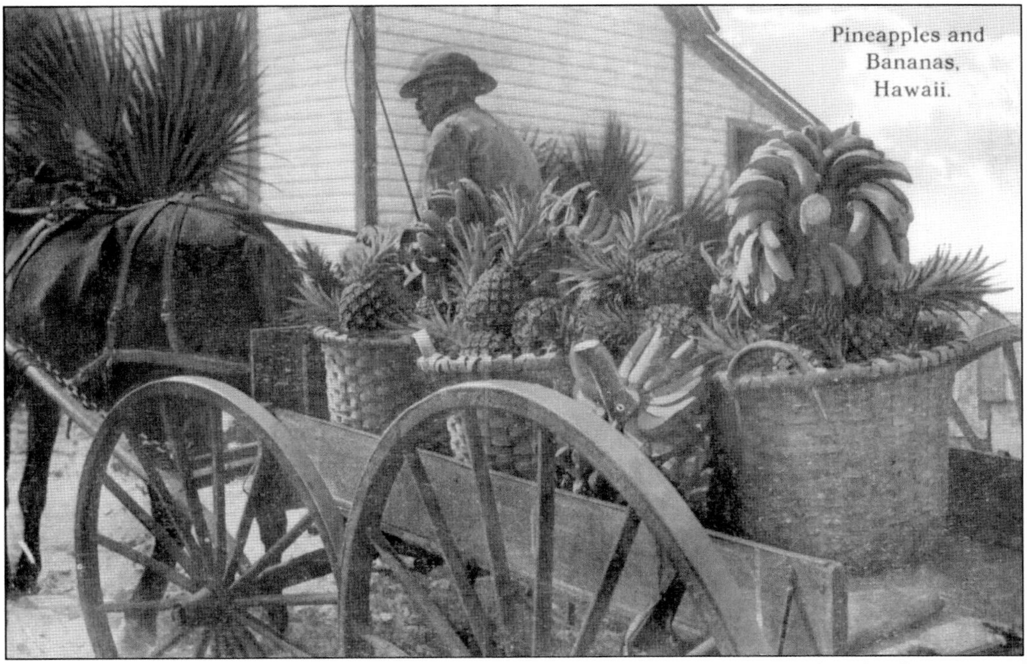

This 1920 postcard states that pineapples and bananas are, next to sugar, the chief exports of the Hawaiian Islands. Bananas are sent in bunches and sold fresh. Pineapples are mostly canned for shipment. The Hawaiian pineapple is known for its large size and exquisite flavor and has a worldwide reputation. (6.)

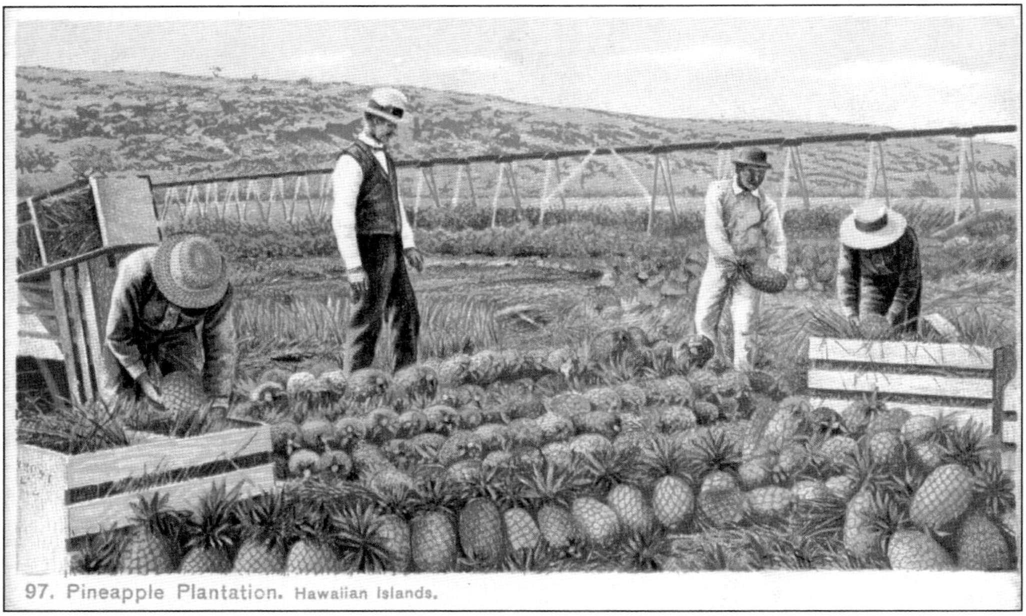

Unlike bananas, pineapples did not come to the islands with the original Hawaiians. Pineapples were introduced possibly as early as 1527. Many believe a ship carrying pineapples broke apart off the coast of the Big Island. It is also known that Francisco de Paula Marin, a Spaniard who came to the islands in 1794 and became an advisor to King Kamehameha I, raised pineapples in the early 1800s. (4.)

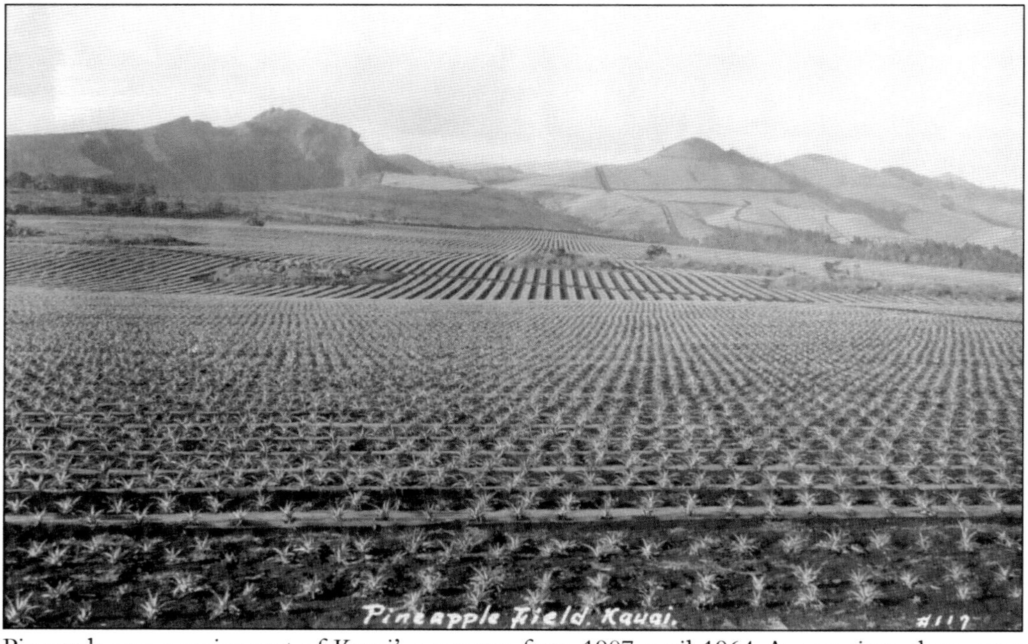

Pineapple was a major part of Kauai's economy from 1907 until 1964. At one time, there were three canning plants: one in Lawai and two in Kapaa. Pineapple production was the territory's second largest industry. (0, A.)

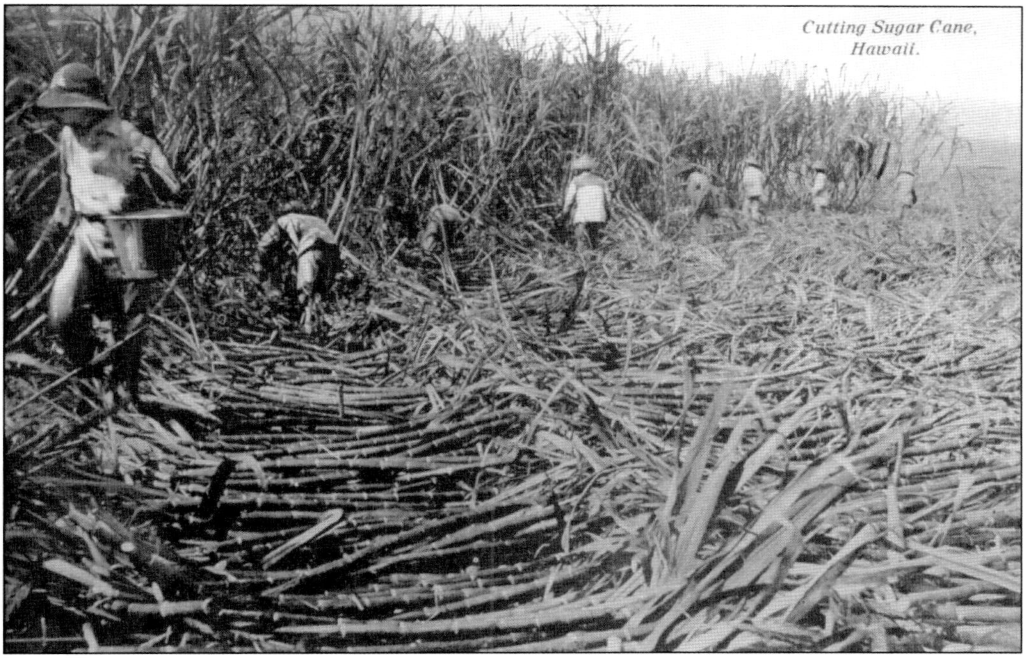

The main industry of the Hawaiian Islands for over 100 years sugar production. All the main islands had immense sugar plantations and some of the largest sugar mills in the world. The science of the cultivation and milling of sugarcane was always looking to find ways to increase production. (6.)

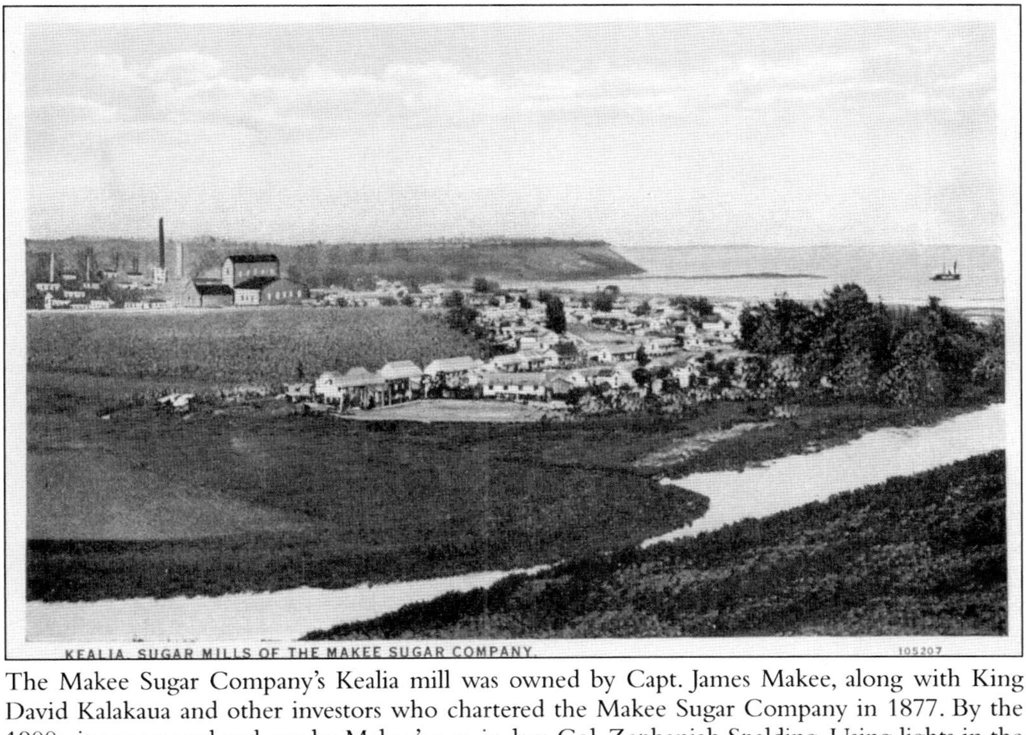

The Makee Sugar Company's Kealia mill was owned by Capt. James Makee, along with King David Kalakaua and other investors who chartered the Makee Sugar Company in 1877. By the 1900s, it was owned and run by Makee's son-in-law, Col. Zephaniah Spalding. Using lights in the fields to increase production, Spalding was the first to bring night manufacturing to Hawaii. (7.)

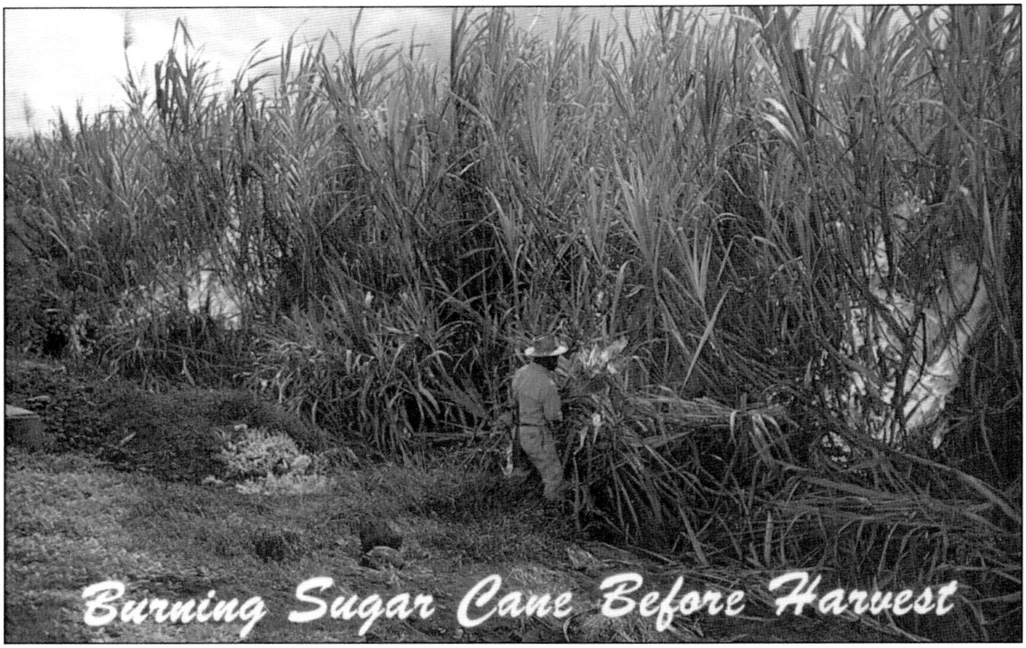

This 1950s view was an unusual sight for mainlanders. It is the burning of the foliage on the mature fields of sugarcane before harvesting. The fire-blackened stalks are then gathered and transported to the mills for processing into raw sugar. Beginning in 2010, no sugarcane will be commercially grown on Kauai. (8.)

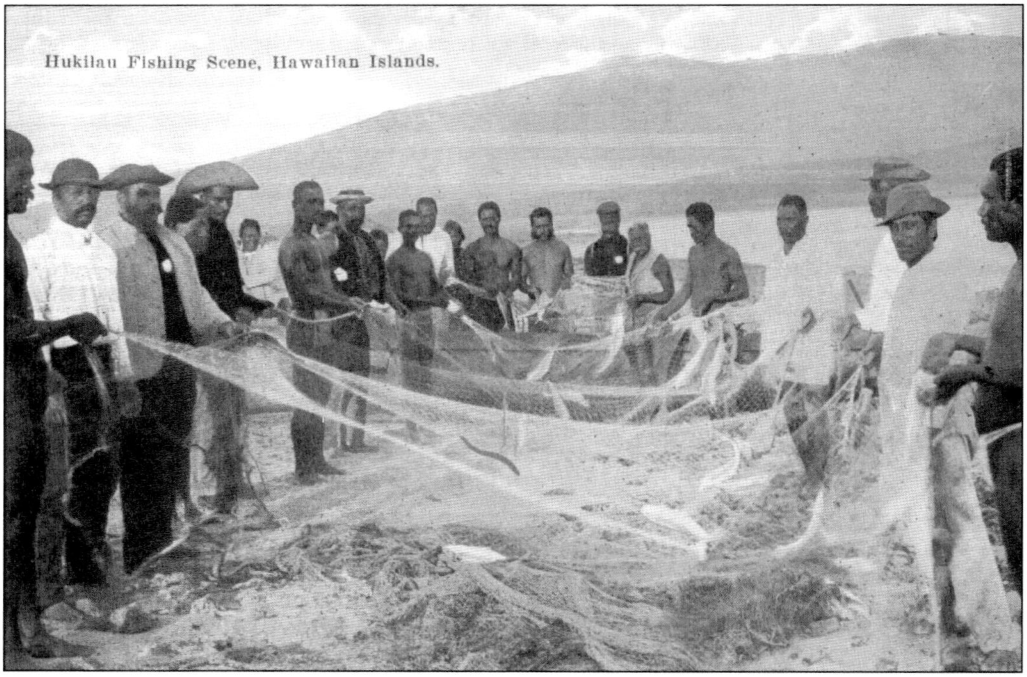

Another part of Hawaiian life that has always intrigued visitors is the food. Net fishing uses a net around 120 to 130 feet long and requires a group of people working together to pull in a catch of fish. All who participate in the *hukilau* can take a share of the fish. This 1915 postcard shows unidentified men displaying their good catch. (3.)

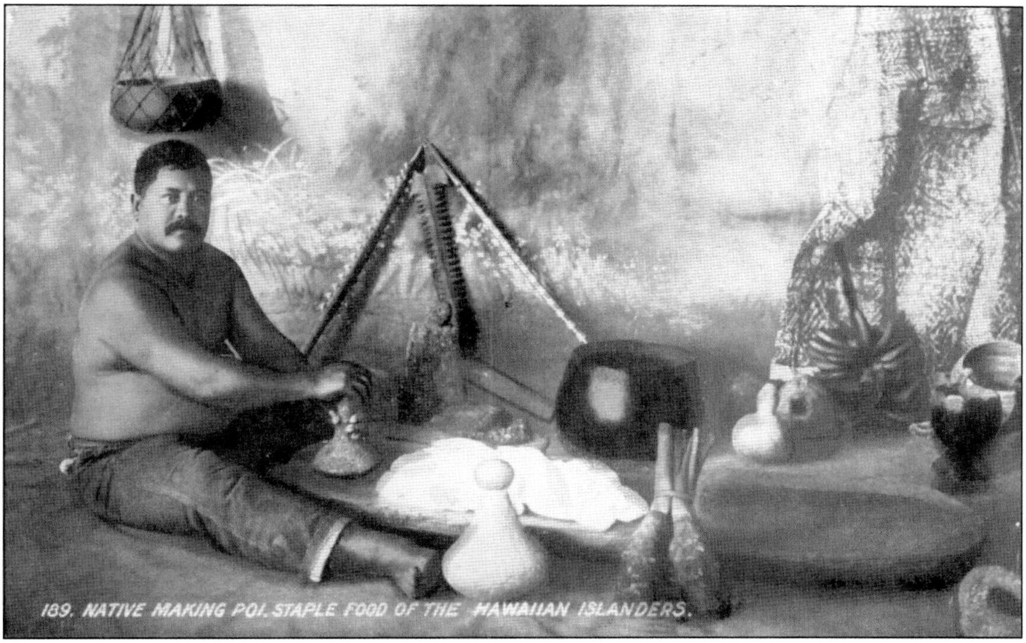

Made from the taro plant, poi is a staple food of the Hawaiians. The taro must be boiled and mashed similar to a potato, and taro is rich in fiber, vitamin E, vitamin B6, potassium, and manganese. Also shown are three wooden calabashes, bowls, and large amounts of tapa, cloth made from paper mulberry tree bark. Tapa is surprisingly durable, water-resistant yet washable, and warm. (9.)

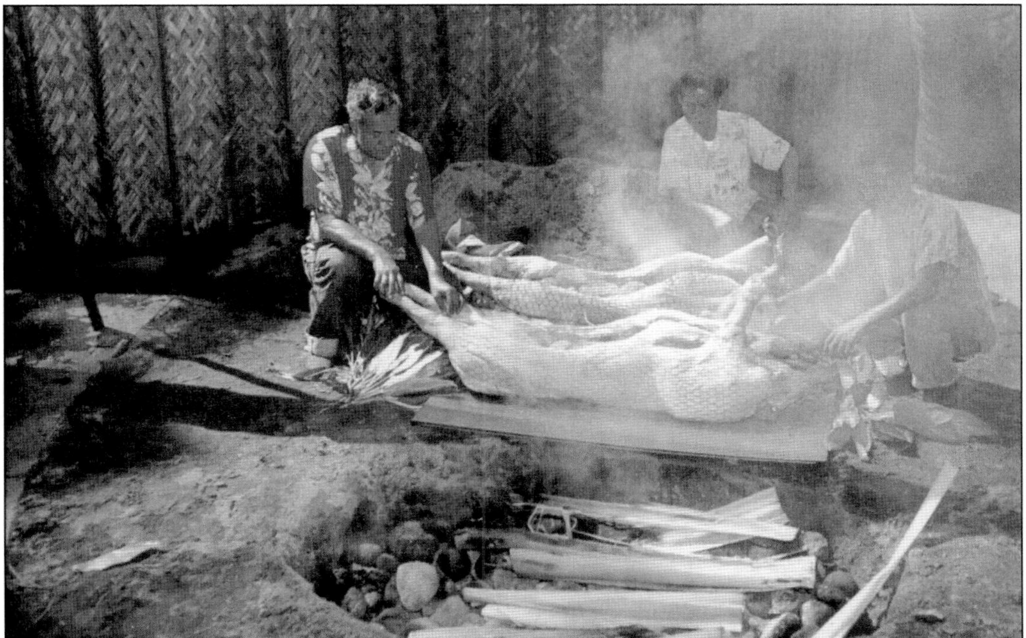

Once the fish has been caught and the poi has been made, the pig must be roasted. Here, pigs are being prepared for the *imu* (oven) with red-hot stones covered with leaves and earth to roast for several hours before serving. (10.)

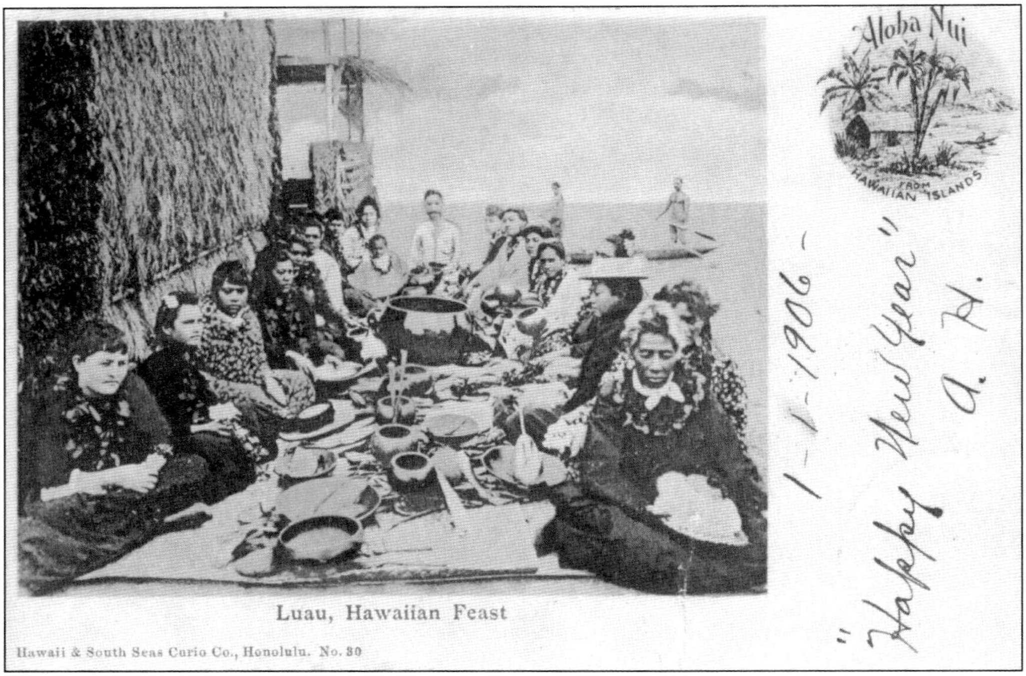

From the initial postcards depicting Hawaiian life, luaus fascinated travelers, as this 1906 card shows (above). Most early visitors, however, would not have seen a luau unless they were considered very important or invited to a special occasion where all the relatives and friends share in preparing the feast. Below, a 1920s card shows continued curiosity. "A Luau or native feast is a feature of the sojourn of the traveler in Hawaii. The principal food of the natives is *poi* and quantities of this is consumed at this feast; other food is *pua'a* or pork and *limu* or seaweed and sweet potatoes and all food is eaten with the fingers. Music accompanies all luaus as well as *Hula Hula* dancers and among the tropical surroundings, these feasts are particularly attractive." (Both, 6.)

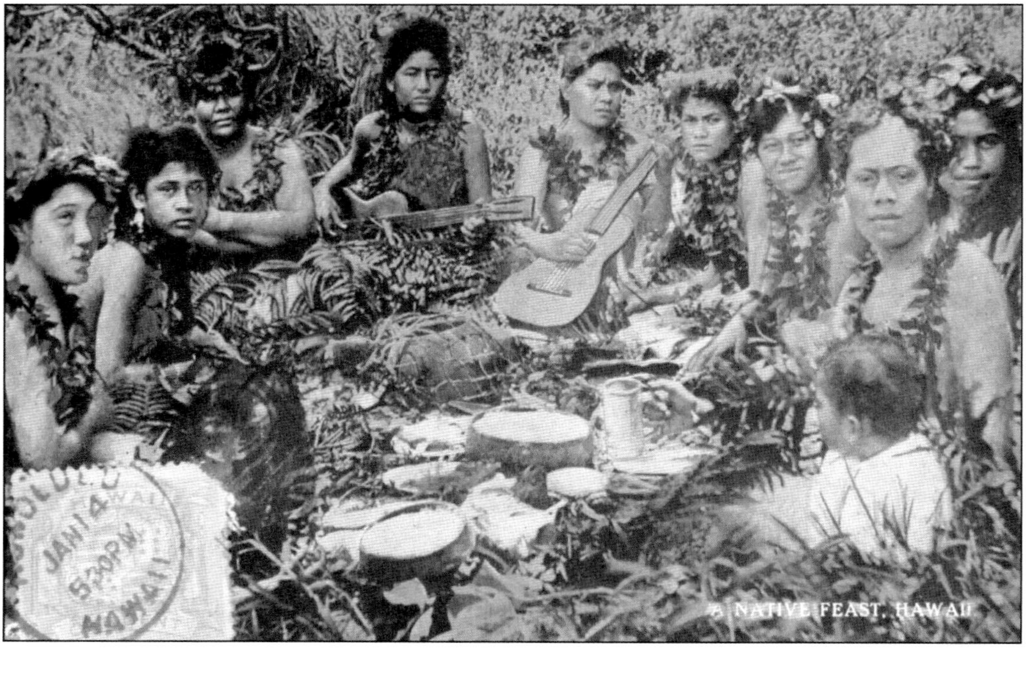

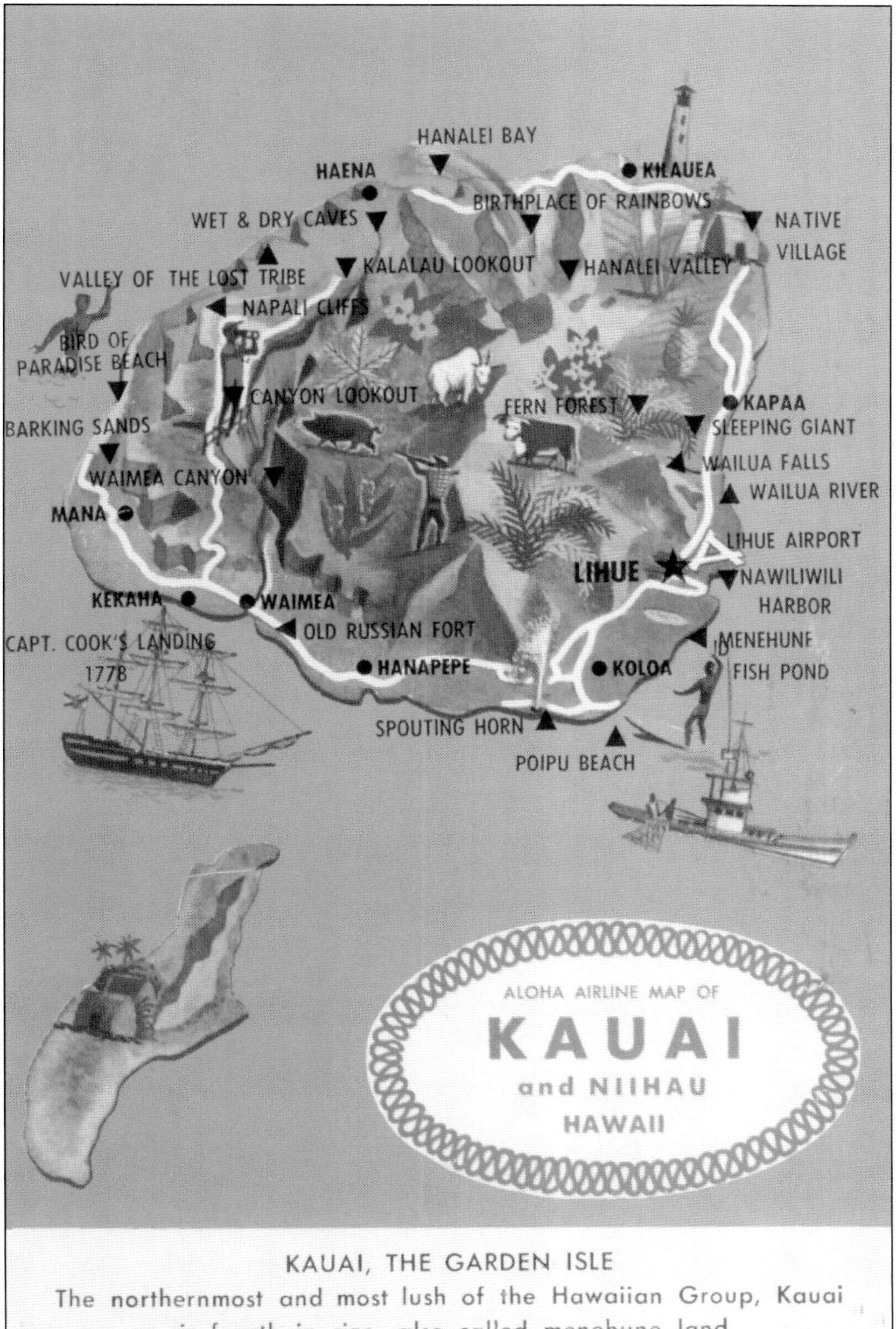

This Aloha Airlines map shows "Kauai, The Garden Isle / The northernmost and most lush of the Hawaiian Group, Kauai is fourth in size, also called menehune land." The author has never heard the term used in this way, but it added to the myth in 1961. (10.)

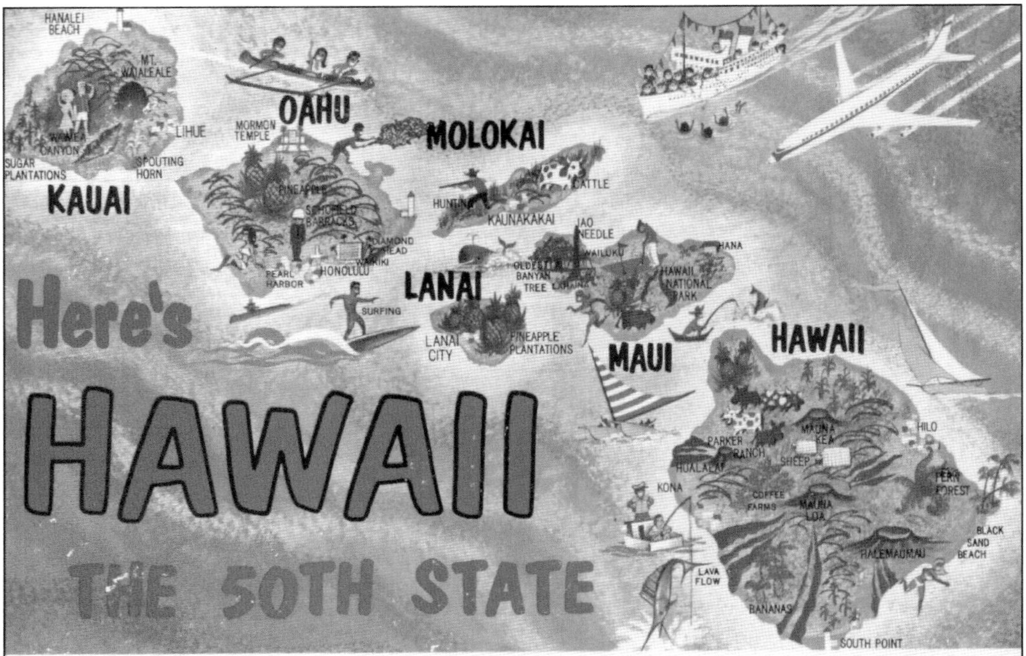

Here's Hawaii, The 50th State

As Hawaii became a US state, 1959 brought much excitement to the islands. In 2009, Hawaii celebrated the 50th anniversary of statehood. Again, there was a strong push to sell the Hawaiian mystique to visitors around the world. (11.)

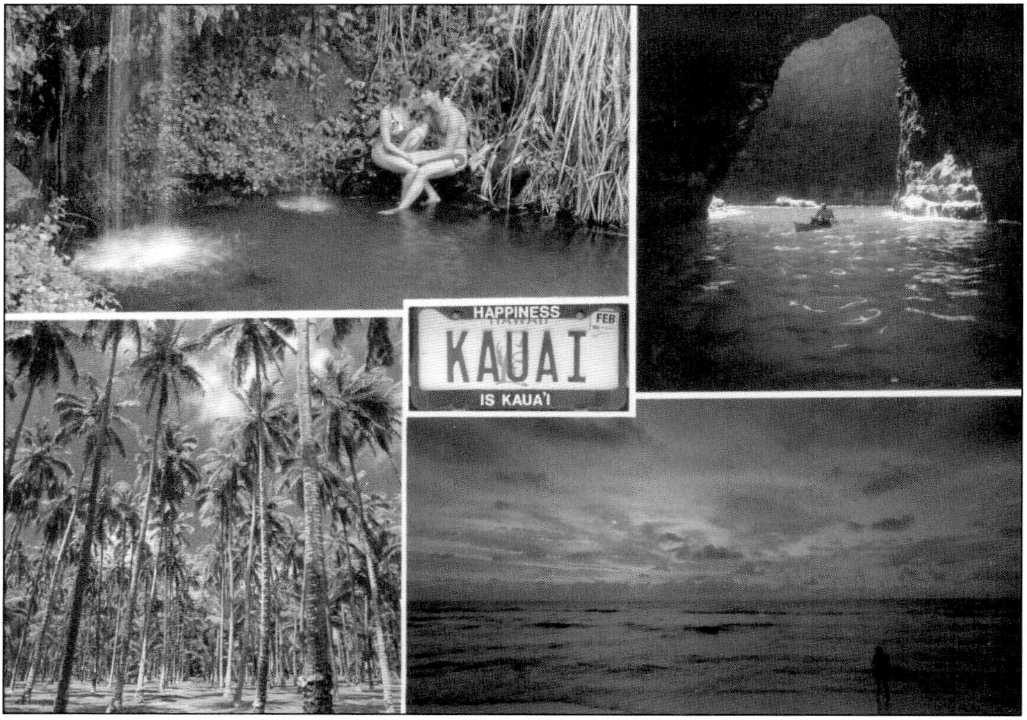

This 1985 postcard states, "Wish you were here." With a romantic couple by a waterfall and a glorious sunset, The message is clear. Kauai is beautiful, and it will likely make visitors happy. (12, B.)

Two

COMINGS AND GOINGS

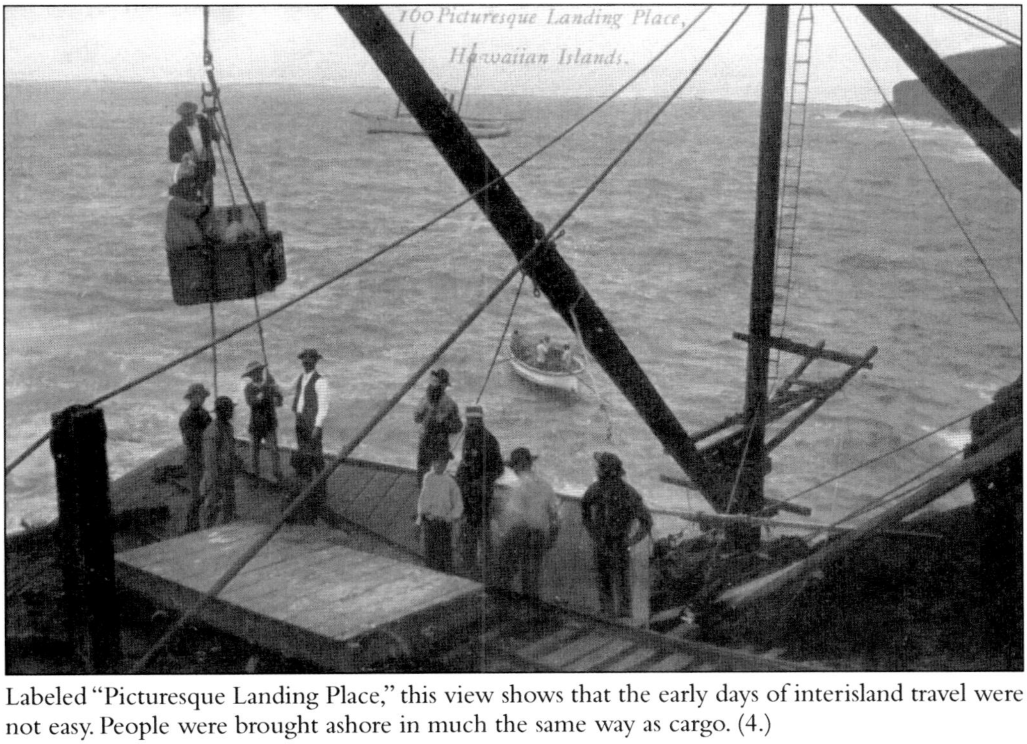

Labeled "Picturesque Landing Place," this view shows that the early days of interisland travel were not easy. People were brought ashore in much the same way as cargo. (4.)

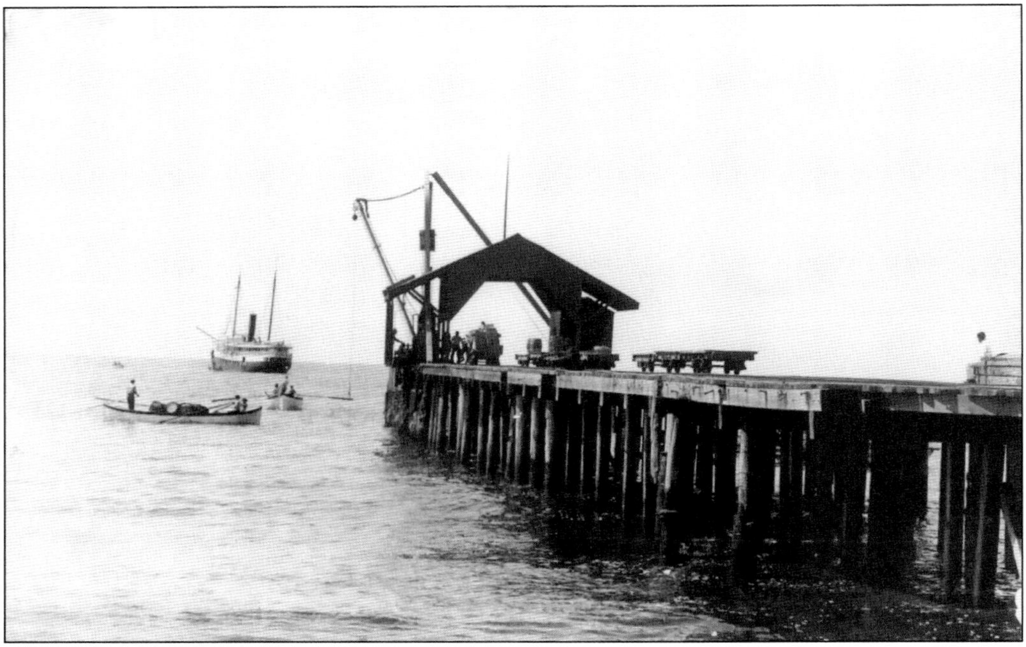

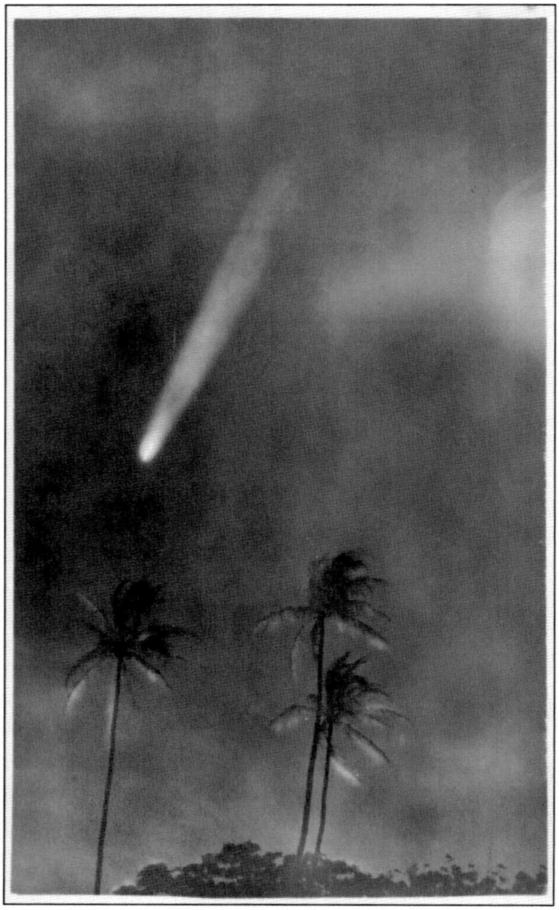

The steamship *Claudine* belonged to the Wilders Steamship Company. In the 1880s and 1890s, all mail between the islands, including private mailing cards, came by steamships like this one. The *Claudine*'s usual route was to Maui, but this postcard is of the steamer off Waimea, Kauai. (0.)

Halley's comet was viewed in the sky between March 1 and mid-May in 1910. Hawaii was said to perhaps be the place to have the best views. The comet's rare appearance occurs about every 76 years. This postcard shows light from the comet illuminating the palm trees against the night sky. (0.)

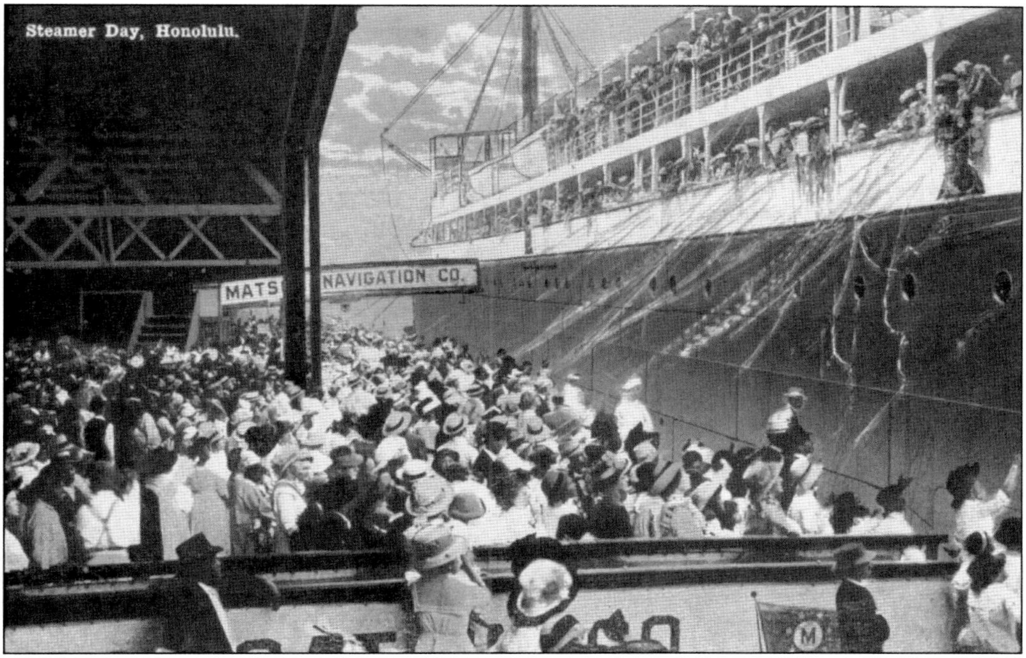

With the arrival of the Matson steamer, boat day was always a festive occasion in Honolulu, as in this 1915 postcard (above). For most, this was the end of voyage. Only the more adventurous continued on to the outer islands onboard smaller boats. Matson Navigation began its long association with Hawaii in 1882, when Capt. William Matson sailed his three-masted schooner from San Francisco to Hilo carrying food and supplies. Matson died in 1917. Matson Navigation had a major expansion during the 1920s and 1930s, adding ships and terminals. The SS *Malolo* commissioned in 1927 cruised at 22 knots, making it the fastest ship in the Pacific. Below is the Hawaiian Interisland Boat, the steamer *Waialeale* that began interisland service to Kauai in 1928. At the time, steamers were the primary form of travel between the islands. (Above, 3; below, 0, A.)

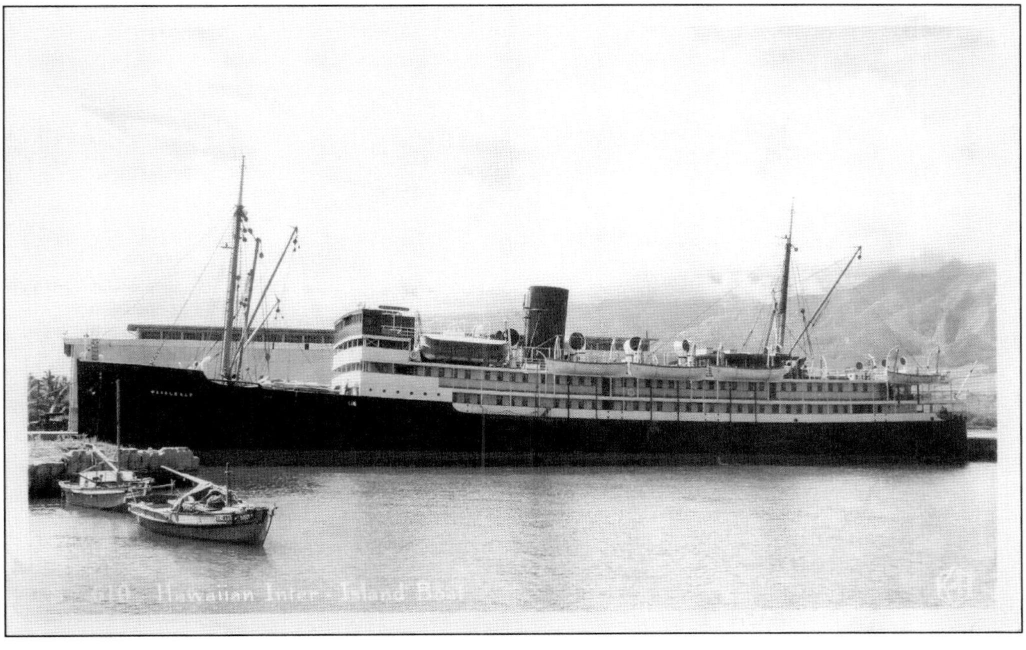

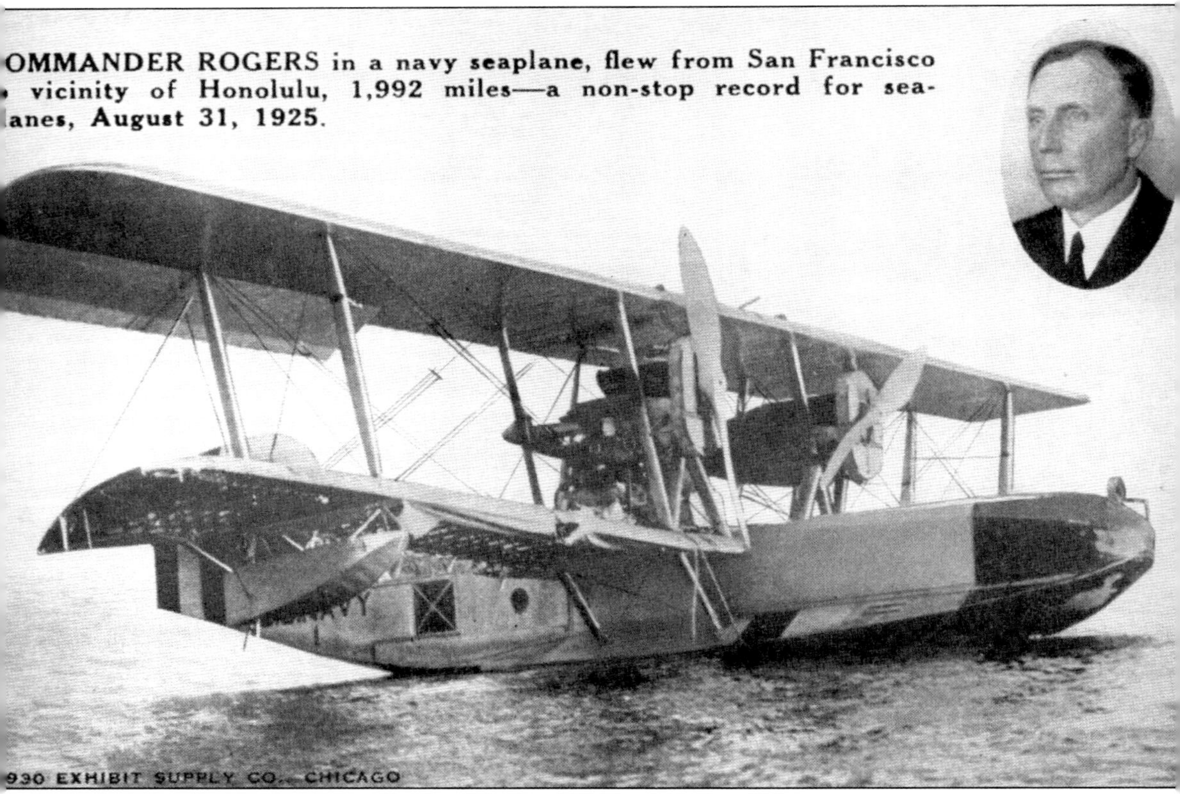

Interesting, but not mentioned on this postcard, is the fact that the seaplane ran out of fuel and landed well out to sea. The ditched Curtiss PN-9 did set a record for a nonstop flight of 28 hours and 35 minutes from San Francisco to Hawaii, but it was actually 400 miles short of its destination. John Rodgers and his crew survived nine days at sea. On September 10, a submarine spotted the plane and towed it into Nawiliwili Harbor. After an overnight on Kauai, a destroyer picked up Rodgers and his crew and delivered them to Honolulu. It was a historic flight with a brief visit to Kauai. Rodgers's heroics were recognized, and he was appointed assistant chief of the Bureau of Naval Aeronautics. But working at a desk in Washington did not suit his style. He was about to command an experimental seaplane squadron when he died on August 27, 1926, in a plane crash a year after his flight across the Pacific. (13.)

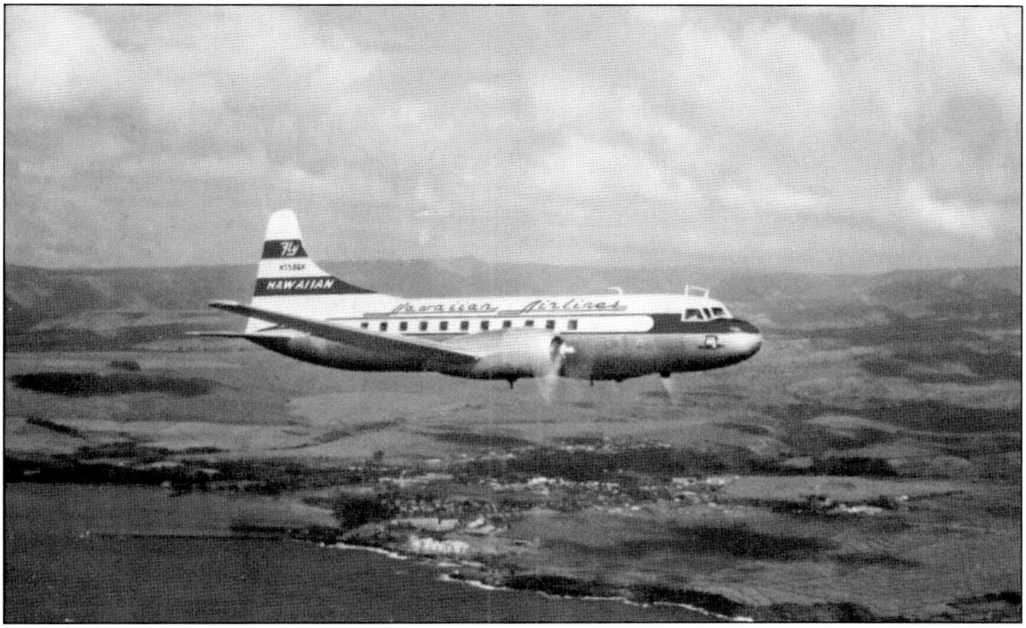

In 1952, Hawaiian Airlines began flying 44 passenger Convair 340s interisland. These pressurized, air-conditioned aircraft flew at 300 miles per hour. The aircraft pictured is flying over Port Allen, Kauai. (0.)

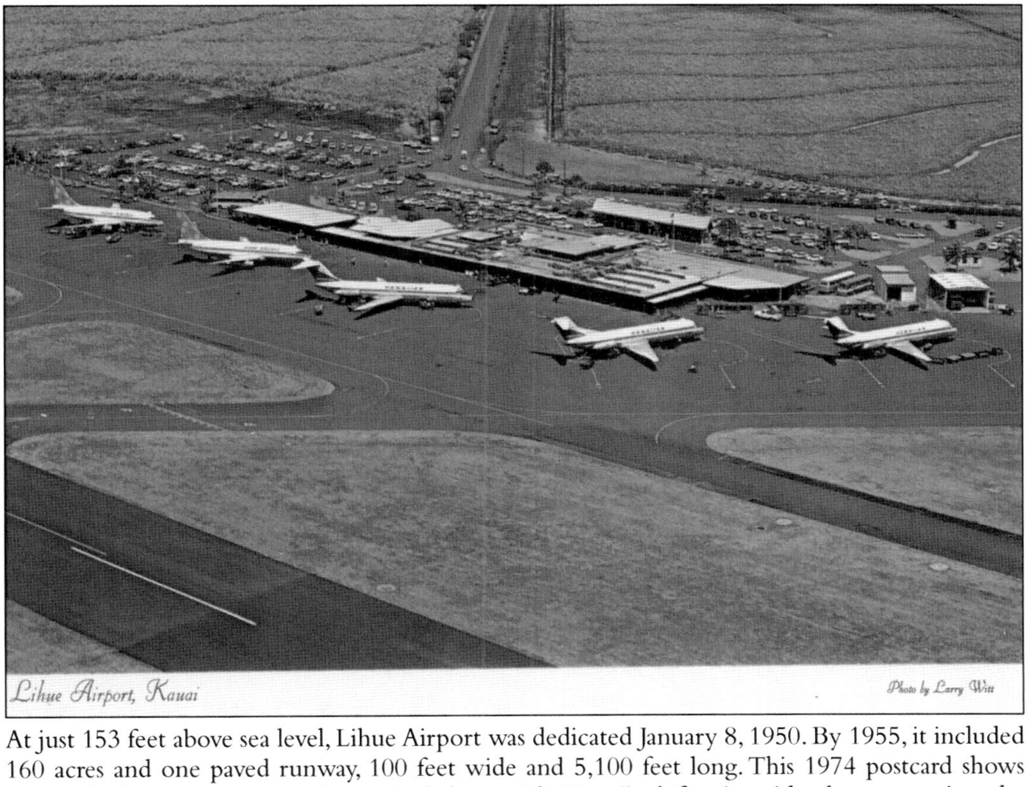

At just 153 feet above sea level, Lihue Airport was dedicated January 8, 1950. By 1955, it included 160 acres and one paved runway, 100 feet wide and 5,100 feet long. This 1974 postcard shows the original one-story, open-air terminal along with Hawaiian's first interisland passenger jets, the DC-9-10s. (14.)

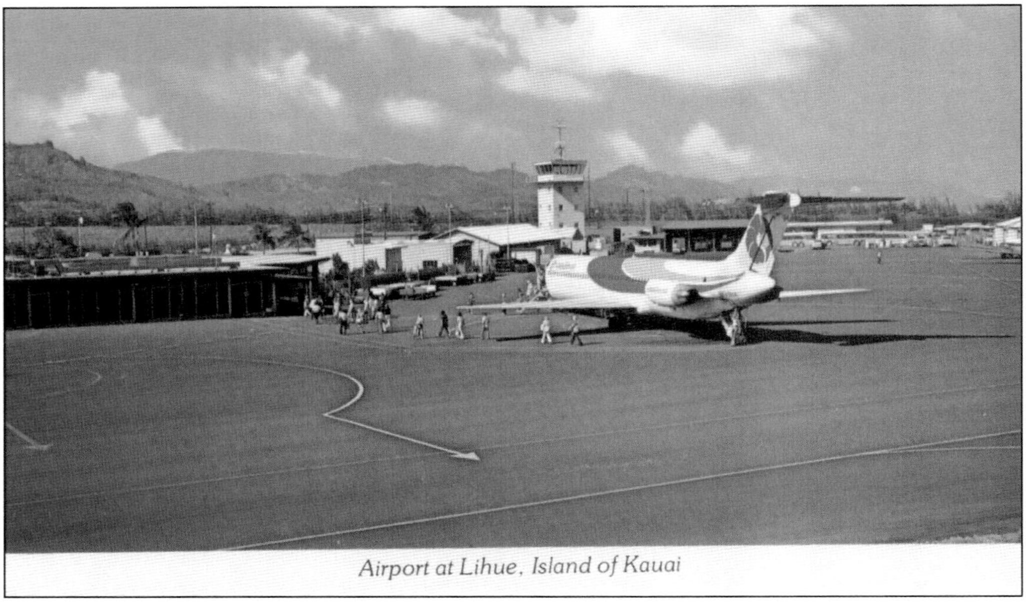

This view of Lihue Airport from the tarmac shows passengers deplaning a Hawaiian Airlines 130-passenger DC-9-50, added to the fleet in 1975. The logo, Pualani ("flower of the sky") was also introduced in 1975. A new terminal with Jetways was dedicated on February 25, 1987. The airport now covers 879 acres and has two active runways, each 6,500 feet long and 150 feet wide. (15.)

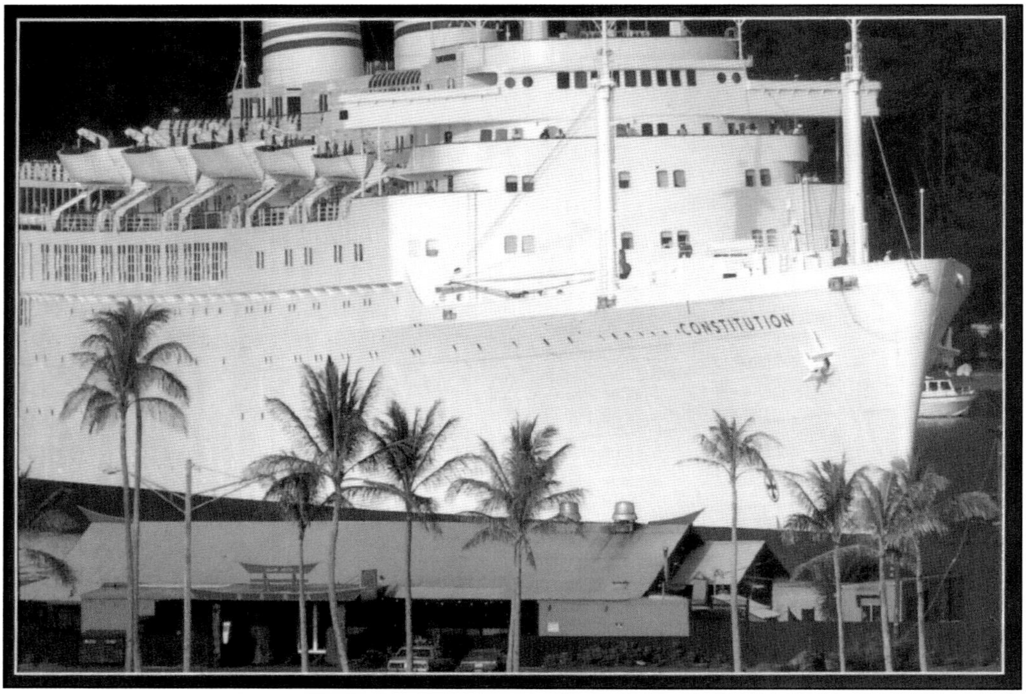

From 1982 to 1996, the SS *Constitution* sailed between the Hawaiian Islands. On September 11, 1992, Hurricane Iniki destroyed the famous Club Jetty, shown here dwarfed in size by the ship. The ship was retired in 1996. While being towed to Japan to be sold as scrap, it took on water and sunk 700 miles north of Hawaii. (16.)

Three

Churches and Other Buildings

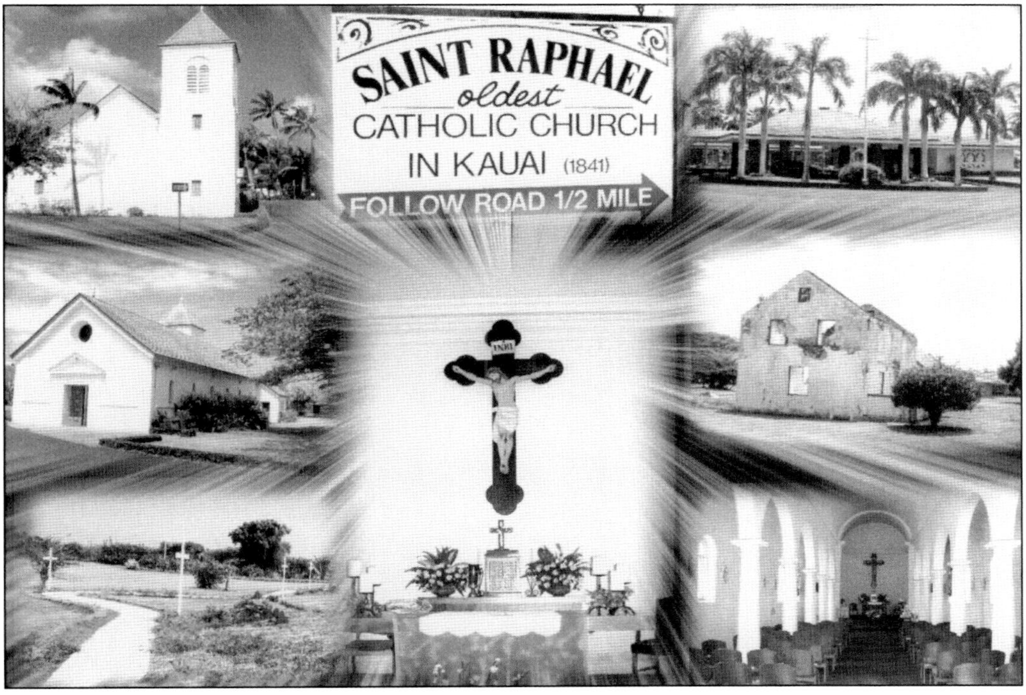

Established in 1841, St. Raphael's Church in Koloa is the oldest Catholic church on Kauai. Fr. Arsene Walsh was given 17 acres of land from King Kamehameha III on December 18, 1843. Clockwise from top right are the new Gathering Hall built in 1996; the old rectory that has now been torn down; the interior sanctuary; a close-up of the altar; a walkway along the Stations of the Cross to a grotto; the front of the original building with its three-foot thick walls that were blessed in 1856; and St. Raphael's from the back. (O, D.)

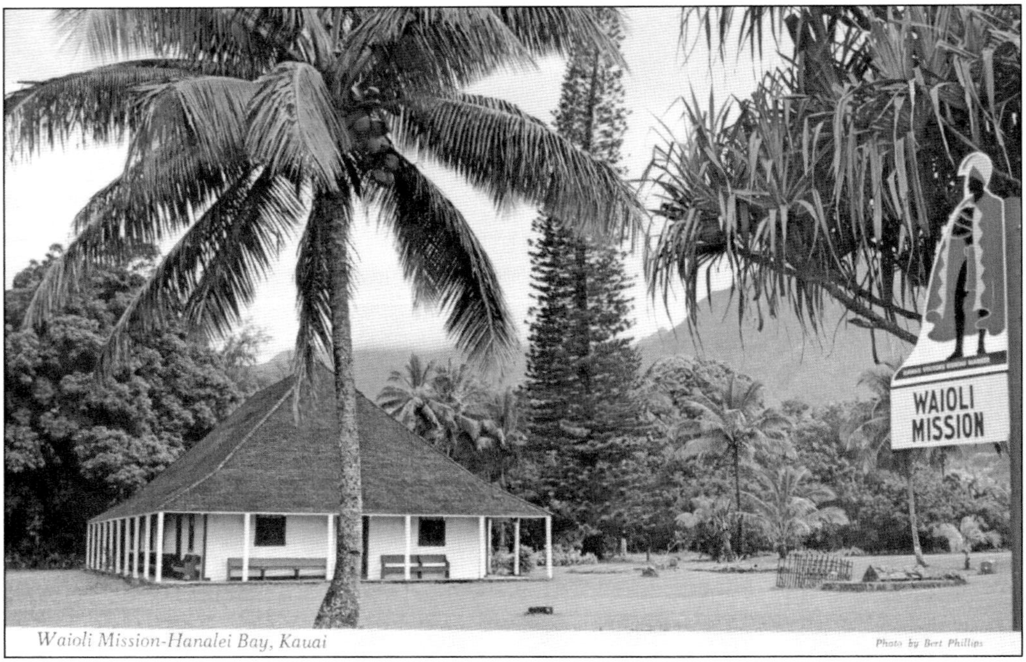

Waioli Mission Hall was established in 1834 as one of the early mission stations. William and Mary Alexander arrived by double-hulled canoe from Waimea and began the mission as a thatched building, which later burned down. A replacement building blew away., and a wooden mission was built in 1841. It suffered severe damage in Hurricane Iniki and was rebuilt. The mission is listed on both the Hawaii and National Registers of Historic Places. (17, E.)

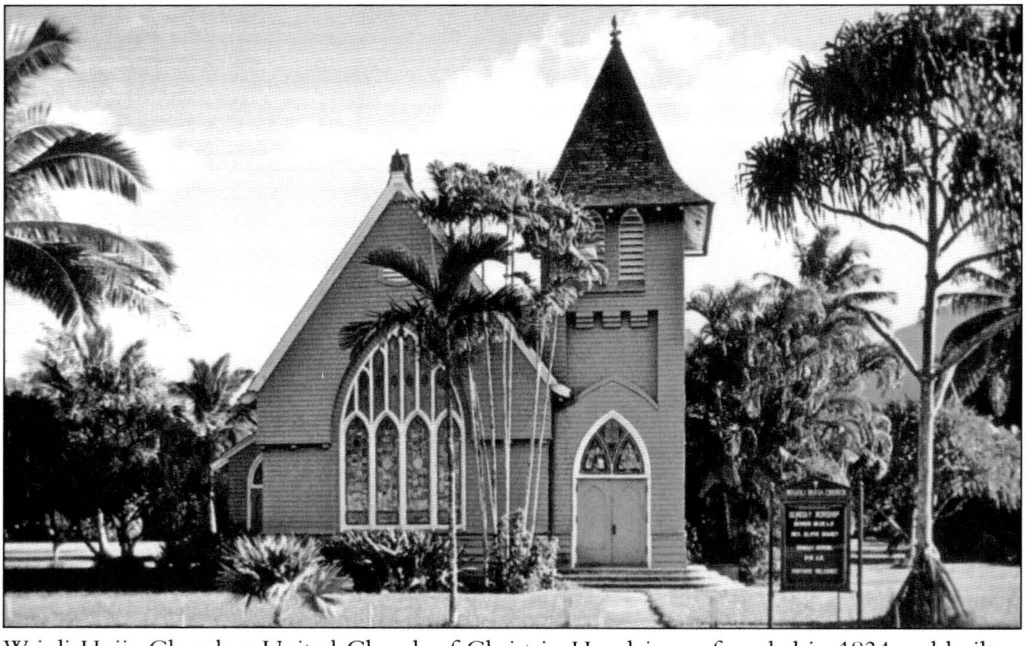
Waioli Huiia Church, a United Church of Christ in Hanalei, was founded in 1834 and built as it stands today in 1912. Three sons of educational missionaries Abner and Lucy Wilcox—Sam, George, and Albert—financially supported the building. The memorable stained-glass windows are done in the opaque opalescent style of John LaFarge and Louis Comfort Tiffany. (18.)

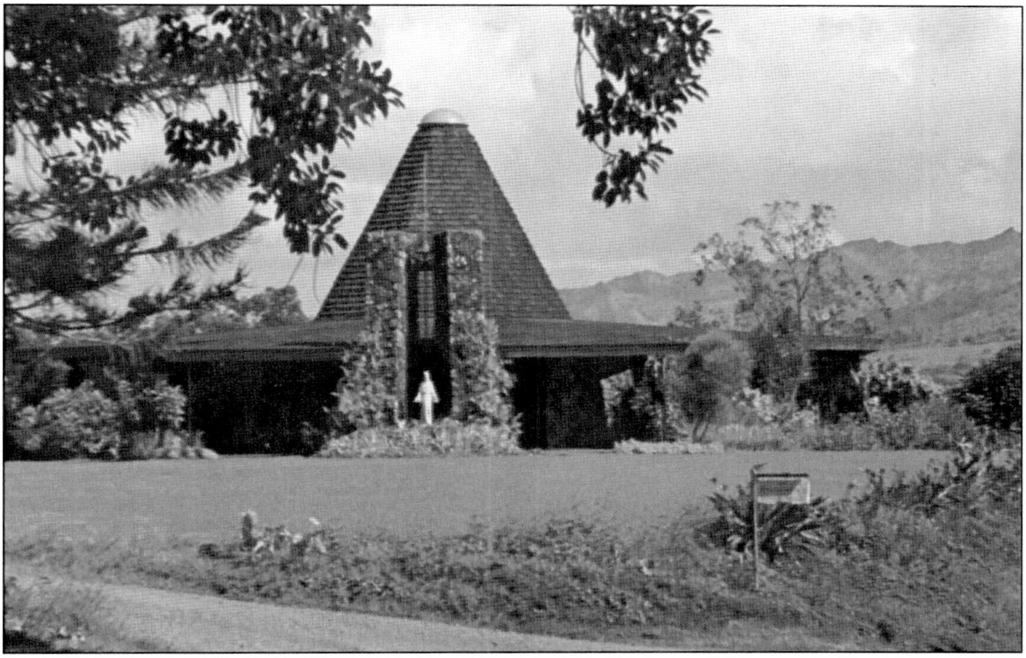

St. Sylvester's Catholic Church in Kilauea was dedicated February 10, 1957. Its unique use of lava rocks both outside on the facade and inside at the altar create a surprisingly airy feel despite the use of the dark rock. (19.)

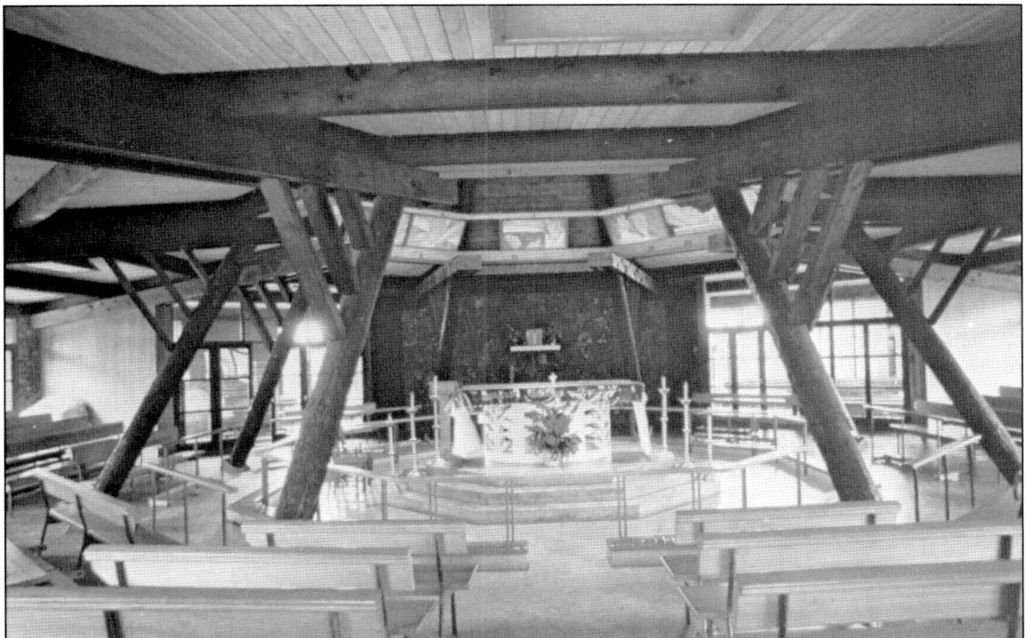

The interior of St. Sylvester's Church is graced by 14 two-foot-by-four-foot frescoes, the *Way of the Cross,* painted by the world-renowned French artist Jean Charlot in 1956. Three of the frescoes are visible above the altar. Charlot died March 20, 1979, in Honolulu at the age of 81. (19, F.)

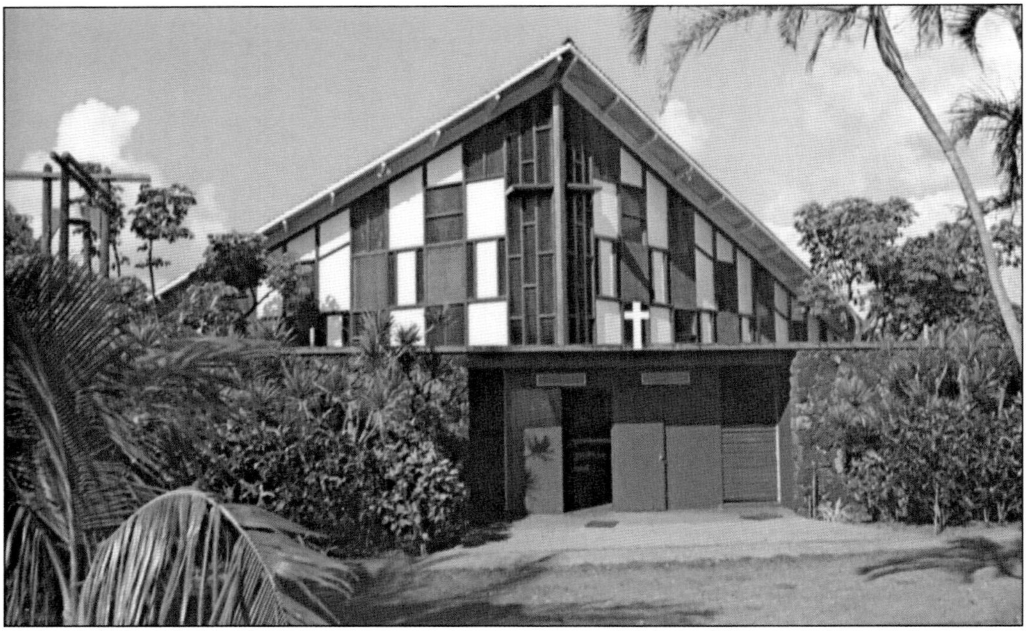
St. Catherine's Church in Kapaa was dedicated April 20, 1958. It is noted for its celebrated art: the frescoes *Compassionate Christ* and 14 ceramic tile panels titled *Stations of the Cross* by Jean Charlot; *The Hawaiian Madonna* by Hawaii-born artist Juliette May Fraser; and *Francis Xavier, Apostle of Asia* by Tseng Yu Ho. Due to Fr. John McDonald's ability to promote his choir to movie producers, St. Catherine's choir was cast in both *South Pacific* and *Blue Hawaii*. (19.)

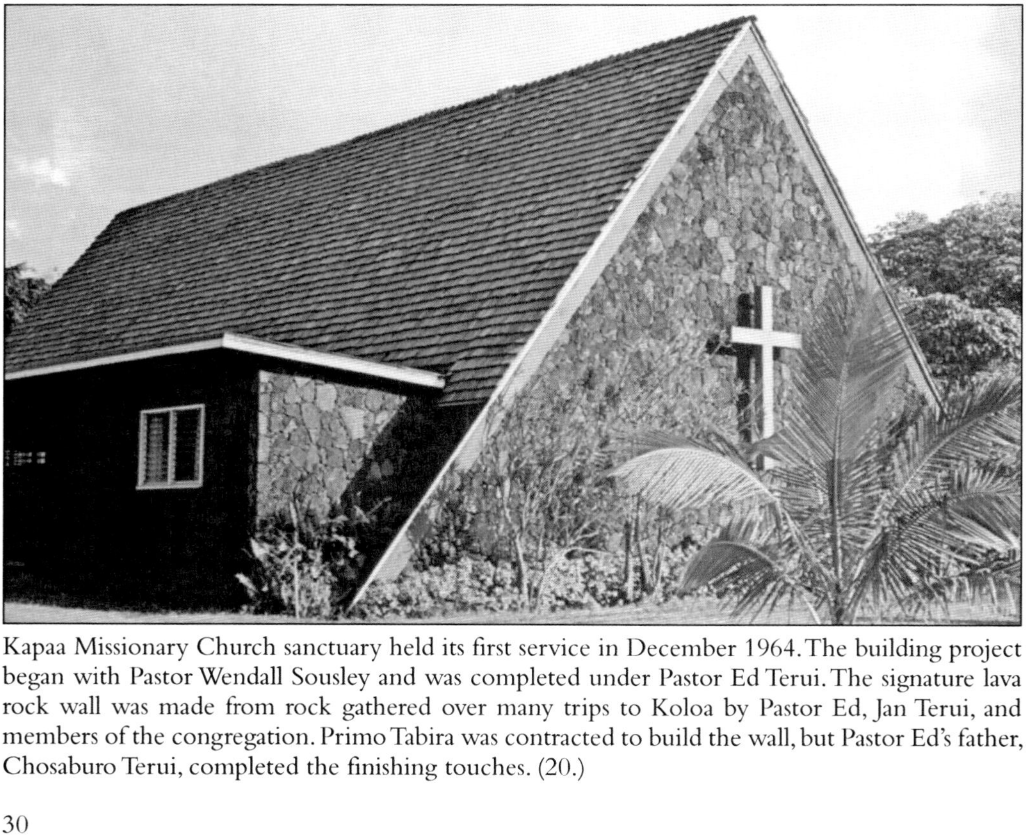
Kapaa Missionary Church sanctuary held its first service in December 1964. The building project began with Pastor Wendall Sousley and was completed under Pastor Ed Terui. The signature lava rock wall was made from rock gathered over many trips to Koloa by Pastor Ed, Jan Terui, and members of the congregation. Primo Tabira was contracted to build the wall, but Pastor Ed's father, Chosaburo Terui, completed the finishing touches. (20.)

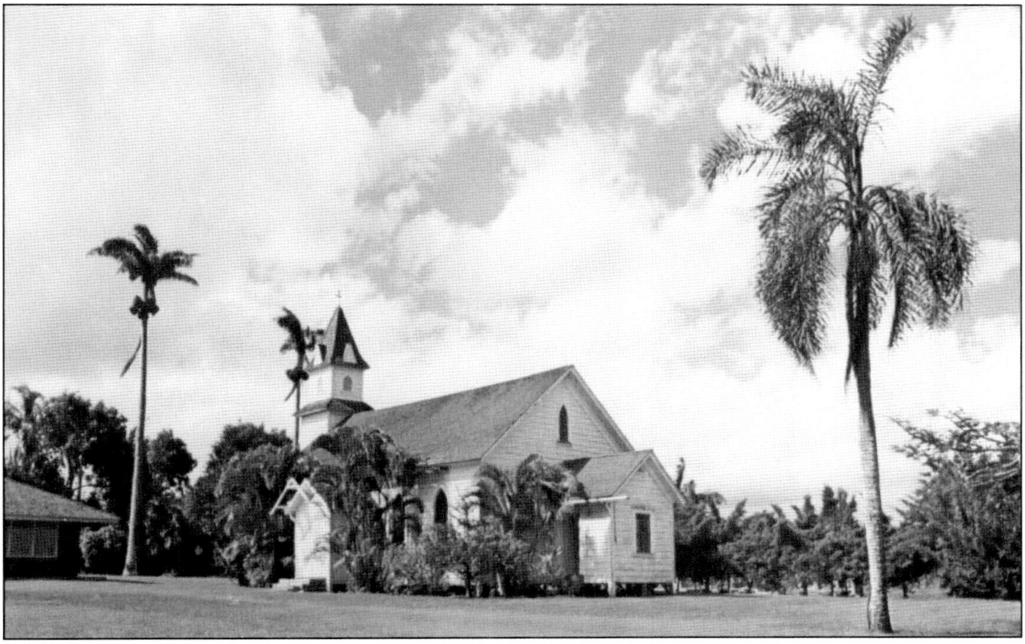

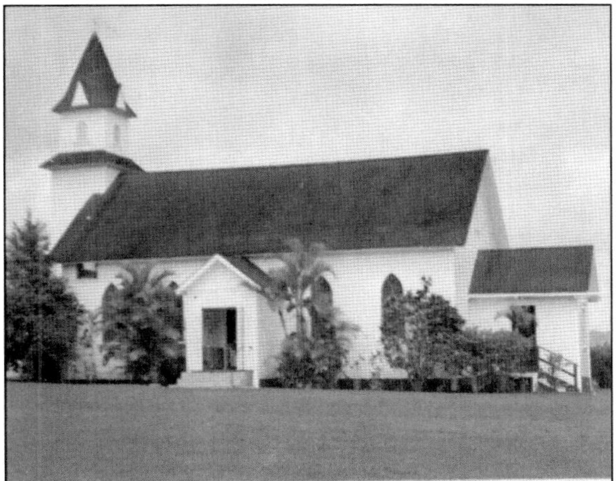

Lihue Lutheran Church dates back to 1881. It is the oldest Lutheran church in the Hawaiian Islands. Paul Isenberg came to work at the Lihue Plantation and became its president. His younger brother Hans, an ordained Lutheran pastor, served this church from 1887 until 1918. This postcard commemorated the church's 100th anniversary in 1981. Unfortunately, Hurricane Iwa destroyed the church the next year, and it was rebuilt to look the same. (19.)

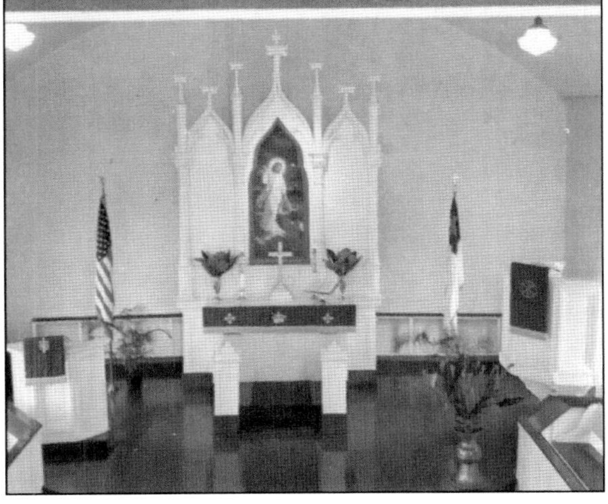

The German immigrants who founded the Lihue Lutheran Church in June 1881 had sailed around Cape Horn, a trip that took them six months. The church's interior architecture is rich with ship symbolism, from slanted floors similar to the deck of a ship to the pulpit as the forecastle. The altar painting is an original work by Ernst Marx. (21.)

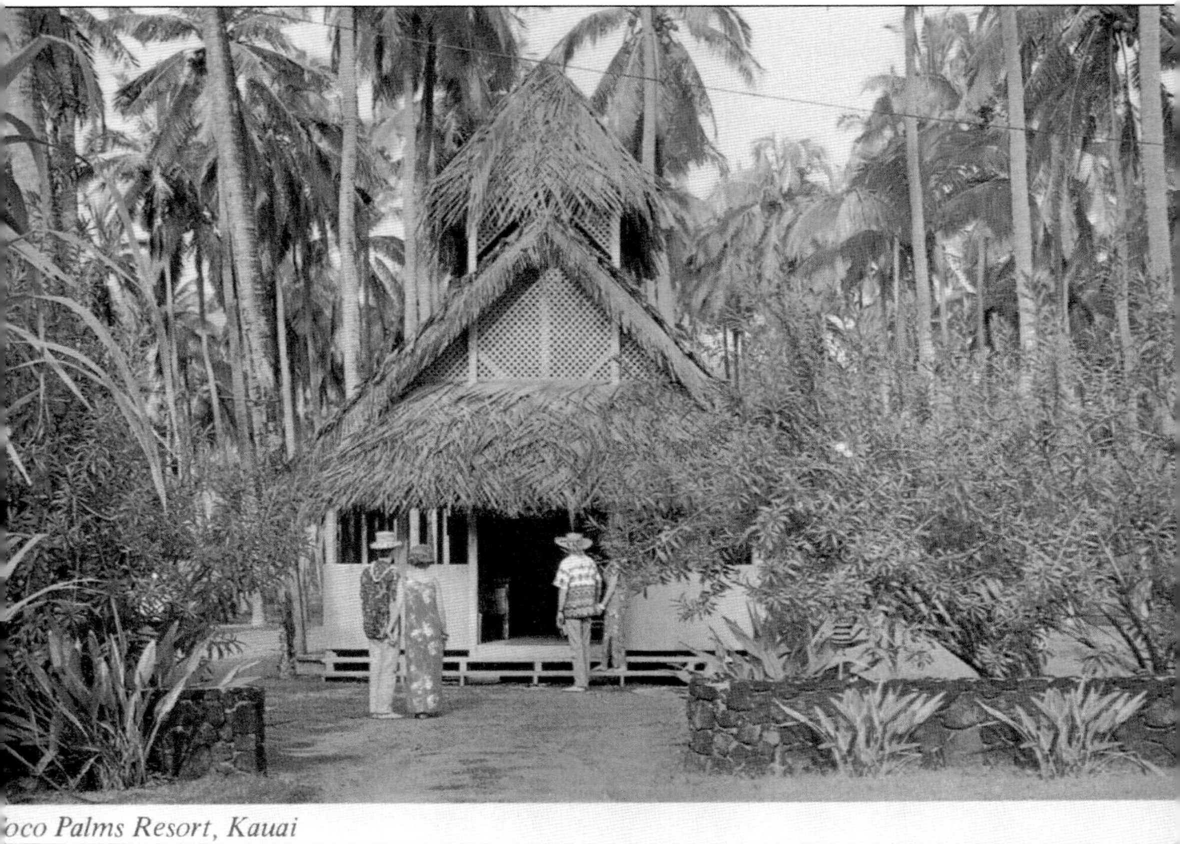

Chapel in the Palms is situated in the palm grove on the Coco Palms property. This building, however, was erected in May 1953 for the movie *Miss Sadie Thompson*, starring Rita Hayworth and Jose Ferrer. Later, the hotel took the structure and improved upon it. Sunday church services were held weekly for guests. Even though the hotel has been closed for many years, weddings are still performed today thanks to Larry Rivera, who keeps the memory of the once great hotel alive. (11.)

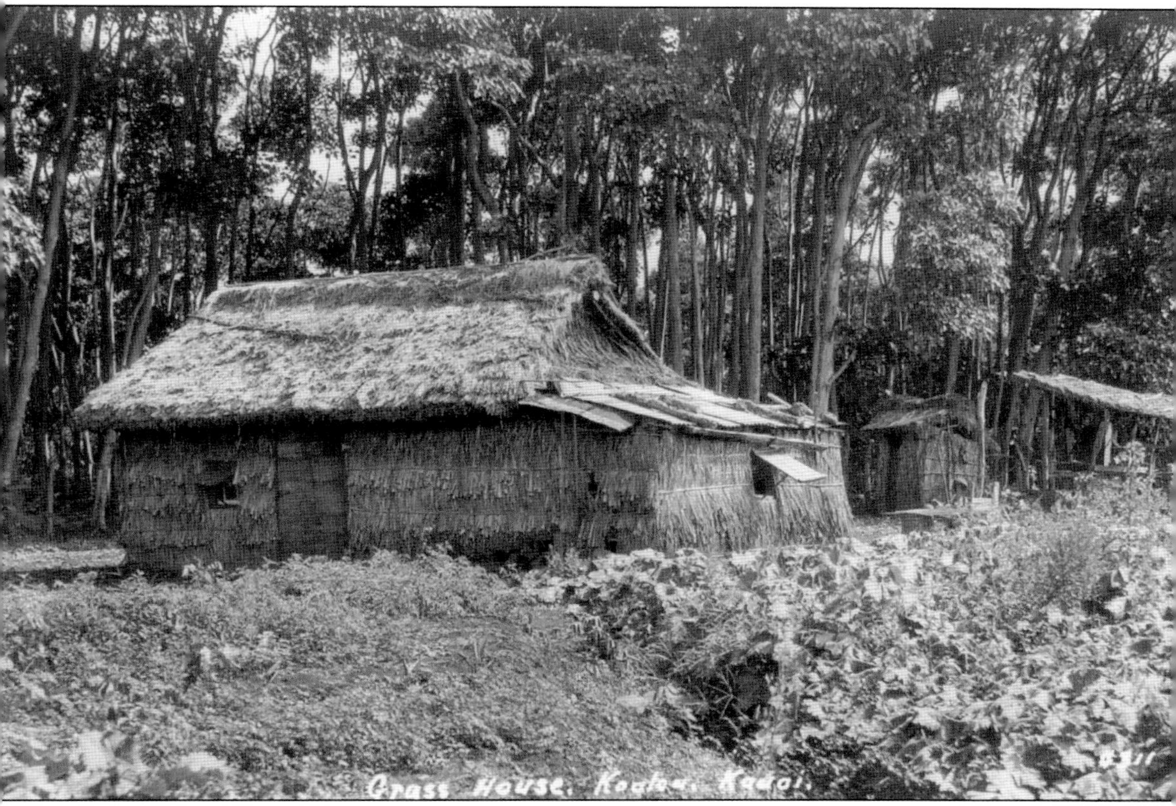

This *hale pili* was erected in Koolau District, probably in Anahola Valley, according to those who live in that area and considering the dense vegetation and the large grove of Kukui nut trees in the background. It would have been rare to see such a home in the 1930s when Kauai photographer W. J. Senda photographed it. It was probably one of the last left on the island at that time. (0, A.)

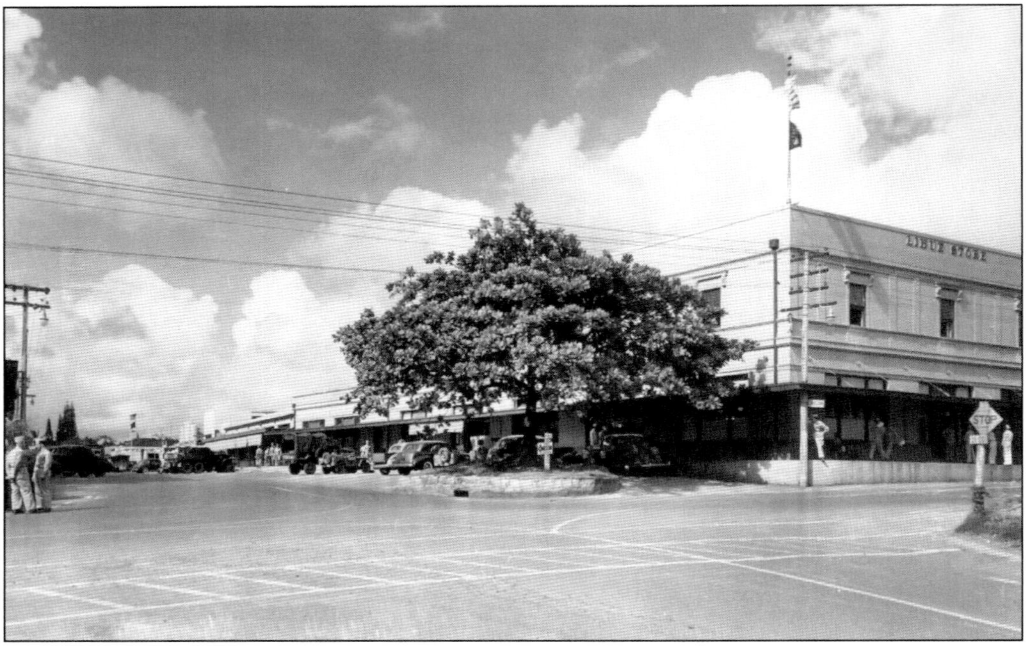

The corner of Government Road and Rice Street shows the Lihue Store in the 1940s with a number of soldiers milling about. Lihue Store, also known as Kauai's Emporium, was the primary place for shopping needs. A false Kamani tree still stands guard at the store's entrance. As the town grew, it became a traffic hazard, and not wanting to cut it down, kind-hearted tree-lovers had it moved to Wilcox Hospital grounds. (0, A.)

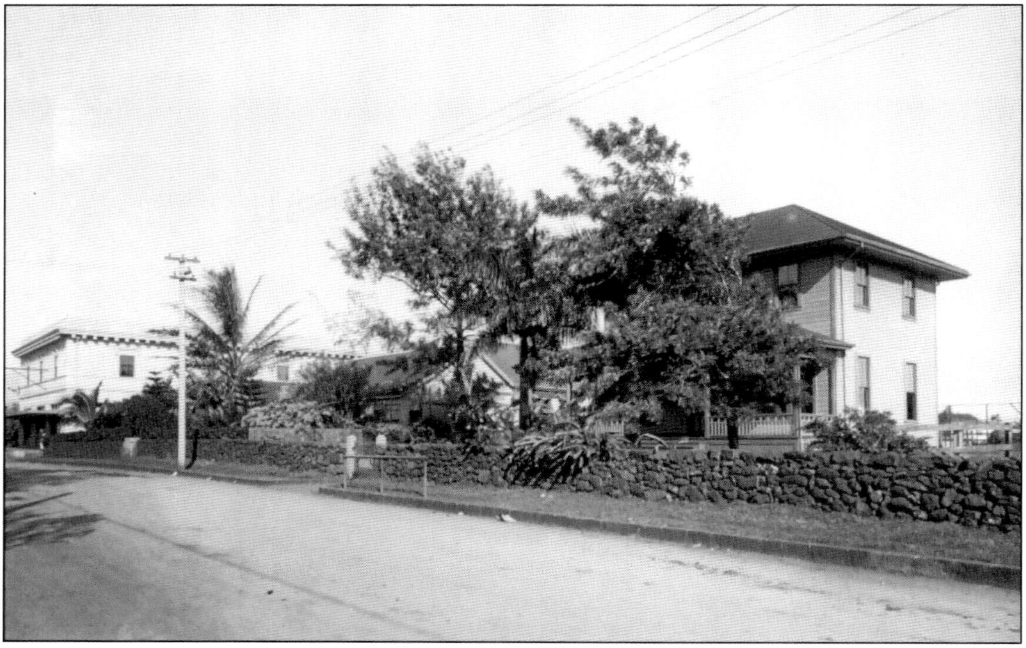

The Herman Rohrig House on Rice Street in Lihue stood between the Lihue Store, the white building at left center, and the Lihue Plantation building, the tall two-story building at right. None of these structures exist today. Now, this entire area is the Lihue Shopping Center parking lot. Herman Rohrig had been a manager for Lihue Plantation. (0, A.)

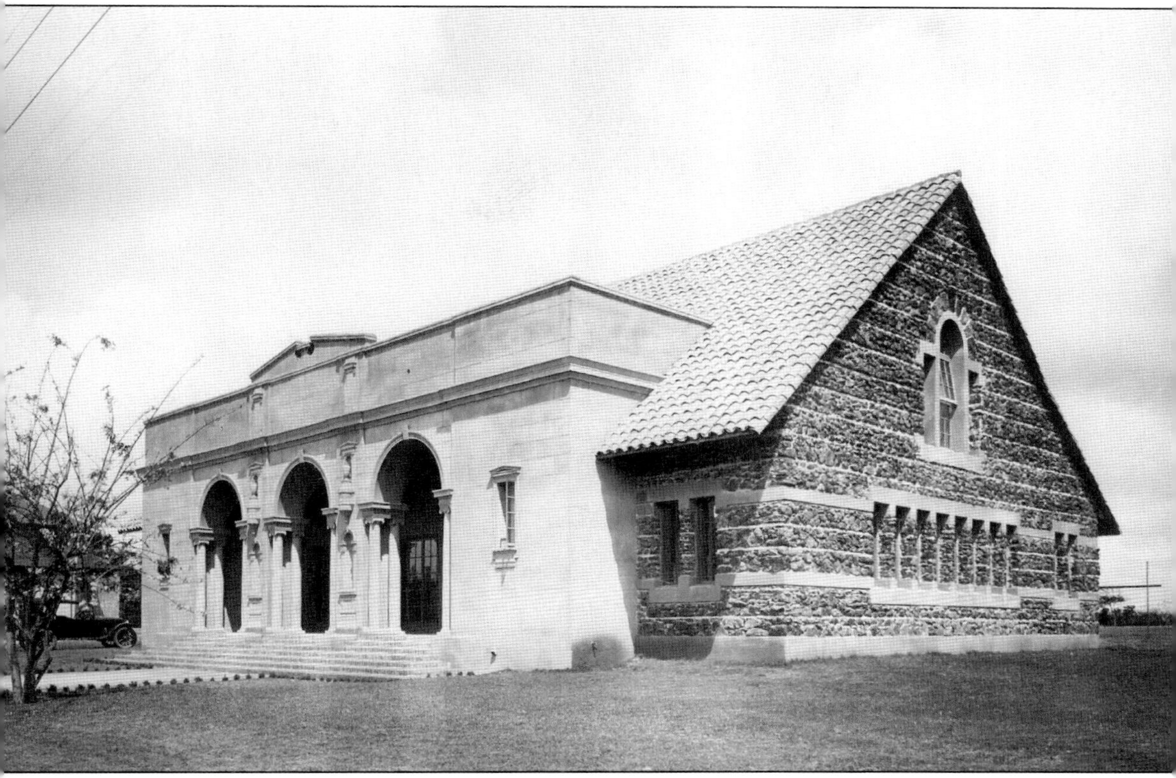

The Albert Spencer Wilcox Memorial Library was constructed in 1922. One of Hawaii's foremost architects, Hart Wood, designed it emphasizing the use of local lava rock and a signature blue tile roof. This is one of the few surviving Hart Wood–designed buildings left in Hawaii. Lihue Plantation sold the library site to the building association for $1. Emma Kauikeolani Wilcox donated $75,000 for the building. Rev. J.M. Lydgate donated his collection of books, and he encourages his friends to do likewise. Through the efforts of Juliet Rice Wichman, a museum was added adjacent to the library opening on December 3, 1960. When the library outgrew its space, a new facility was built on Hardy Street in 1969. The museum expanded to include the area the library vacated. Today, both buildings are the home of the Kauai Museum. (0.)

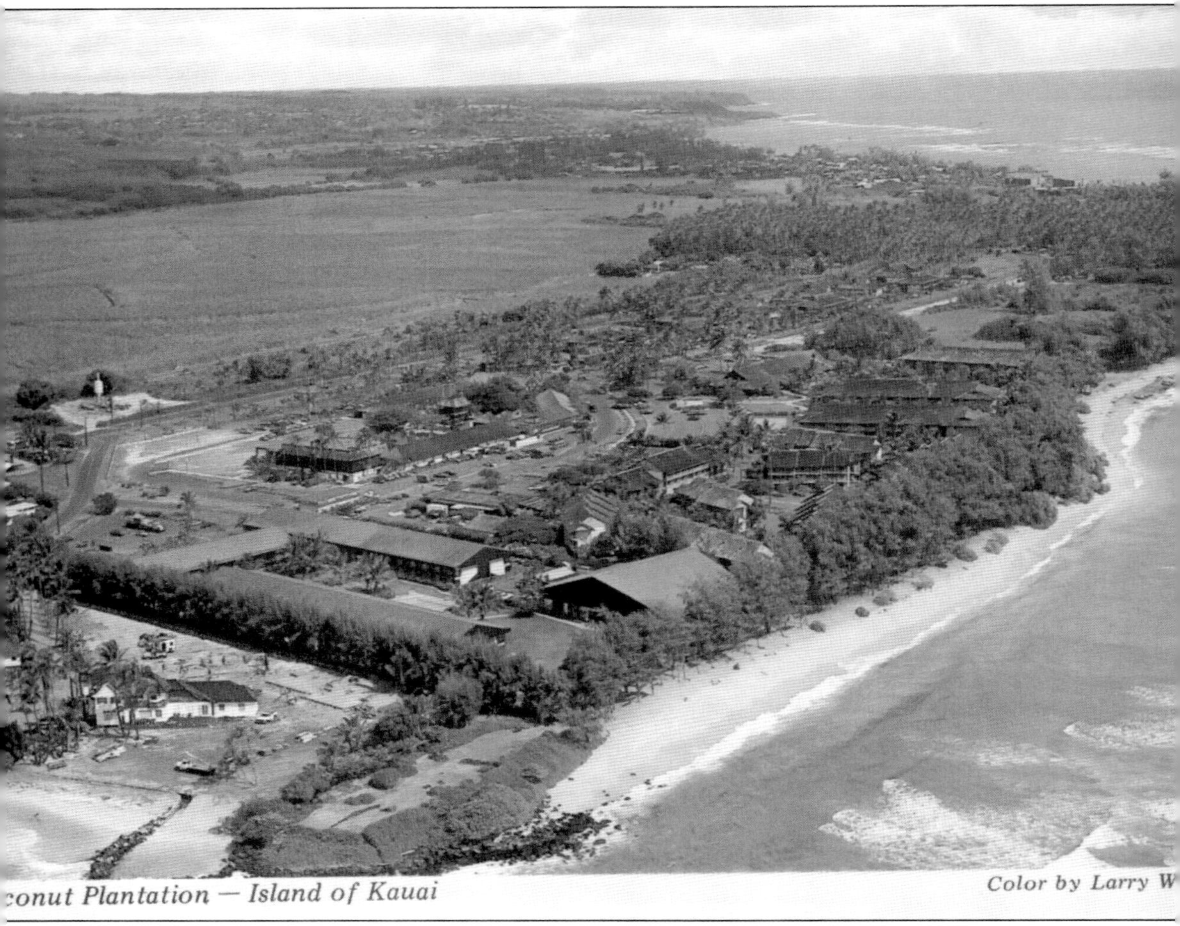

Coconut Plantation Marketplace was built in three phases starting in 1972 near several hotels: the Islander Inn, Kauai Beach Boy, and the Kauai Sands Hotel. Phase II began in 1976, and Phase III commenced in 1978. The center then contained 64,000 square feet of shopping area with over 70 stores and restaurants. The house visible in the lower left-hand corner once belonged to Albert Horner Sr. and, later, to Albert Horner Jr. Both men were involved with the Hawaiian Canneries Company, a pineapple cannery in Kapaa. The house was featured in the 1950 film *Pagan Love Song*. In 1976, the house was sold to Pauline and Mel Ventura and moved to another location. The house site is now the location of the Lae Nani Condominium. (22, G.)

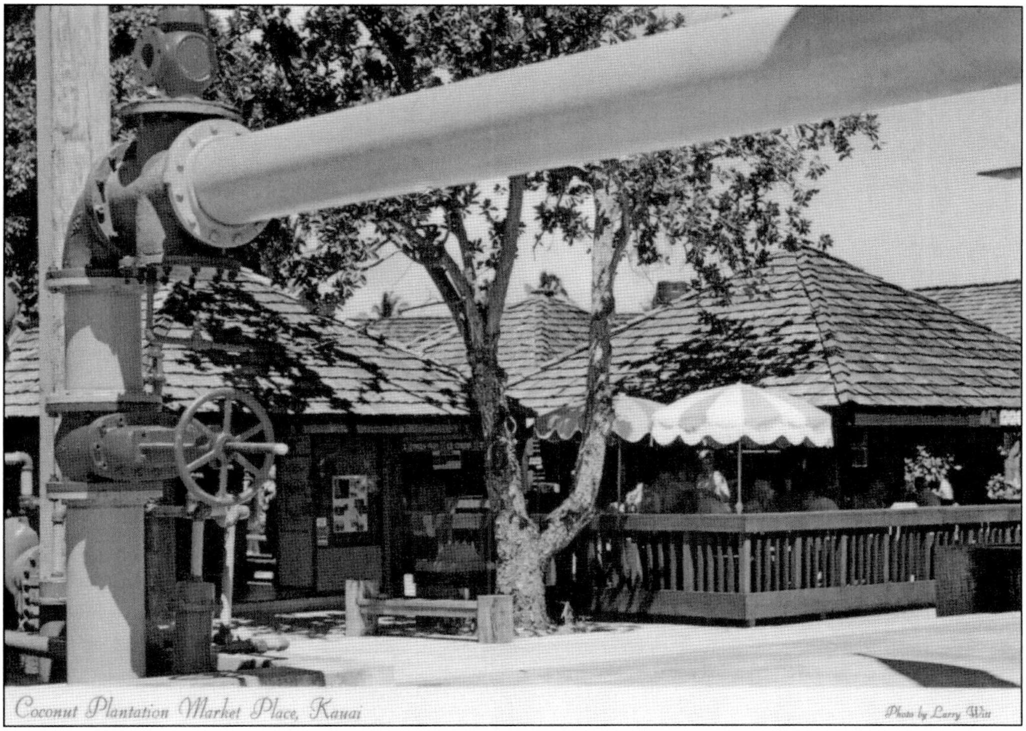

Coconut Plantation Marketplace was a favorite place to visit, as the writer of the above 1984 postcard states, boasting "I bought 10 T-shirts at Crazy Shirts alone!" The center was built using antique sugar-mill machinery as an architectural feature. The image on the card below was taken after Phase I was built. But after multiple painting of the metal, rust became more and more of a problem. The sugar mill look was taken out in a remodeling in 2007. (Above, 22, G; below, 23.)

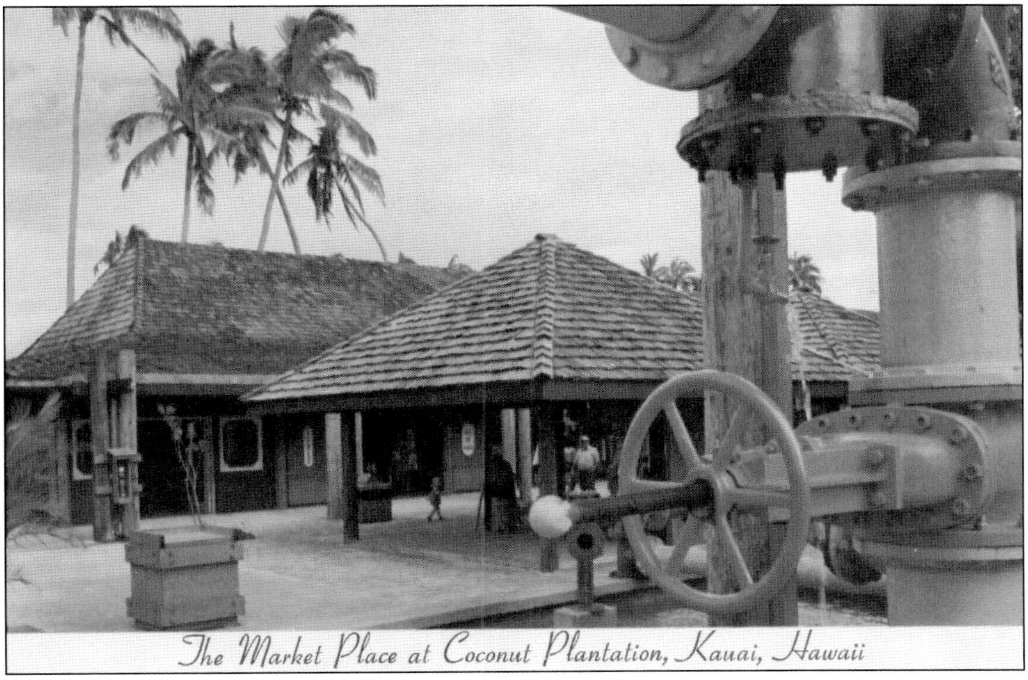

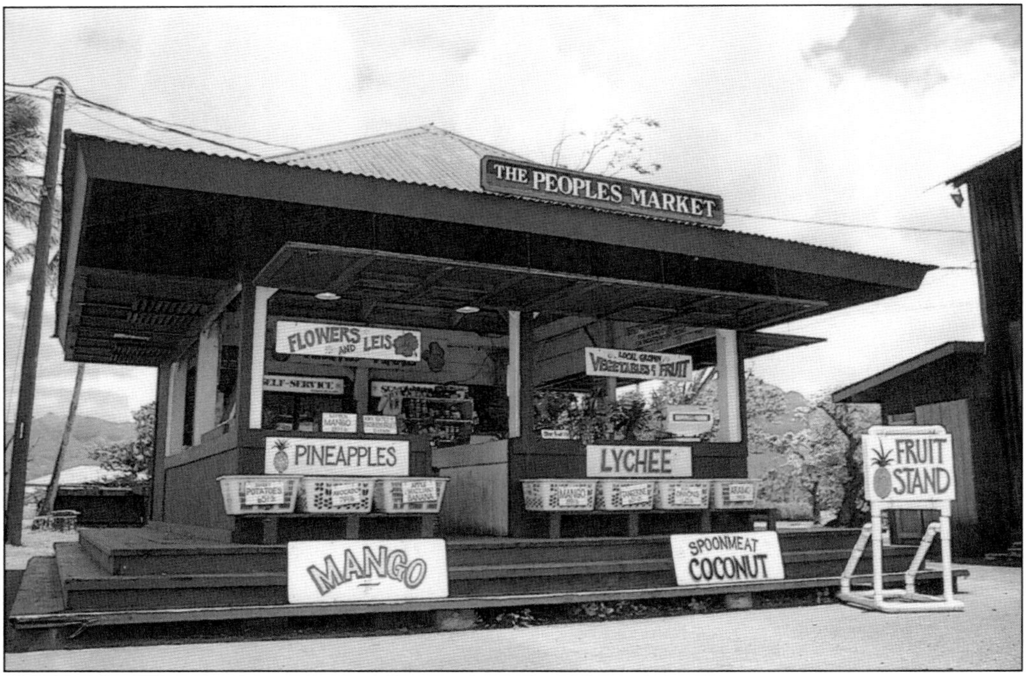

The People's Market belonged to the Masaki family. Michael Miyuki Masaki started the fruit and flower business in Puhi in 1981. It was removed in 1998 to make way for a small shopping center across from Kauai Community College. The building now stands vacant in Waimea. (24, H.)

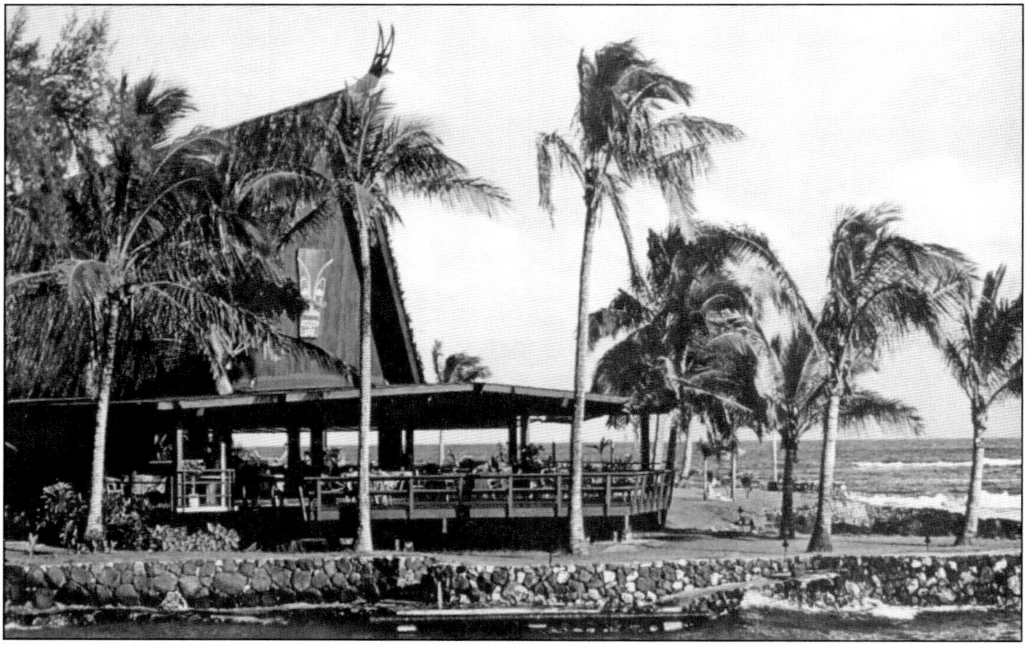

Paul Sandifur's Metropolitan Mortgage and Securities built the Tahiti Longhouse for $70,000 back in the 1960s. The restaurant had spectacular views of both the ocean and south shore sunsets. Unfortunately, Hurricane Iwa washed it away in 1982. The owners rebuilt it, and renamed it the Beach House, but Hurricane Iniki destroyed this structure in 1992. It has again been rebuilt and remains a favorite south shore eatery known for awesome food and sunsets. (25.)

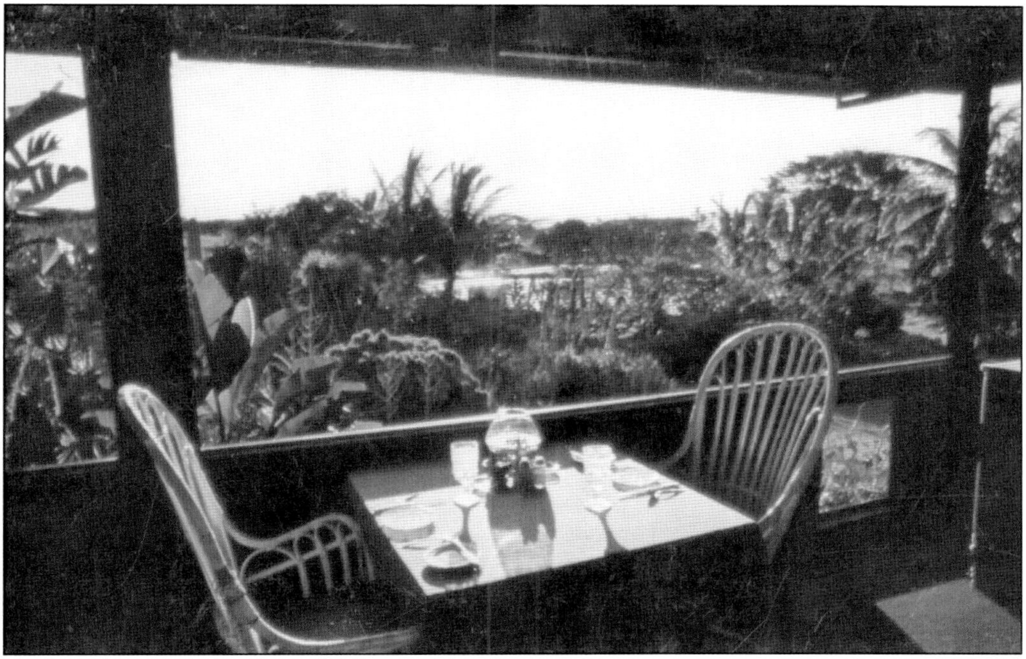

The Plantation Gardens Restaurant was once the home of the Moir family. The dining area looks out over quite an extensive collection of cacti planted by the Moirs. The restaurant is not visible from the road but is surrounded by the Kiahuna Plantation. (0.)

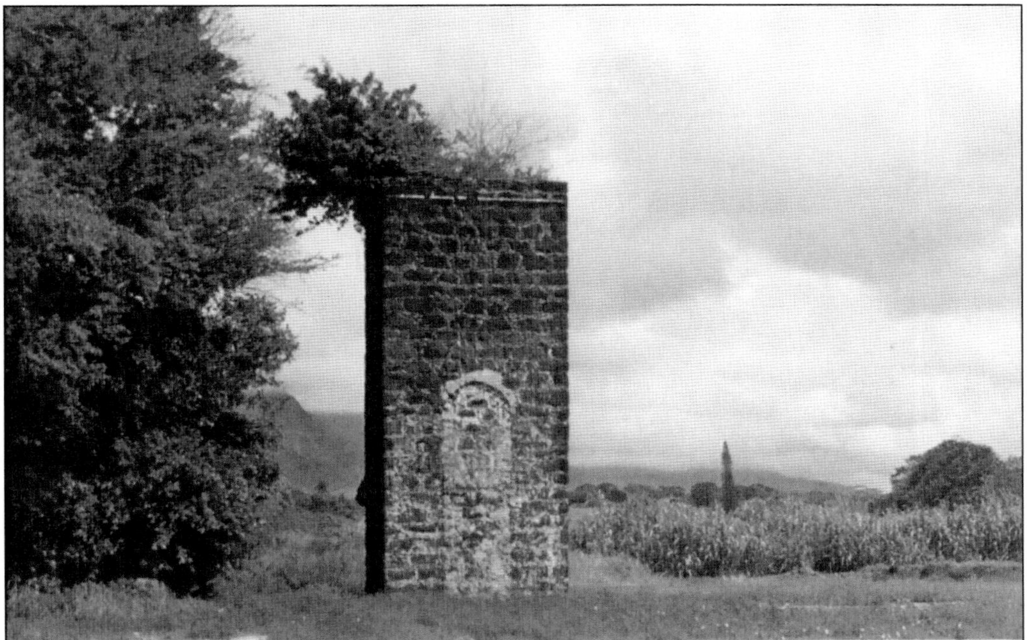

The Last Standing Remains of Hawaii's First Sugar Mill

The last standing remains of Hawaii's first sugar mill are located at the intersection of Maluhia Road and Koloa Road. The first successful sugar mill was started by Ladd and Company and later known as the Koloa Sugar Company. It later moved a few miles away. (11.)

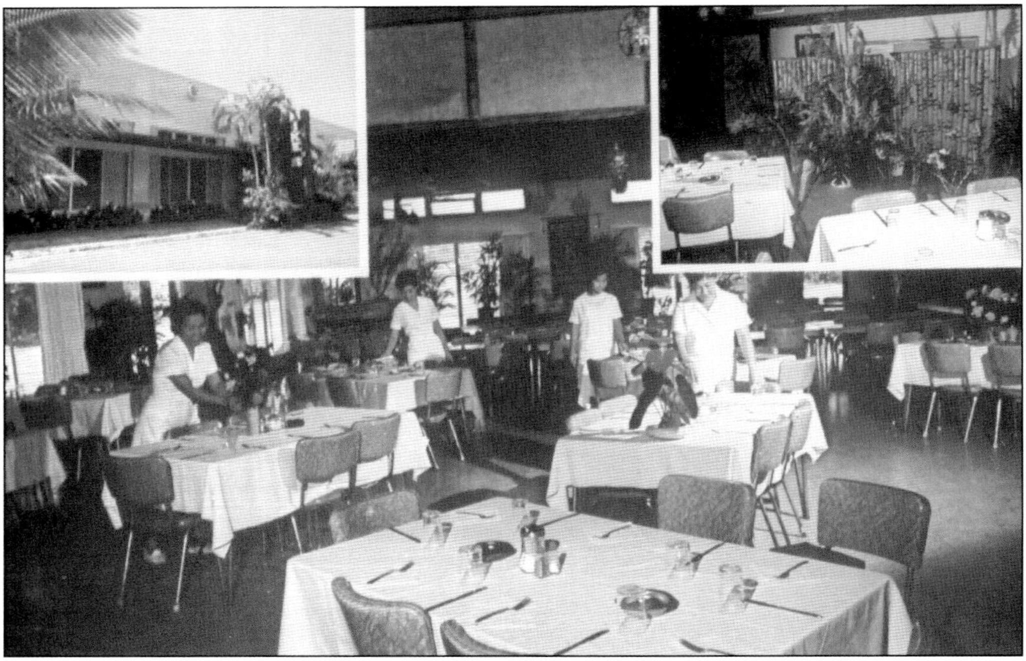

Mike Yoshinobu started Mike's Café in Hanapepe in the 1950s. From the start, it was known for its Lilikoi chiffon pie, a family recipe that became a restaurant favorite. Later, the eatery became known as Conrad and Wong's; Conrad Nonaka and Jackson Wong were the owners. Today, it is known only as Wong's and owned by Jackie and Jo-Ann Wong. (19.)

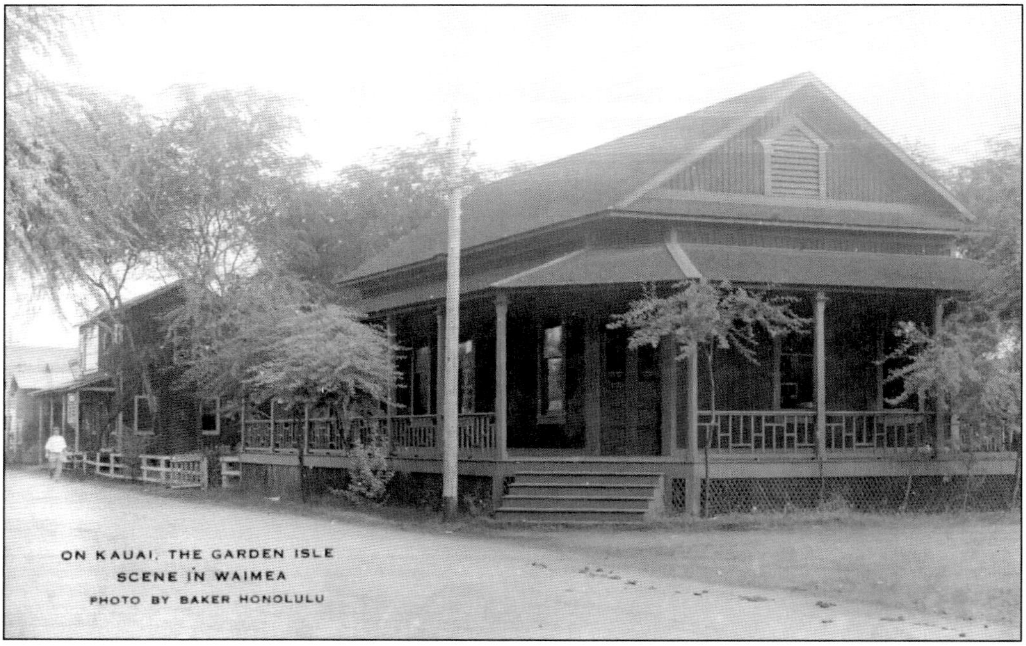

This Waimea building was the first Kauai branch of First Hawaiian Bank, which opened in 1911. First Hawaiian Bank was founded August 17, 1858, by Charles Reed Bishop and known as the Bishop & Co. Bank. The current Neoclassical cement building that replaced this one was built in 1933. (0, L.)

Four

Beaches and Town Views

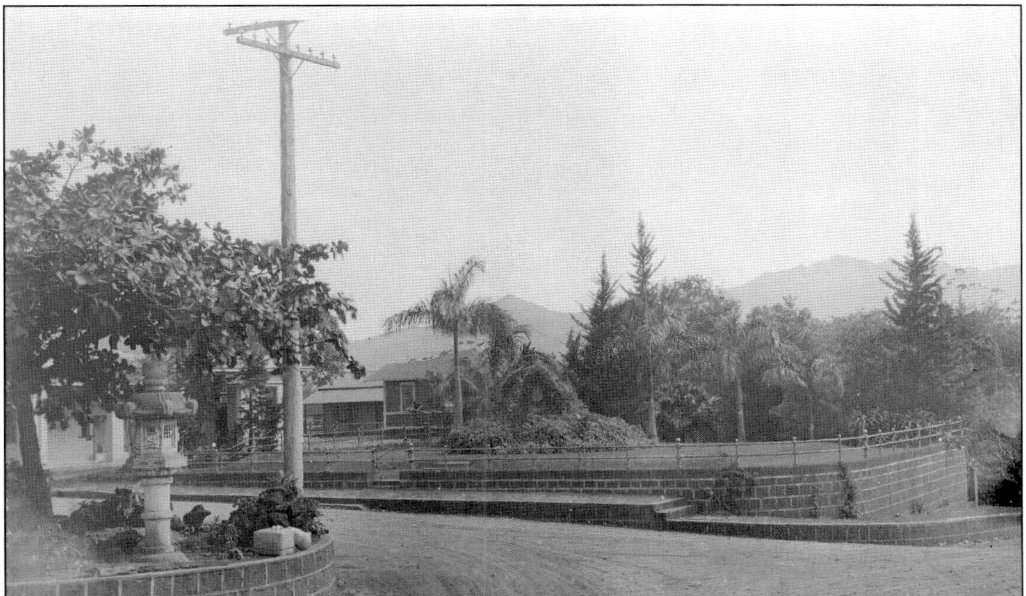

This 1910 postcard is of the Isenberg Memorial, dedicated April 15, 1904. Paul Isenberg was a manager of Lihue Plantation for 16 years from 1862 to 1878. Barely visible through the leaves at left is what was the Lihue Bank, now a Bank of Hawaii branch. It is one of only a few landmarks not lost when the Round building was built in 1965. (O.)

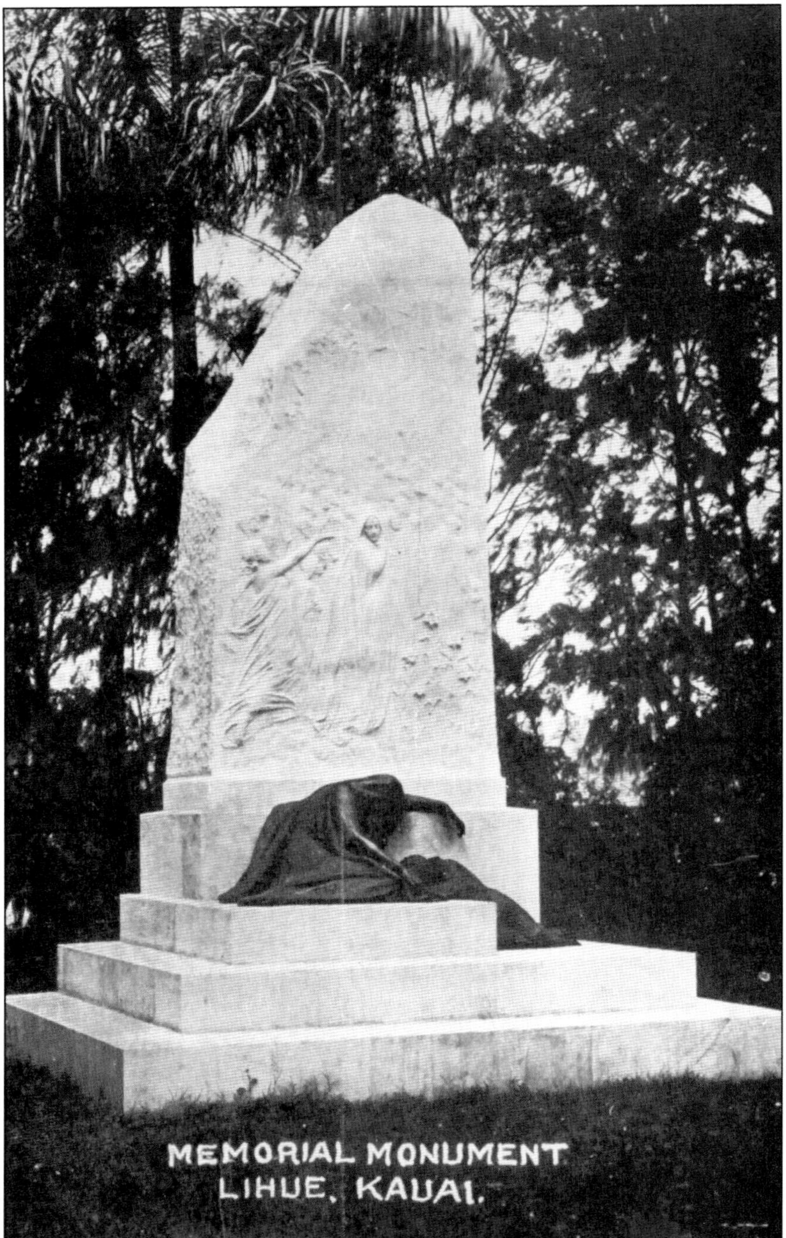

Hannah Marie Rice was born February 17, 1842, and died April 7, 1867, at age 25 after a short marriage to Paul Isenberg, the Lihue Plantation manager. Besides being a memorial to Hannah Maria Rice Isenberg, the memorial also lists seven other family members who died before its 1911 unveiling: William Harrison Rice, May 1862; Mary Sophie Hyde Rice, May 1911; Paul Isenberg, Jan. 1903; Mary H. Rice, Sept. 1870; H. Alexander Isenberg, Nov. 1905; Charles M. Cooke, Aug. 1909; and Emily Dole Rice de La Vergne. June 1911. The sculptor was Stephan Sinding, born in Trondheim, Norway, in 1846. He finished the sculpture in 1910, exhibited it in Paris and Bremen, and then had it sent by ship around Cape Horn to Kauai. W. Schieber, head mason of Lihue Plantation, set it up. On Sept 1, 1911, Anna C. Rice Cooke unveiled it to family and friends. (29.)

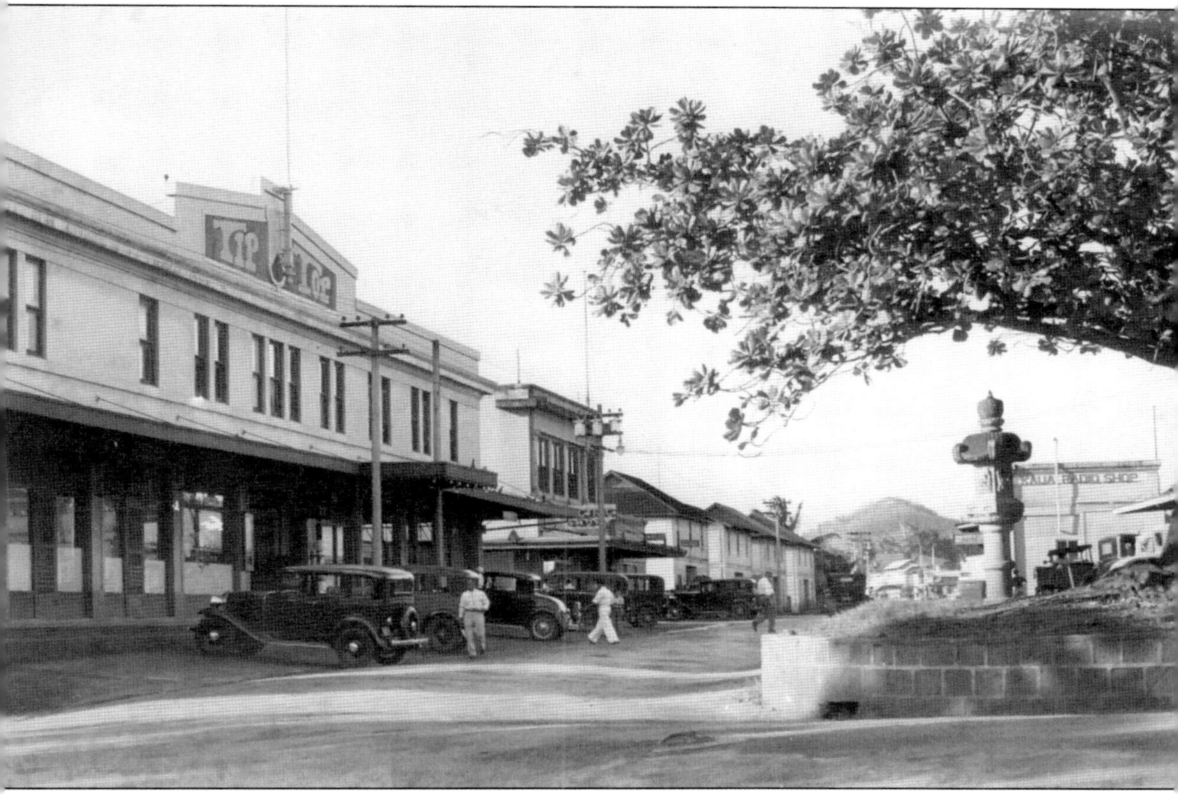

In 1933, the Tip Top Bakery looked like this. In November 1916, the building was constructed by Lihue Plantation for its offices. It was Lihue Plantation that named it the Tip Top Building, so Denjiro Ota, who started the bakery and café, named his business after the structure. Ota had been a cook for the plantation manager and was asked to open a business so Lihue residences could have breakfast and coffee in the morning. The bakery added bread and delivered it islandwide. In 1965, with the building of the Lihue Shopping Center and the changing of the road, both the Kauai Store and Tip Top Building had to be torn down. The Ota family, led by Mitchell Ota, moved it to its present location on Akahi Street and added a motel to its enterprise. Fourth-generation Jonathan Ota runs the business today. (O, A.)

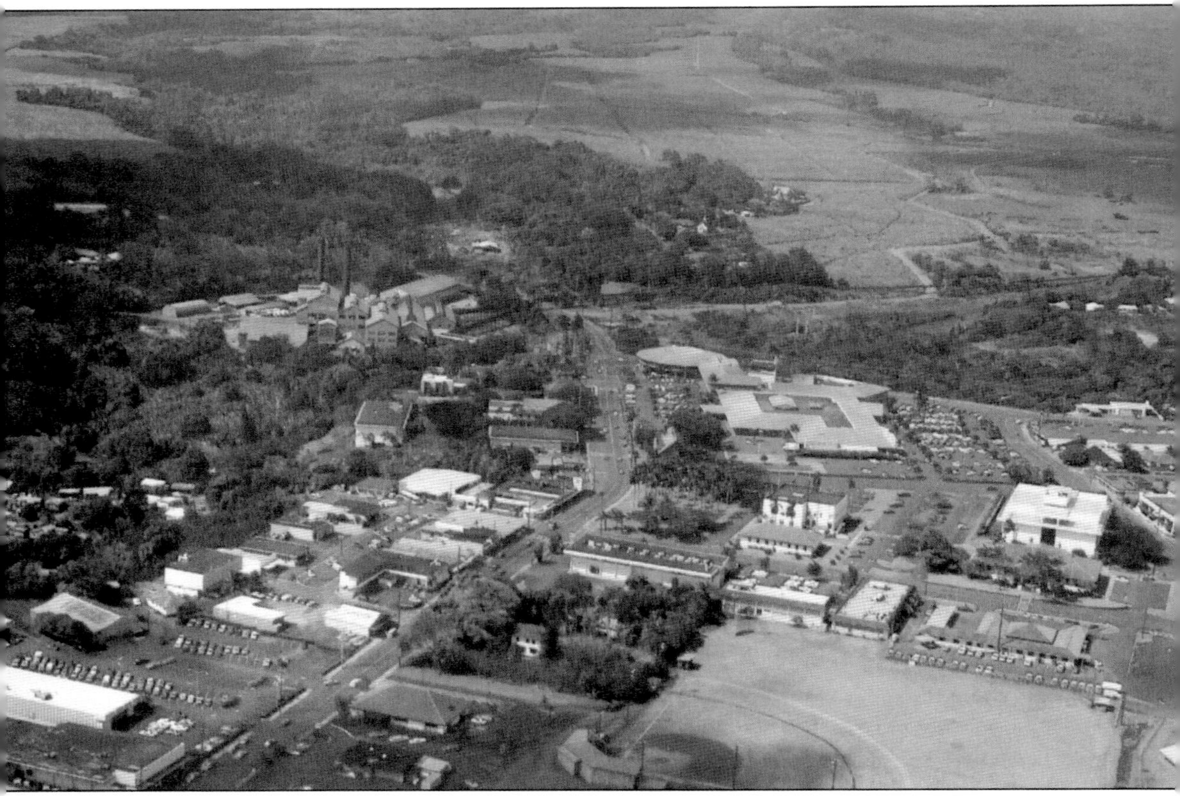

This 1980 aerial view displays the growth of the town of Lihue. Upper center shows the Round building and Lihue Shopping Center. The Tip Top Building was where the Round building is, and Lihue Store was in the parking lot between the Round building and the museum. The white county building is just below and to the right is the very large white state building that dwarfs the courthouse, with its red-tiled roof. In the lower left-hand corner are the white roofs of the Rice Shopping Center. The treed area with a house abutting the ball field is where the Watumull Plaza building will be built and dedicated in 1982. (11, A.)

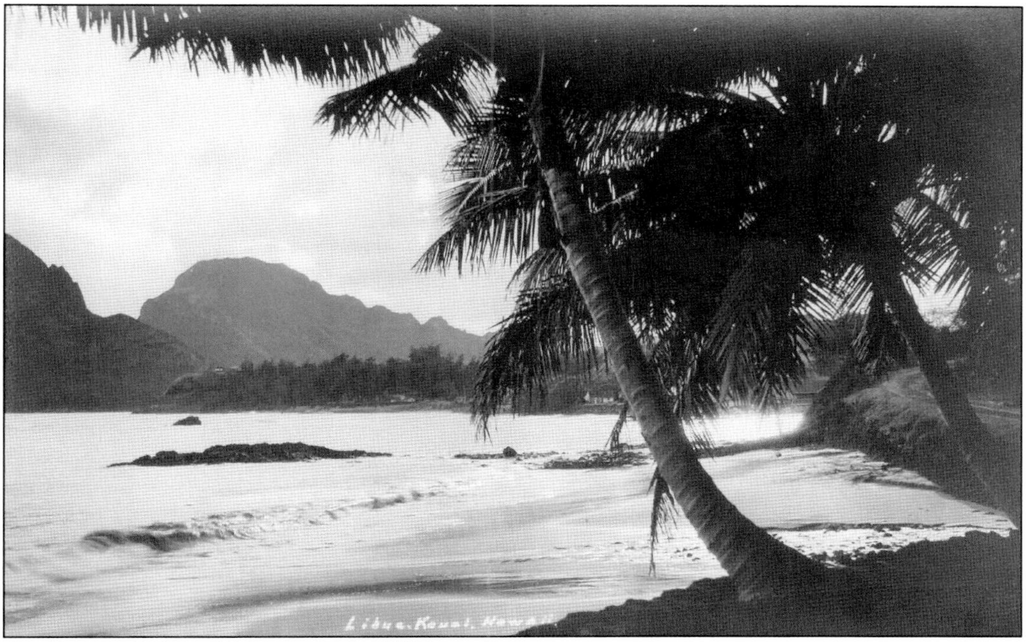

The card above shows Kalapaki Beach in the 1930s, before the heavy influx of tourists, with a coconut palm in the foreground. And below, again in the early1960s, one can see Kalapaki Beach has not changed much, as it has added people and umbrellas and, in this card, the palm has been replaced by a Lauhala tree. (Above, 0, A; below, 27, A.)

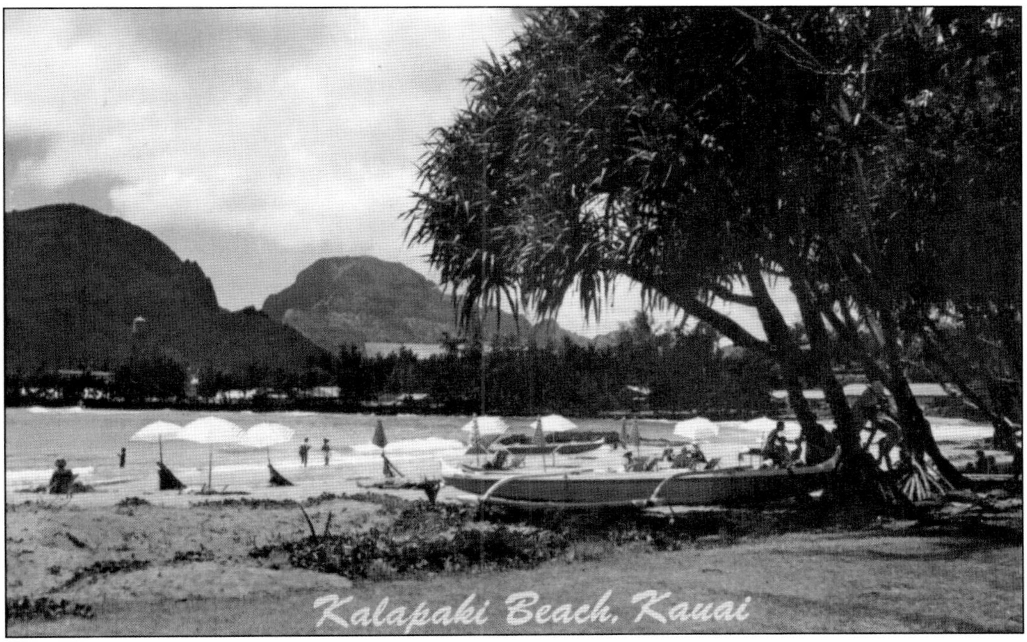

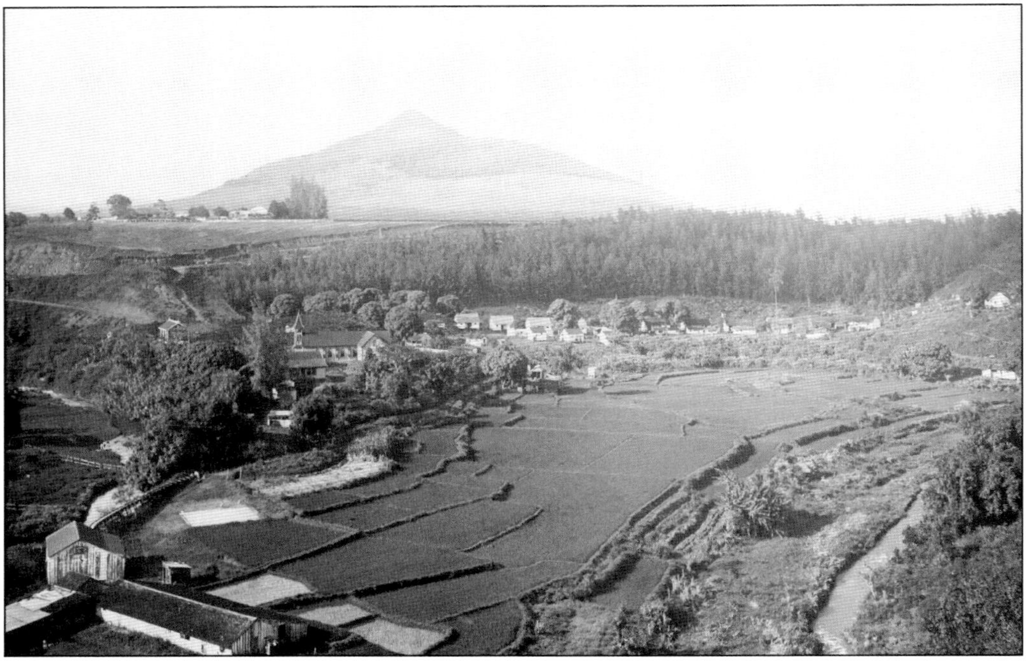

In the 1920s, Kapaia was a sleepy village outside of Lihue planted in acres of rice. Primarily, Chinese and Japanese immigrants settled this area. Center left shows the road coming from Lihue. The first building visible is the Lihue Honwanji and the Immaculate Conception Church. The mountain in the background is Kilohana Crater. (0.)

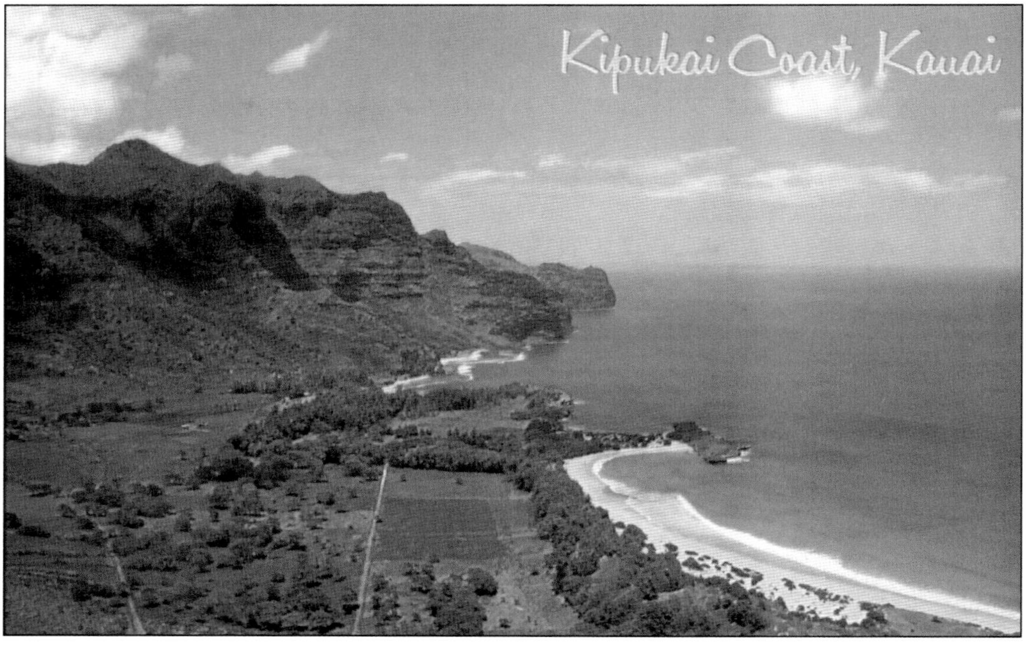

Kipukai is one of prettiest and least accessible beaches on the island. It is part of Kipu Ranch, a 3,000-acre working cattle ranch. William Hyde Rice bought it from the monarchy in 1872. The area is a favorite film location seen in such Hollywood movies as *Raiders of the Lost Ark*, *The Lost World*, *Outbreak*, *Islands in the Stream*, *Mighty Joe Young*, *Diamond Head*, and *The Hawaiians*. (27, A.)

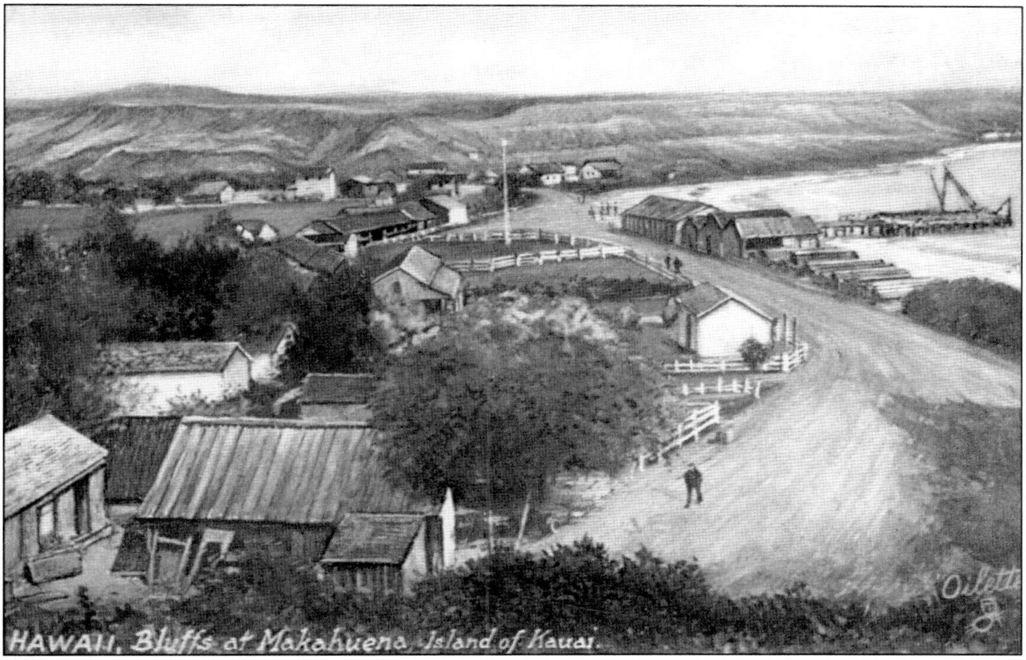

Although labeled "Bluffs at Makahuena, Island of Kauai," this is the fishing village of Nawiliwili. It is not clear how it became mislabeled. As far as anyone knows today, Makahuena is near Poipu, but this view is definitely looking north. Looking at the card below, one can see the same flagpole, bridge, and dock from the opposite direction and at a slightly later timeframe labeled correctly. The card above was printed in England by the famous Raphael Tuck, publisher to the English monarchy. The card below was printed in Honolulu. (Above, 43; below, 7.)

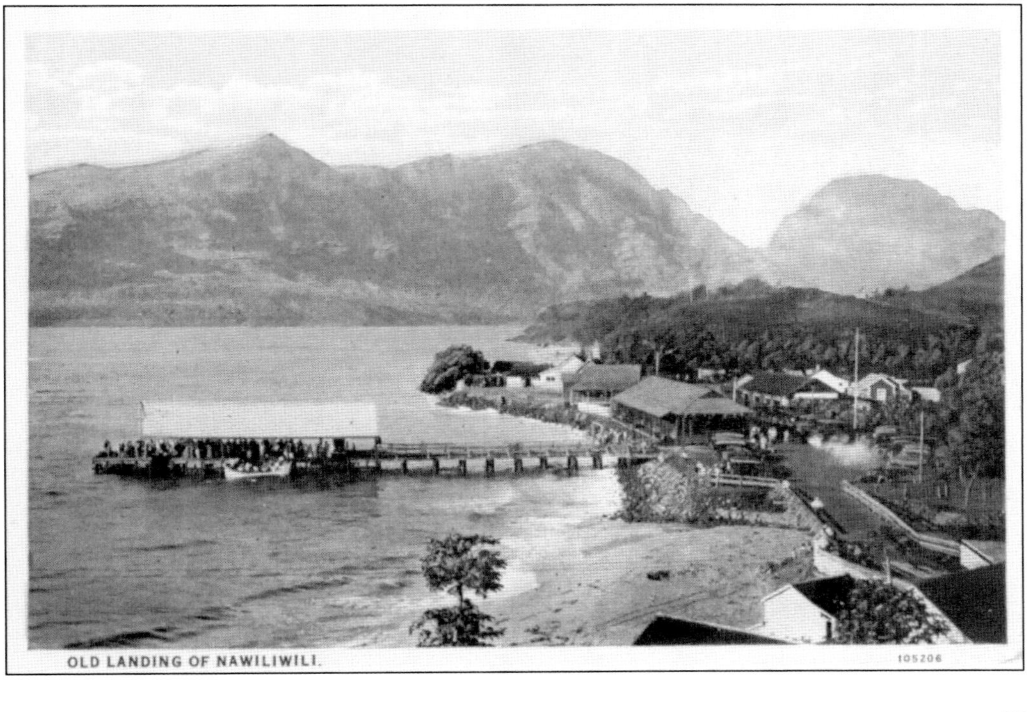

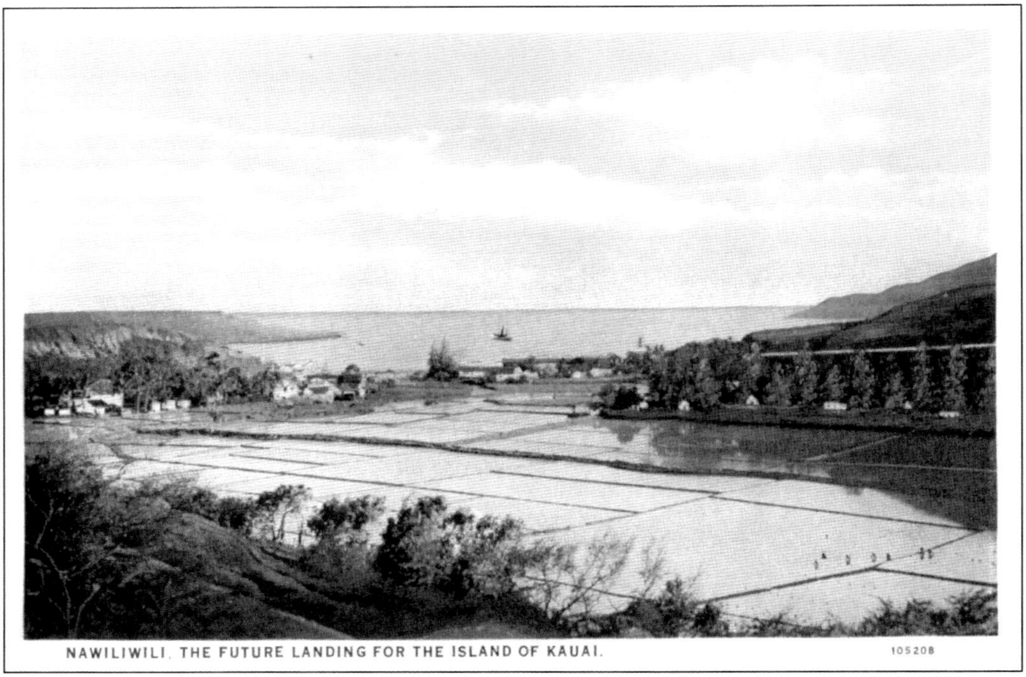

The above card shows the fishing village of Nawiliwili from a high bluff overlooking the Huleia Valley. The road known as Lala Road today is visible at right. The card below is looking back the opposite way, into Huleia Valley that is planted in rice and using the water from Nawiliwili Stream. The ridge with a building seen in outline at left is where Kauai High was established 1914, the first high school on Kauai and the fifth high school in the territory of Hawaii. (Above, 7; below, 0, A.)

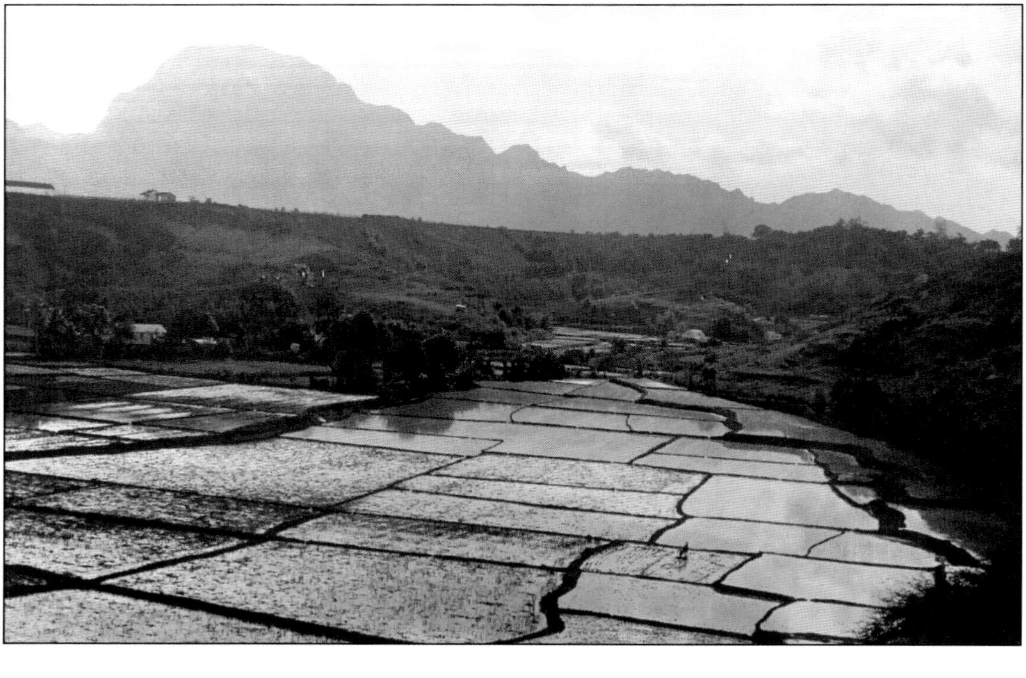

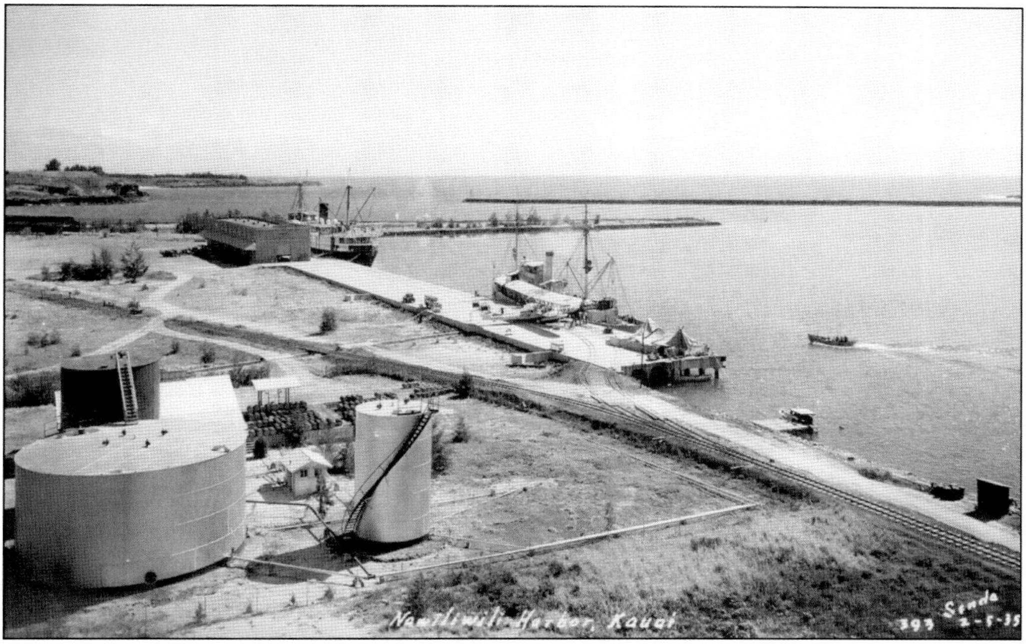

This 1935 postcard (above) was taken to commemorate the newly completed Nawiliwili Harbor. It was dredged, and much dirt was removed from the area to accommodate large ships. The small fishing village that was once there is barely recognizable. Below, the author of this postcard in 1936 writes that they attended a party in "this little village last night". It seems an accurate assessment of Kapaa at the time. Kapaa had a very marshy area that is visible in the center of the card. It was not until after World War II that canals were constructed and the marshland shrank. The tall smokestack at left appears to be left from the old Kapaa Sugar Mill. By 1936, Kapaa supported two pineapple canneries. (Above, 0, A; below, 7.)

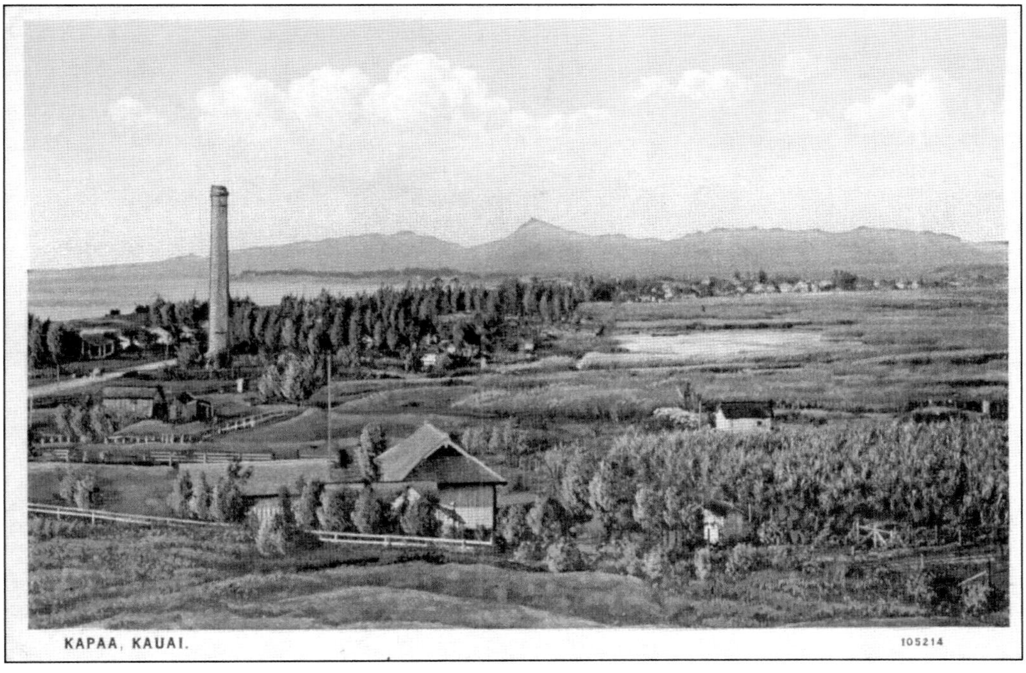

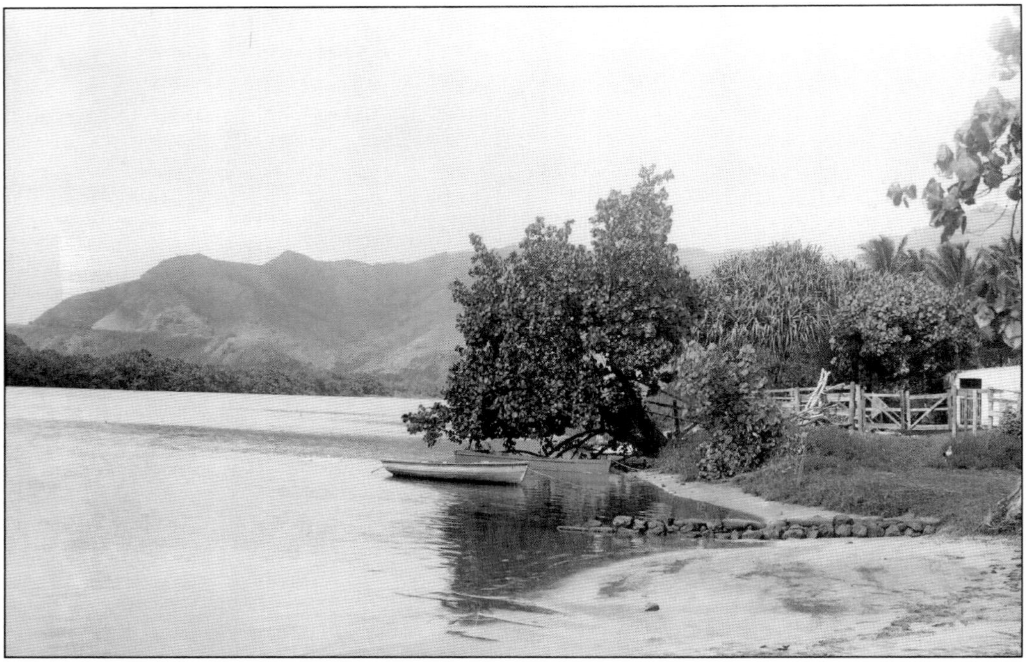

This view of the mouth of the Wailua River (above) is from around 1920, about 30 years before Smith's Boats first set up river tours there. The Wailua Bridge (below) has had many looks. This is the span as it appeared in the 1920s and 1930s. (Above, 0; below, 0, A.)

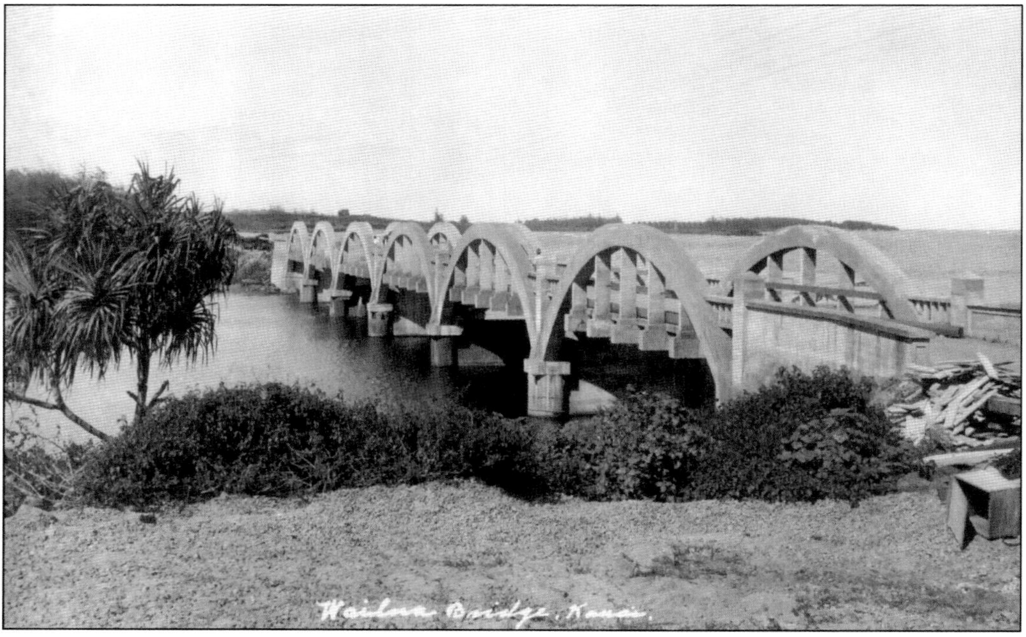

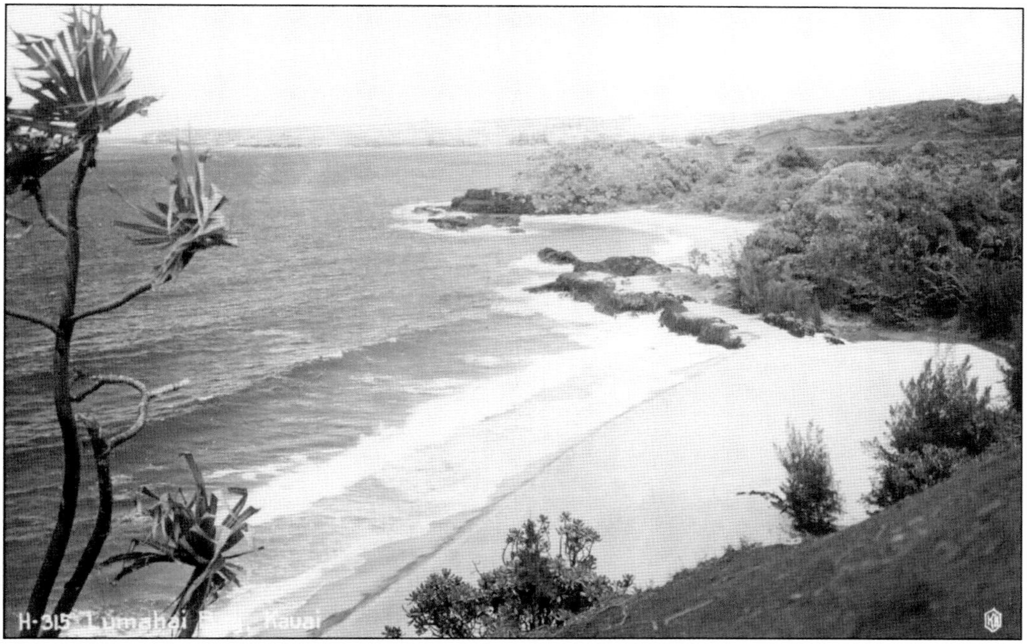

This view of Lumahai Beach (above) is looking back toward Lihue and is far less familiar to people. However, it shows the entire beach that is in two sections; the size of the spit between the two depends on the severity of the winter surf that can take much of the sand away. Lumahai Beach is by far one of Kauai's most picturesque beaches. It is often labeled the most photographed beach on the island. It was used in the movie *South Pacific* as the backdrop for Mitzi Gaynor to sing, "I'm Gonna Wash That Man Right Outta My Hair." For all its beauty, Lumahai is not a very safe beach, particularly during the winter season. The safest section, shown below, is the area sheltered by a rock outcropping. The beach is also known for its multicolored sand that contains bits of olivine. (Above, 0, A; below, 26, J.)

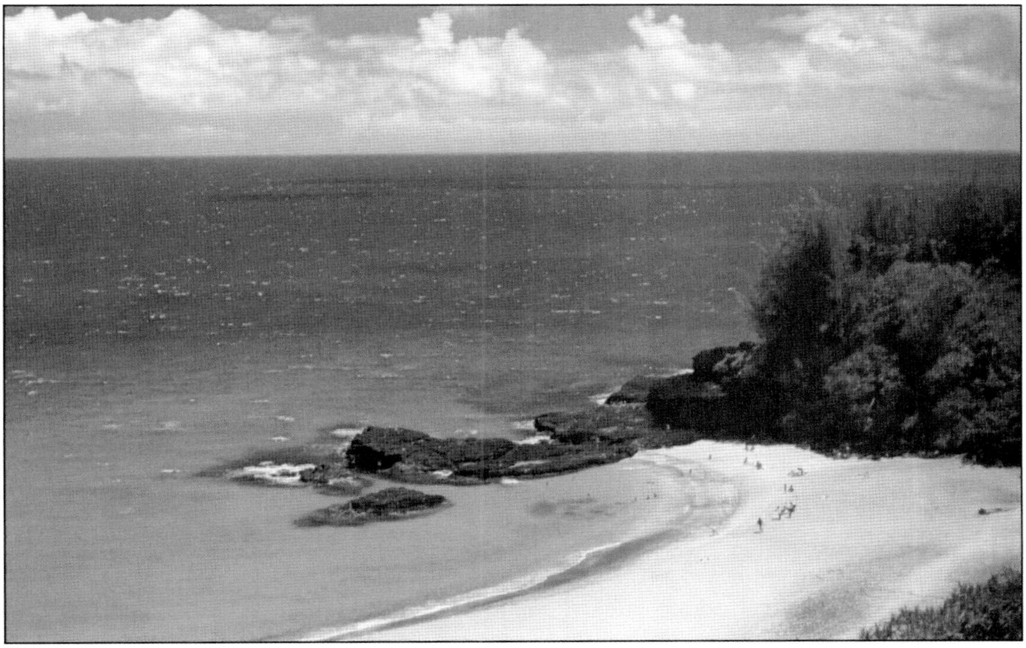

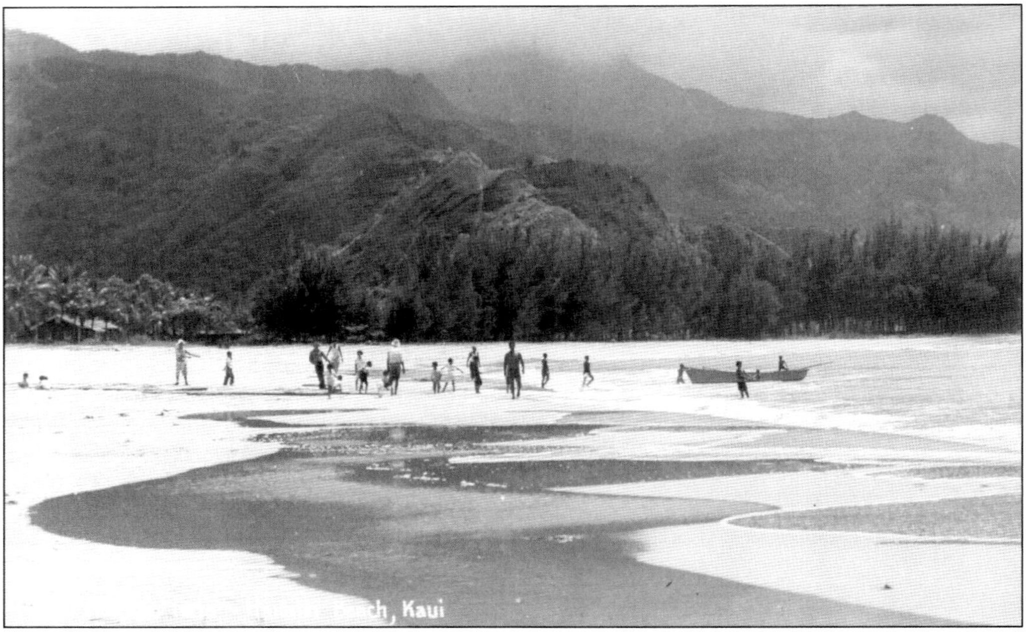

This card captures a *hukilau* in progress in Hanalei Bay. Going along with Hawaiian tradition, anyone who helps with the casting and pulling in of the net is entitled to a share of the catch. (0, A.)

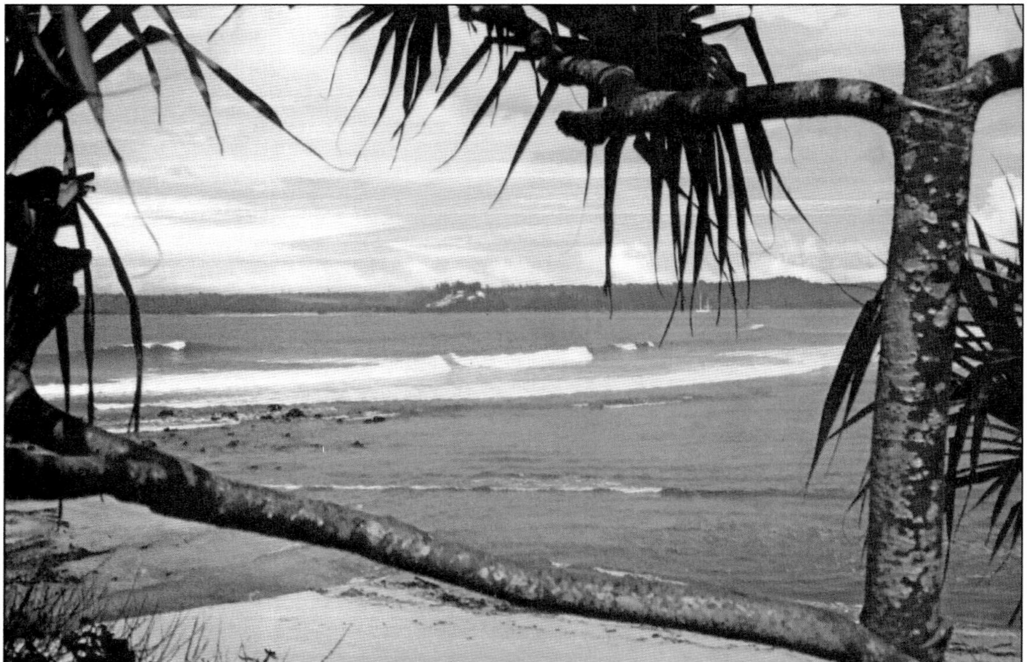

This 1971 view of Hanalei Bay is looking back toward the Hanalei Plantation as it trails down the cliff. *Hanalei* can mean lei work or lei making, or *hana* can mean valley or bay. In any case, Hanalei fits with all those meanings. Its crescent shape is like a lei around the ocean. (22, E.)

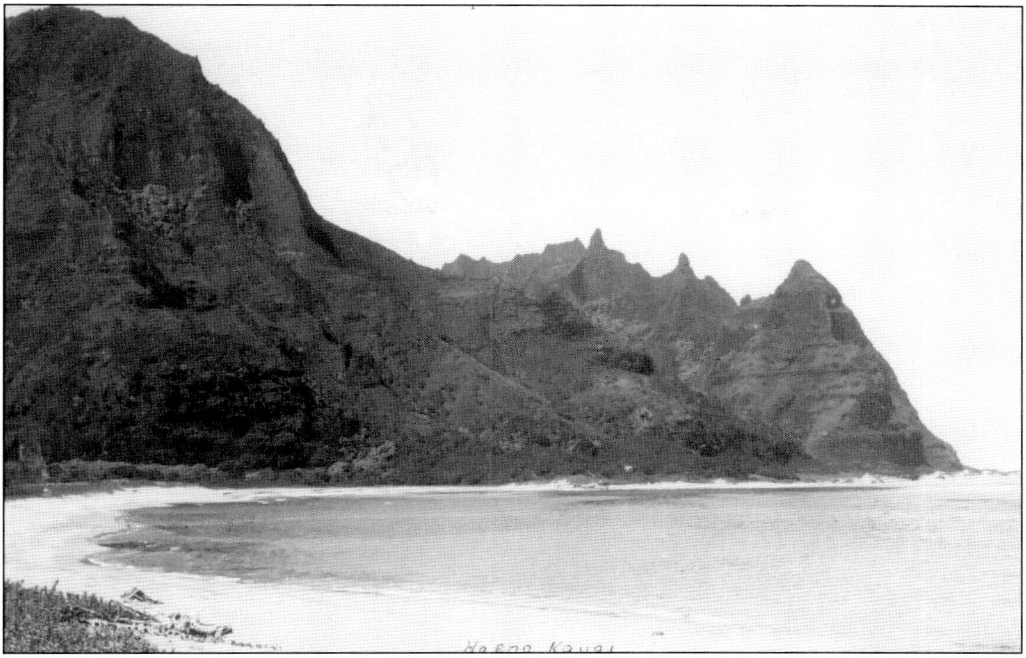

Taken years before the movie *South Pacific* was filmed or the area was dubbed "Bali Hai," this postcard show that the mountains of Haena were very impressive. Just visible in this postcard (below) is the Allerton House above Kee Beach at the end of the road in Haena. It was used as a location in the television miniseries *The Thorn Birds*. In the film, it is a beach on Matlock Island where Fr. Ralph de Bricassart (Richard Chamberlain) and Meggie Cleary (Rachel Ward) have their tryst. (Above, 0, A; below, 16, C.)

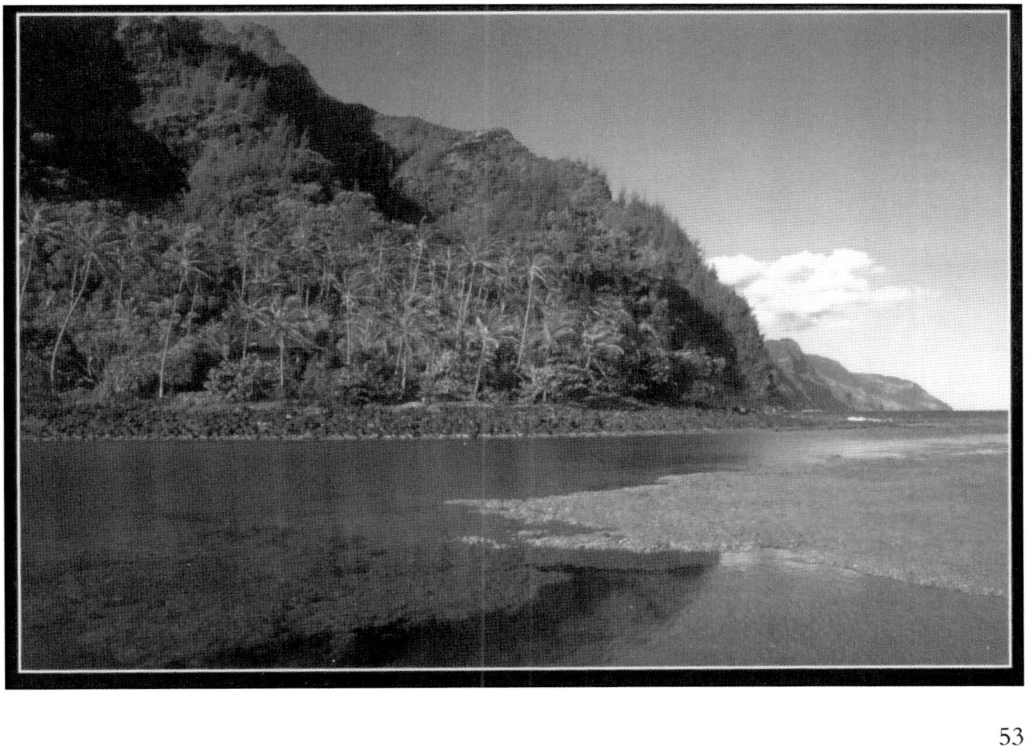

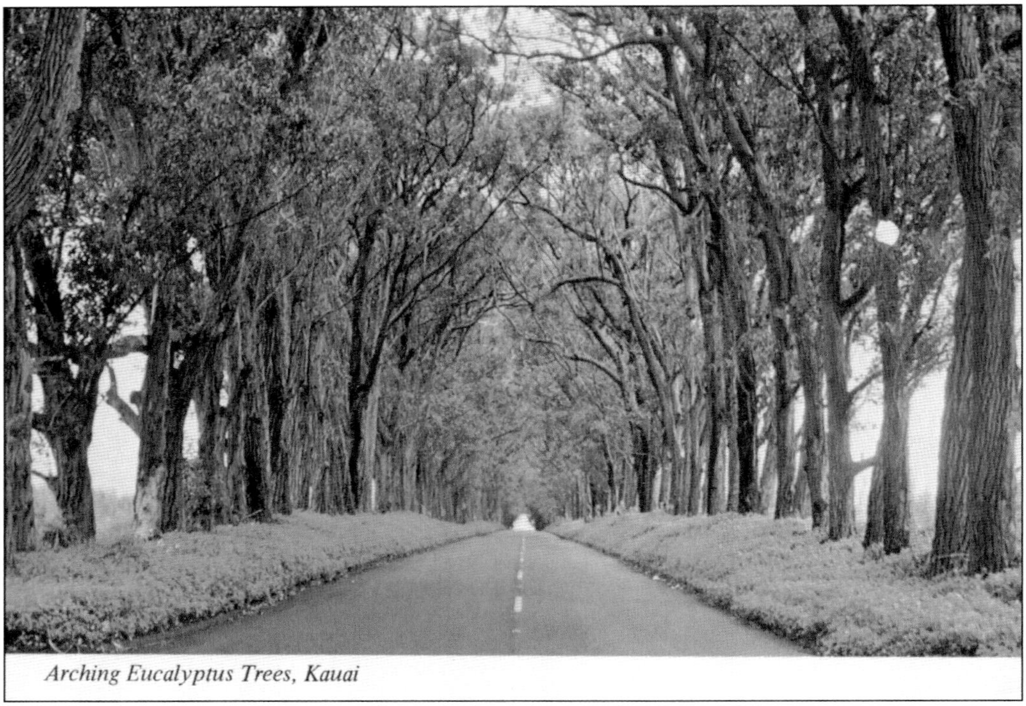

The Tunnel of Trees, part of Maluhia Road, is a favorite view of photographers and painters alike. Since Walter Duncan McBryde planted them as part of a community project in 1911, the canopy has been thinned periodically due to strong winds and two hurricanes. (11.)

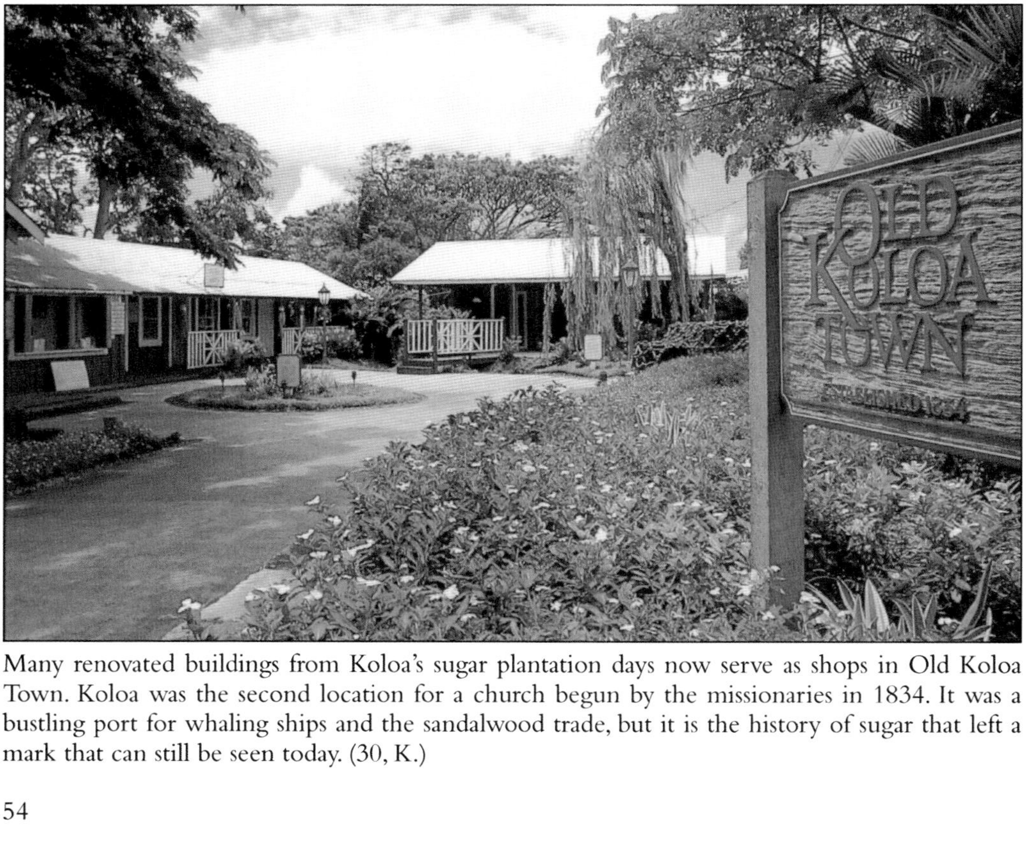

Many renovated buildings from Koloa's sugar plantation days now serve as shops in Old Koloa Town. Koloa was the second location for a church begun by the missionaries in 1834. It was a bustling port for whaling ships and the sandalwood trade, but it is the history of sugar that left a mark that can still be seen today. (30, K.)

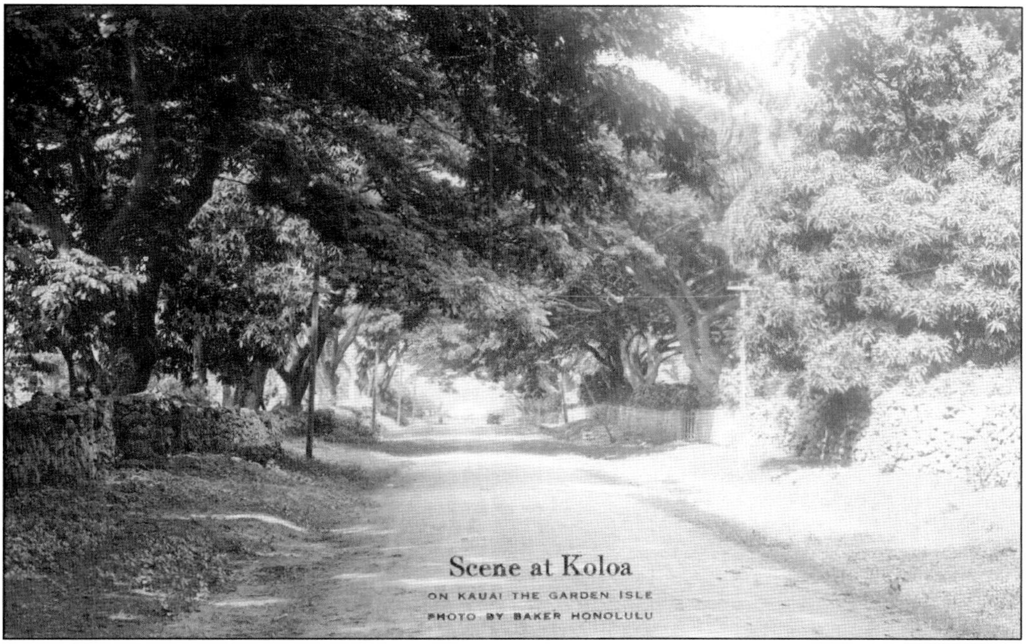

At the turn of the 20th century, each town had its own character that was defined by trees. Koloa was blessed with an abundance of beautiful monkeypod trees that were planted along what is now Poipu Road. This card dates from the 1920s. There are still a few of these old monkeypod trees left, but not the number there once was. (0, L.)

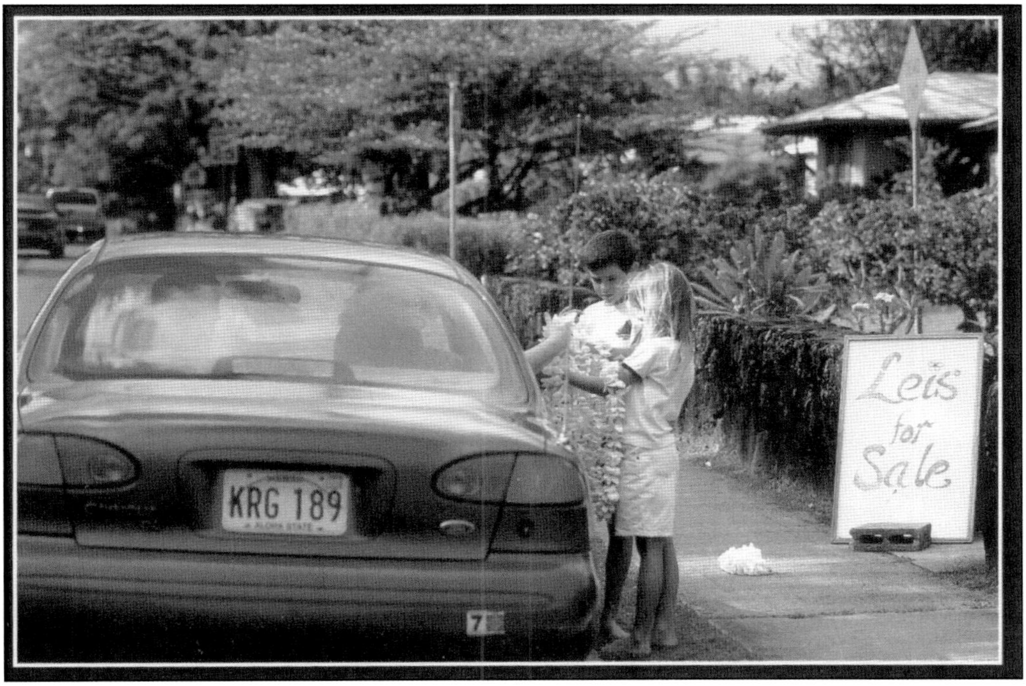

On that same Poipu Road many years later, some unidentified but enterprising children sell leis rather than lemonade to tourists in summer. Mango and avocado stands are also familiar sights. (16, C.)

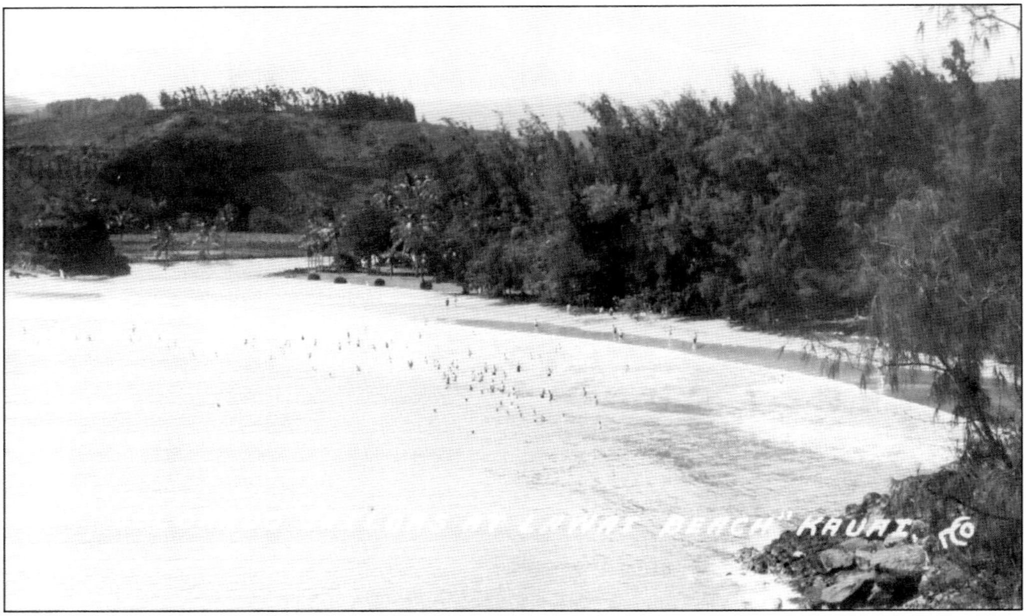

These two views of Lawai Kai were both taken around the time Robert Allerton bought the property at Lawai Kai from the McBryde family. Life partners Robert and John Gregg Allerton moved to Kauai permanently in 1938. In the card above, an aerial view shows the beach and the Lawai river mouth and sailors from the ship USS *Colorado* enjoying some R & R. The area to the right of the river mouth can be seen in the card below from the opposite direction through the grove of coconut palms that shades the lawn running up to the beach. (Above, 0; below, 0, A.)

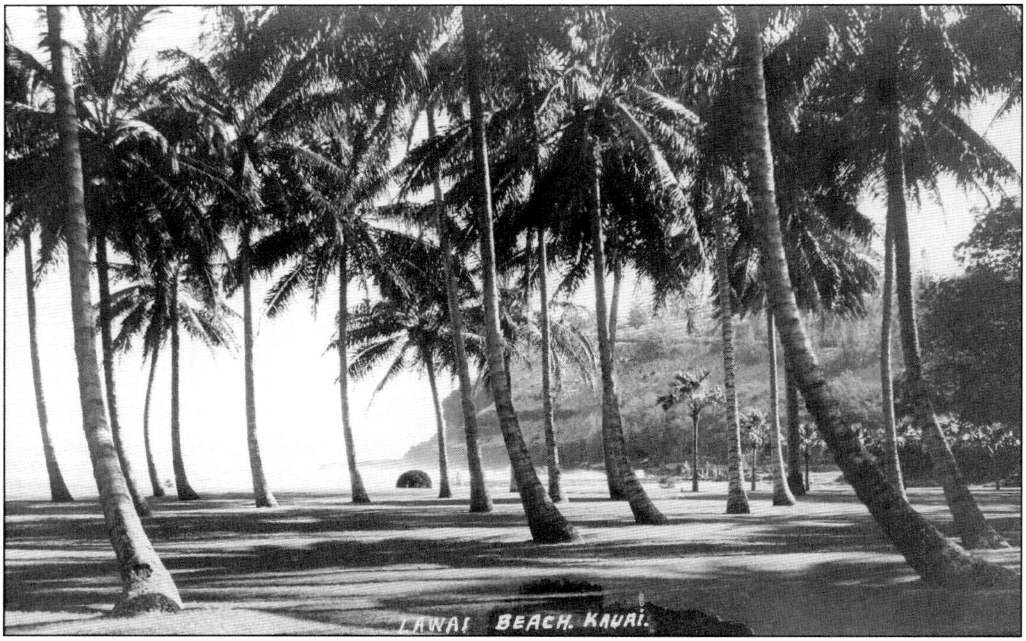

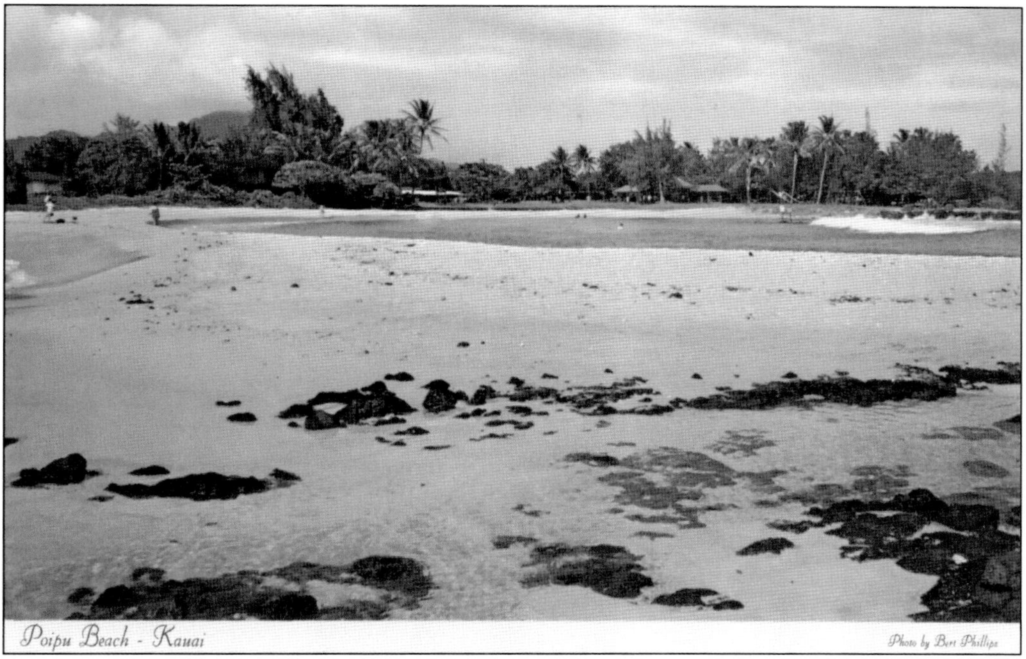

Poipu Beach, on Kauai's south shore, has been voted many times as one of America's best beaches. It is also one of the safest beaches year-round. The spit shown here disappears from time to time due to surf conditions. Before Hurricane Iniki, there were a very large covered pavilion and teeter-totters, shown here, next to the palm trees at right. (22, E.)

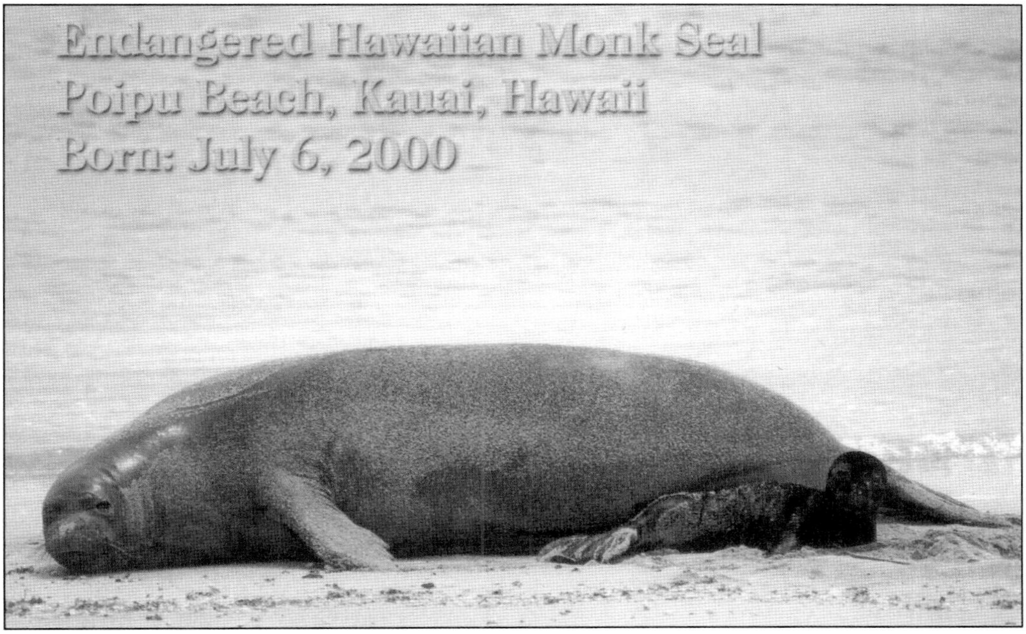

According to the postcard, this Hawaiian monk seal mother and pup were photographed resting just eight hours after birth on July 6, 2000, on Poipu Beach. These seals, found only within the Hawaiian Archipelago, have thrived for 13 million years and are now declining at an alarming rate. It is believed that as few as 1,200 Hawaiian monk seals exist in 2011. The National Oceanic and Atmospheric Administration (NOAA) coordinates semiannual counting of the herd. (16, C.)

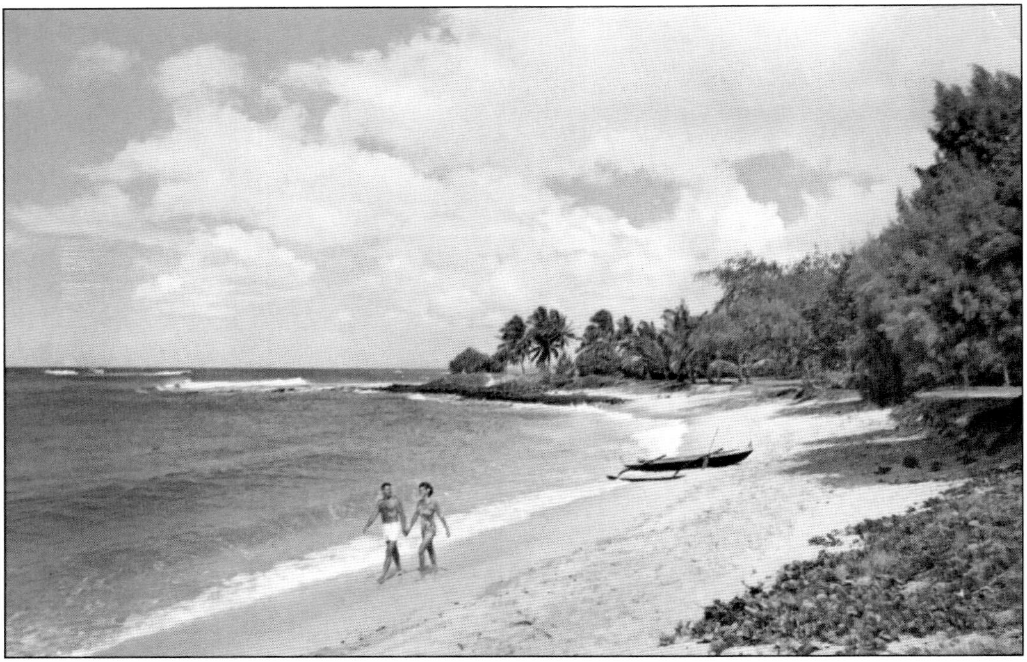

This card from the early 1950s shows the area farthest from Poipu Beach Park. In this timeframe, these beachgoers were walking away from the old Waiohai Hotel. (31, M.)

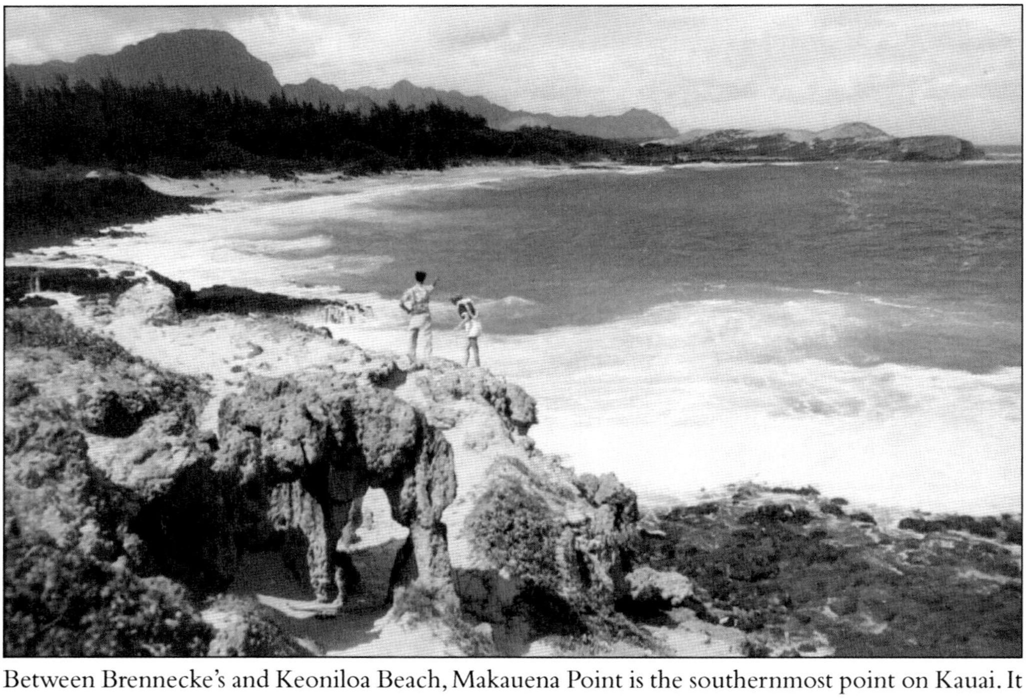

Between Brennecke's and Keoniloa Beach, Makauena Point is the southernmost point on Kauai. It is an ideal spot to watch for whales during the winter season. This was published before the Grand Hyatt hotel was built on the beach visible in the distance. (32, N.)

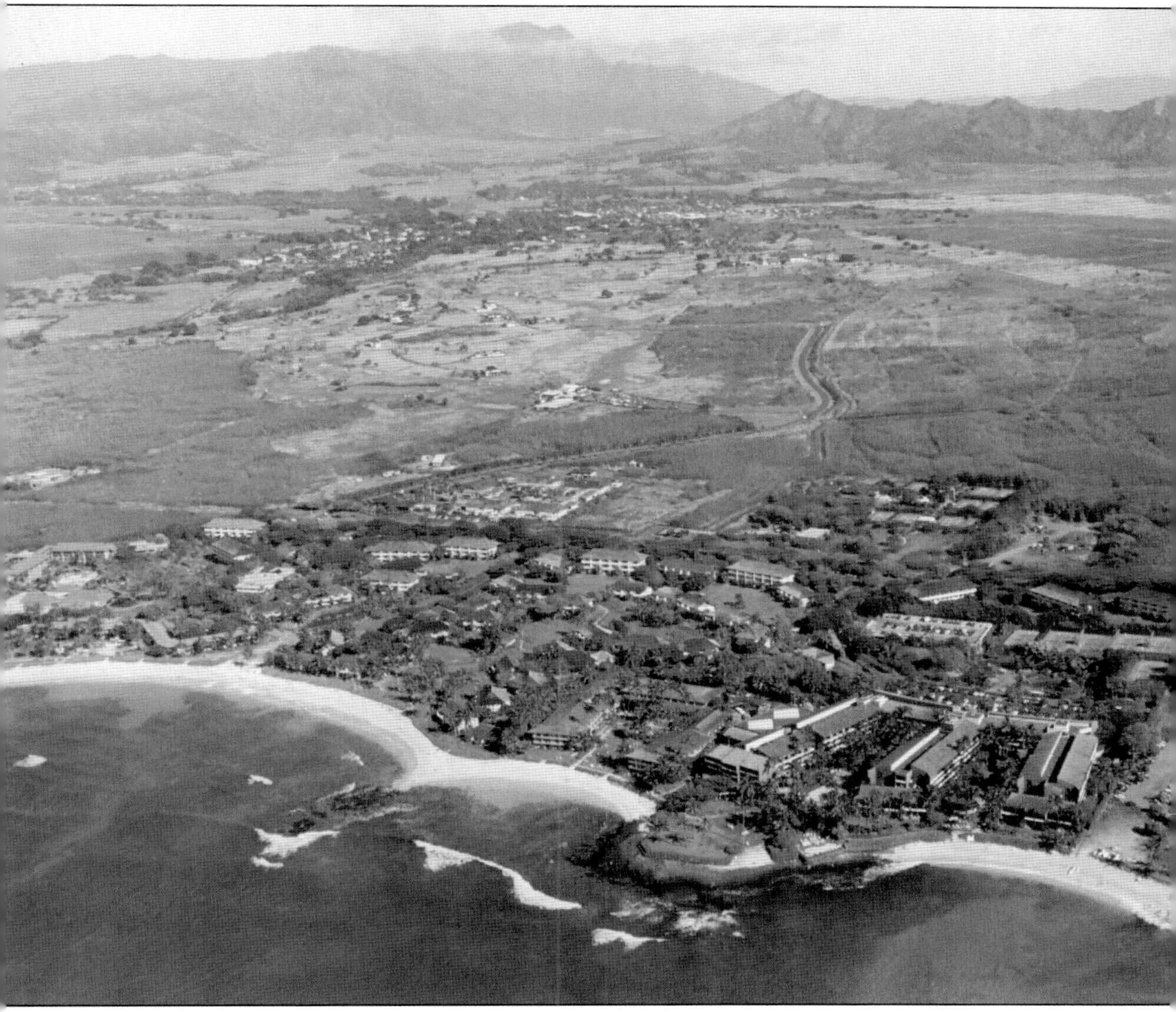

This postcard shows an aerial view of the Poipu area in 1988. Starting in the lower right-hand area and going left, the properties include the following: a very large Waiohai resort complex, with its unique oceanside pool; the Poipu Beach Hotel; the much expanded Kiahuna; the flat square roof of the Plantation Garden Restaurant at the left edge of the property; and the Sheraton, which also has increased in size from its early beginnings. In the center of the card is the Poipu Shopping Village. Up the road from there, the white buildings standing alone are Joe's on the Green. The Kiahuna Golf Course looks very new and is not filled in with homes along the greens. The distant peak surrounded by clouds is Mount Waialeale. (0.)

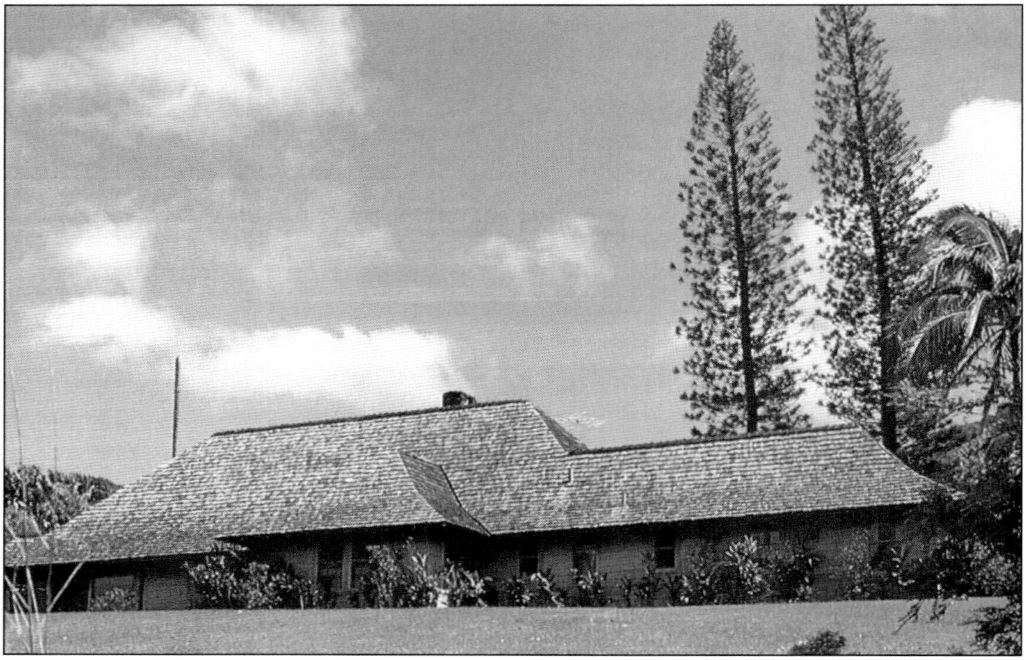

Built in 1932, the main house at Olu Pua Gardens was once the Kauai Pineapple Plantation manager's home. Ray W. Lauchis turned the 12.5 acres into a botanical garden. It was then purchased by Athalie Richardson Irvine Clarke in 1978. While owned by Clarke, it was a popular island attraction. Several renowned guests such as Robert Schuller of the Crystal Cathedral and former president Richard M. Nixon stayed there. (0.)

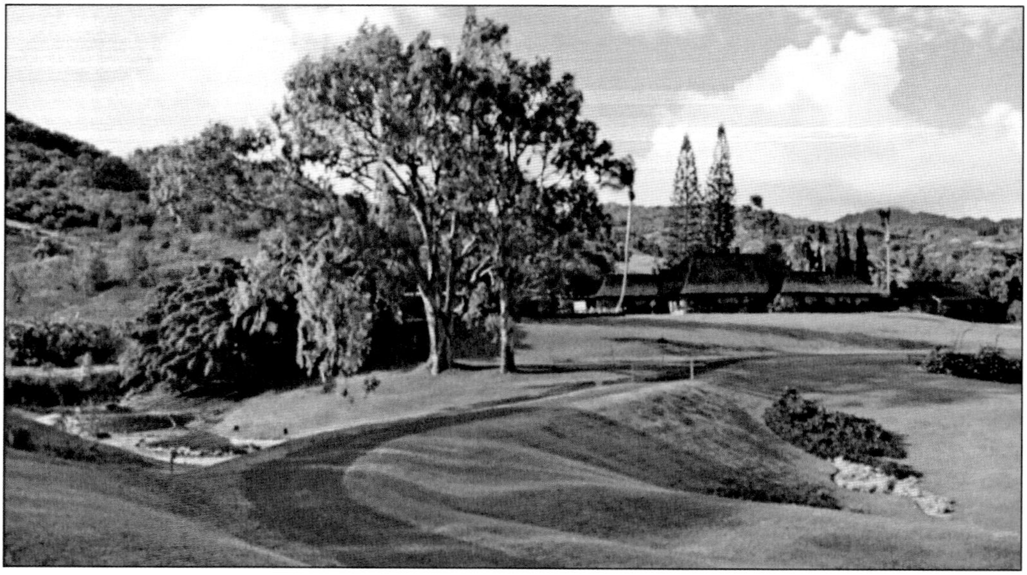

Olu Pua means "at peace among the flowers," and this was once dubbed as *the* garden to see on the way to Waimea Canyon. At one time, it boasted over 5,000 different species of plants, from herbs to orchids to palms. When Athalie Richardson Irvine Clarke owned it, the garden flourished giving educational tours but was also a getaway for her and friends while she lived in Corona del Mar in Newport Beach, California. Unfortunately, Clarke no longer owns the property. The garden no longer gives tours, nor is it open to the public. (25.)

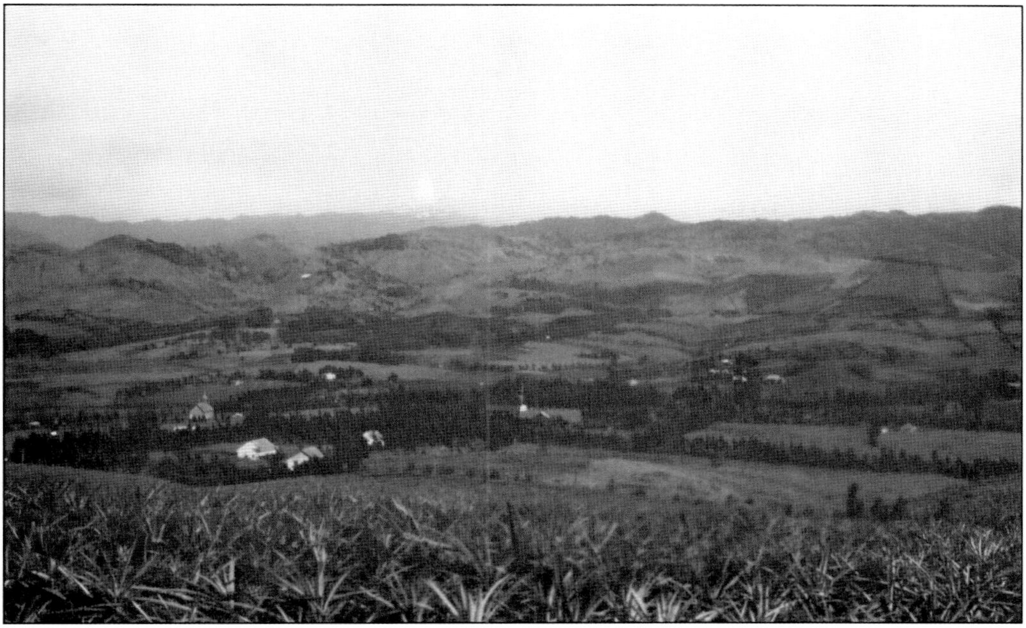

Kalaheo is seen from Kukuiolono Park area about 1910, when it still belonged to Walter Duncan McBryde. The new Holy Cross Church that was established in 1909 is on the left, and in the center is Kalaheo School, which had recently moved to that location. It celebrated its 100th year anniversary in 2004. Note the pineapple in the foreground. Kalaheo, at the time, was planted in acres of pineapple. (0.)

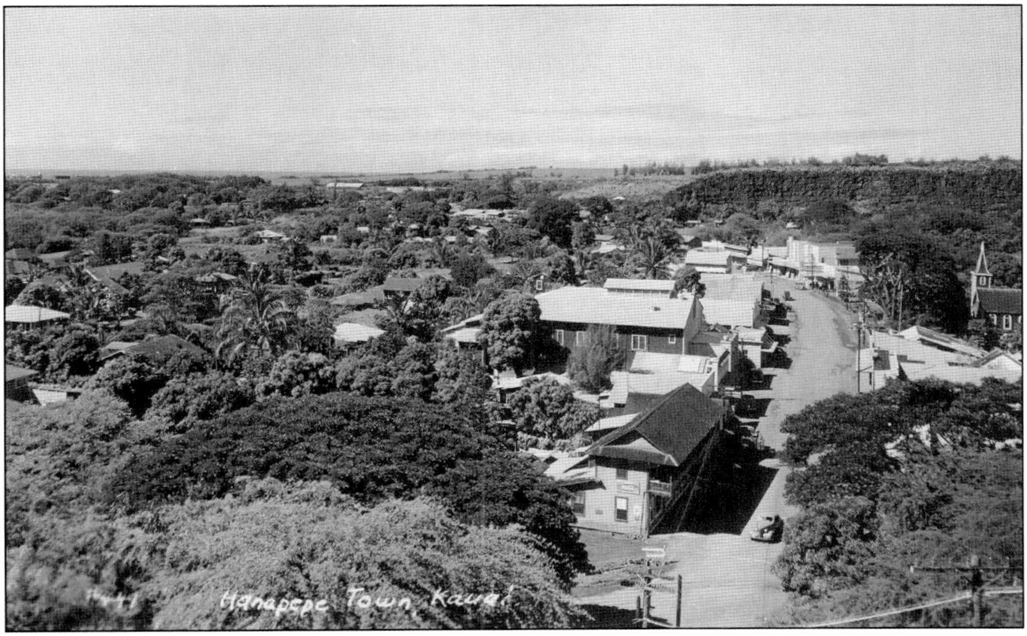

Hanapepe looked like this in the 1940s. The large barn-like structure on the left is the Hanapepe Theatre, and across the street is the Hanapepe Hawaiian Congregational Church. In the distance at right are a Shell gas station and the Aloha Theatre. (0.)

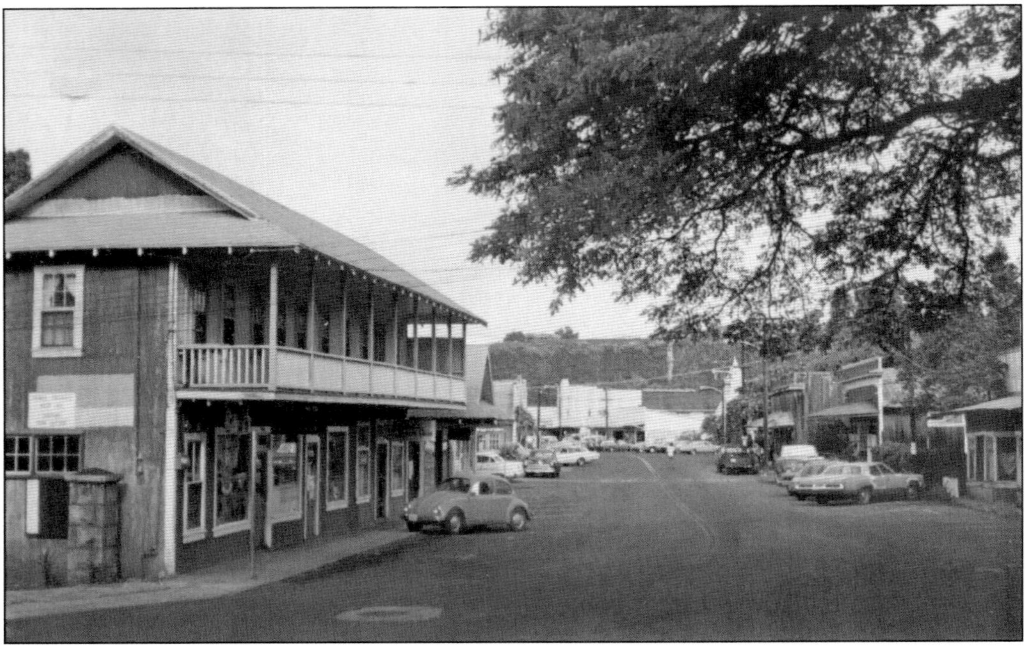

Hanapepe is about 20 years older in this postcard. The same buildings are there but have a more worn appearance. Still known as the "Biggest Little Town on Kauai," it does not have the hustle and bustle of the past except on Friday nights, when the town is alive with live entertainment and many artists showing their crafts in their galleries. In the 1980s, the area shown here became Dungloe Village in north Queensland, Australia, for the miniseries *The Thorn Birds*. (11, A.)

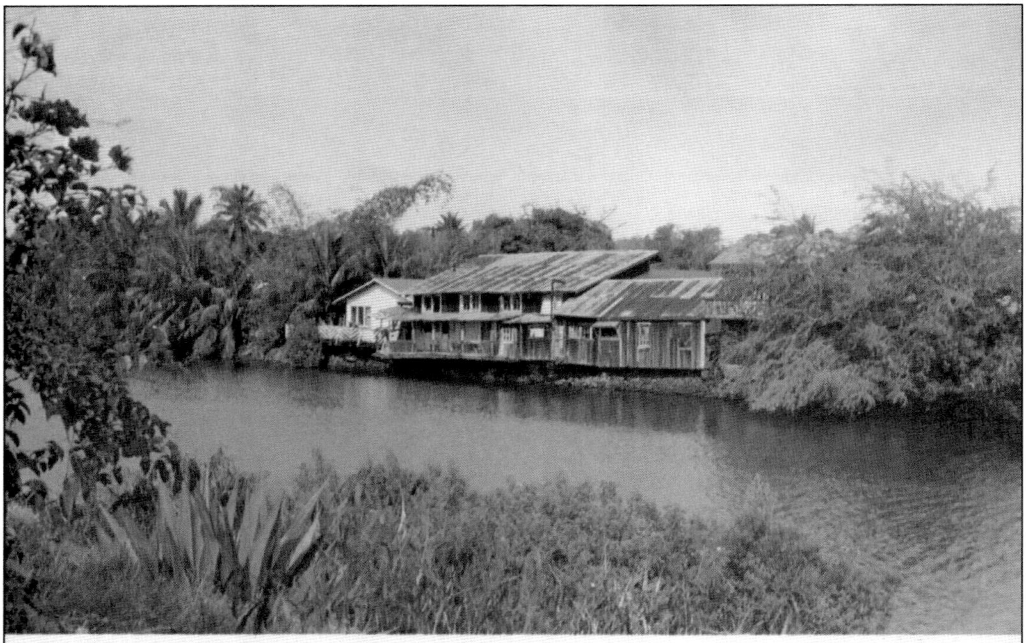

Old Section of Hanapepe Town, Kauai

The old section of Hanapepe still exists and remains picturesque. Most of the tin roofs are now gone. This post–World War II free roofing was no match for two hurricanes that have blown through Kauai since. (11, A.)

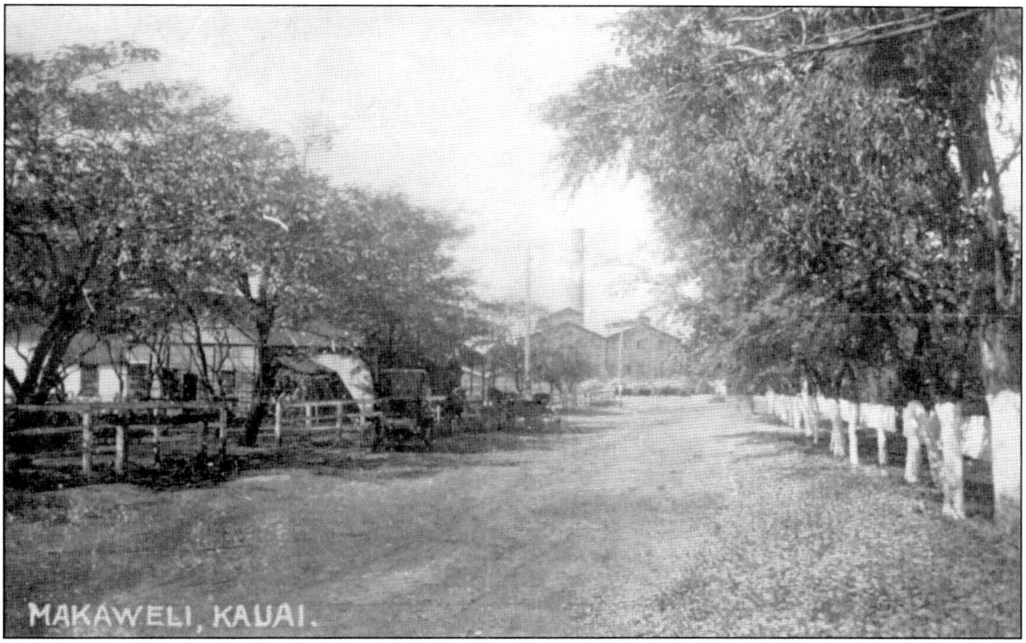

Today, this area is called Kaumakani, but back in the 1920s it was known as Makaweli. Just visible at the end of the road is the Makaweli Mill. This is the same street that today boasts lampposts and sidewalks, a rarity on Kauai. (29.)

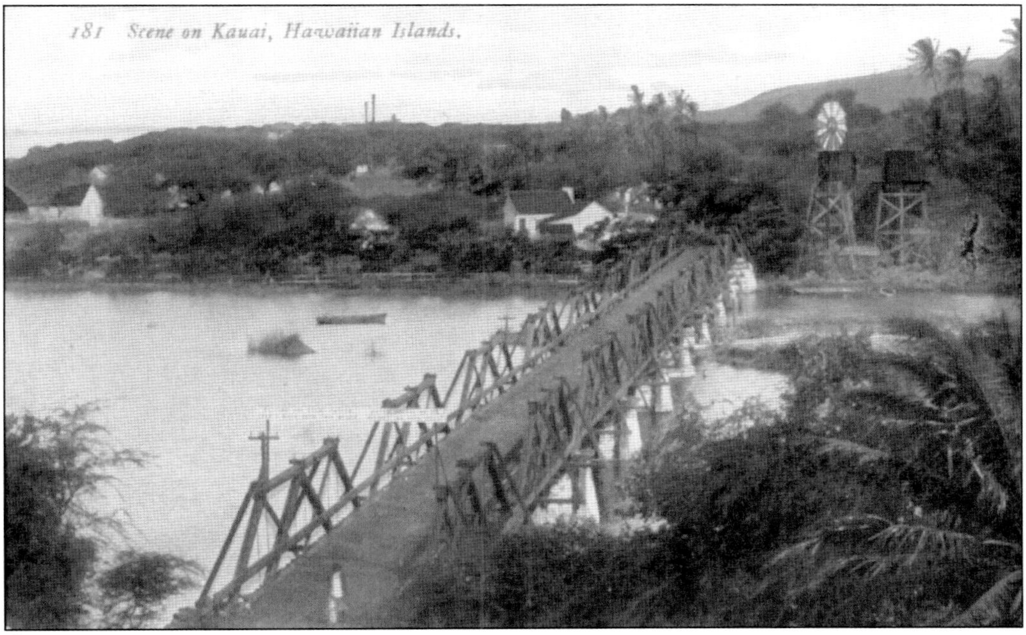

This bridge over the Waimea River dates back to the 1890s. It was further upriver from where the bridge is today. The smokestacks from the Waimea Sugar Mill Company can be seen in the distance. (4.)

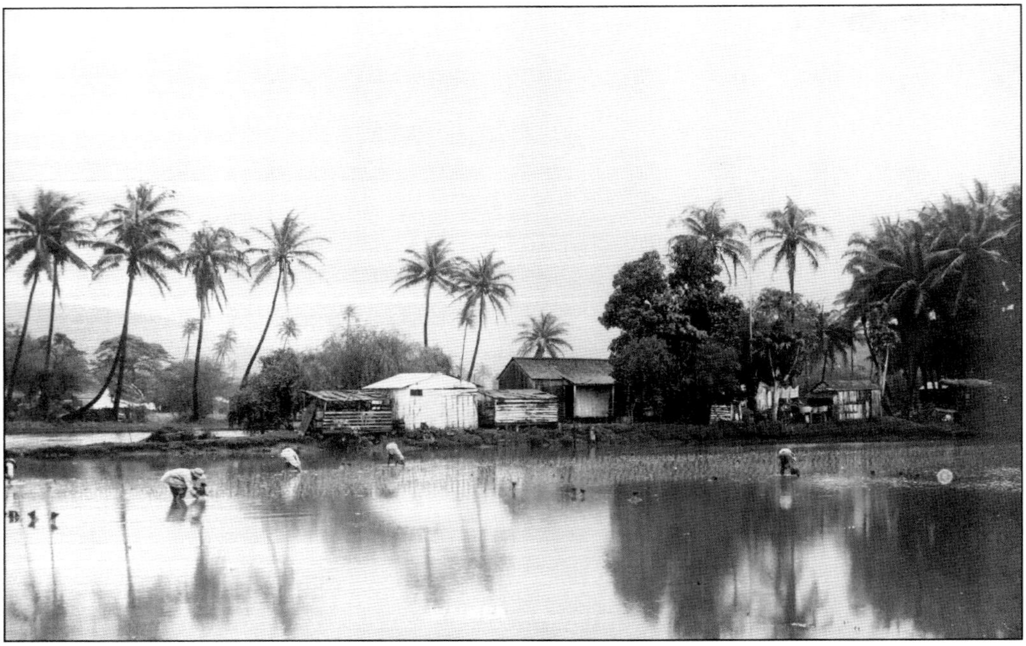

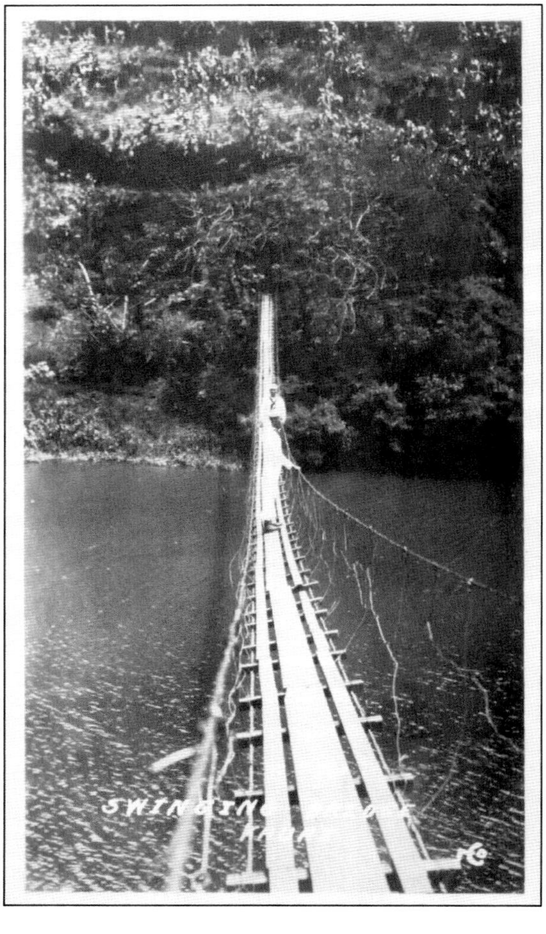

Waimea in the early 1900s had a large portion of town planted in rice. As at Hanalei, taro was replaced by rice in the 1850s. Waimea had a rice mill. Now, the area is once again planted in taro. The area where this photograph was taken is approximately behind where Big Save Market is today. (0, A.)

The Waimea Swinging Bridge was a cable footbridge over the Waimea River in Waimea Valley. It provided the only access to the other side of the river in heavy flooding. The bridge was destroyed in a storm and has been rebuilt as a suspension bridge. (0.)

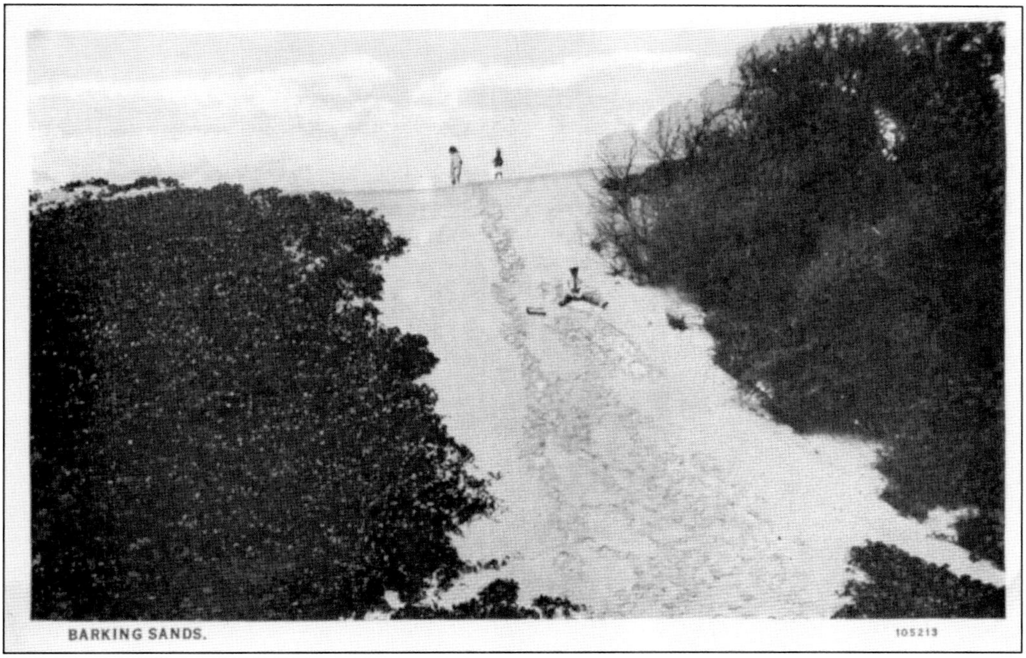

From the earliest days, Keonekani O Nohili, more popularly known as Barking Sands, has lured visitors to this remote area in hopes of hearing the sands "bark," despite an extremely rough dirt road. Actually, the sound is made when the hot sand is compressed. Barking Sands stretches from Nohili Point to the beginning of the rugged Na Pali coast. From this area, there are many great views. (7.)

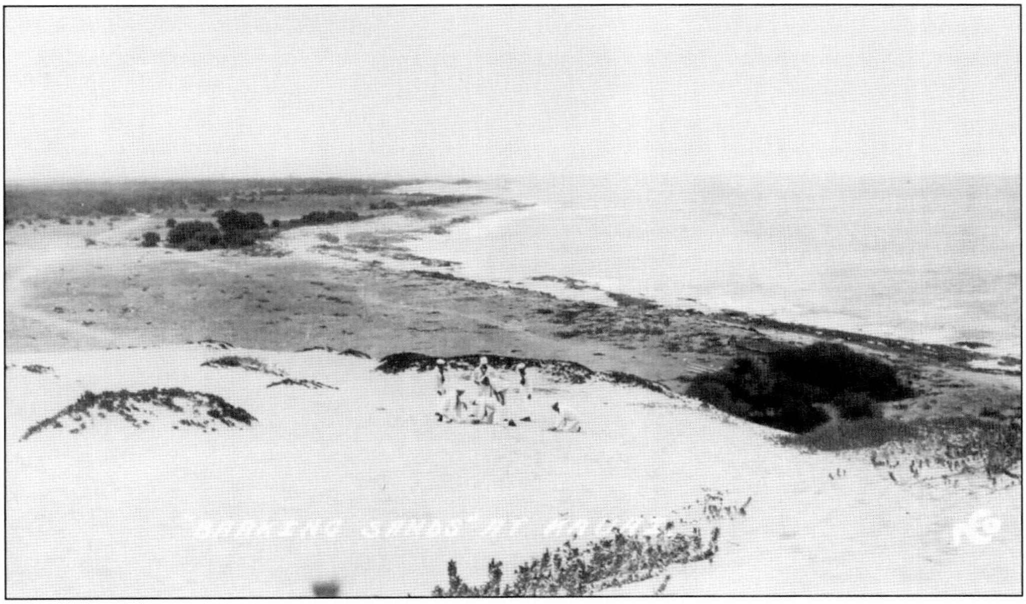

These sailors from the USS *Colorado* appear to be at the Nohili Point Dune area looking south toward Mana Point during the 1940s. The ship missed the attack on Pearl Harbor because it was having a complete overhaul on the West Coast in 1942. It reported for duty at Pearl Harbor a year later. This battleship was then very active in the war in the Pacific. (0.)

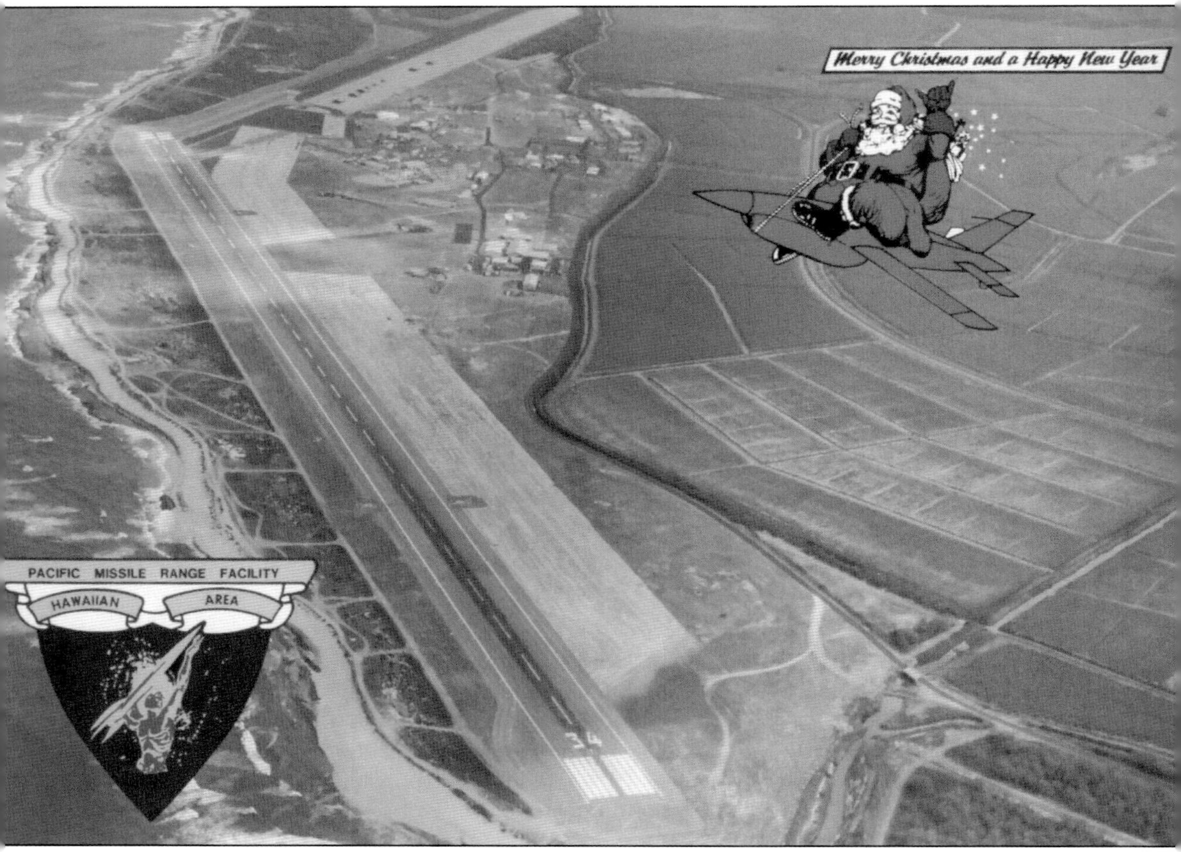

PMRF stands for Pacific Missile Range Facility. The original soil cement runway was constructed in 1930, and the first asphalt overlay was completed in 1941. There have been several additional overlays since, with the most recent being completed in 2010. The runway is 6,006 feet long and 150 feet wide with 100 feet overrun at each side. Even before the first permanent runway was built, Kekaha Sugar prepared a long runway at Barking Sands in preparation for the airplane *The Southern Cross* to fly its 3,180-mile leg to Suva, Fiji, as part of a bid to fly the first trans-Pacific flight from the mainland US to Australia in 1928. Wheeler Army Air Field's runway on Oahu was too short for it to take off fully loaded. The crew of *The Southern Cross* succeeded in its quest. It took them 83 hours and 72 minutes to cover 7,230 miles. (33.)

Five

WATERFALLS AND OTHER NATURAL ATTRACTIONS

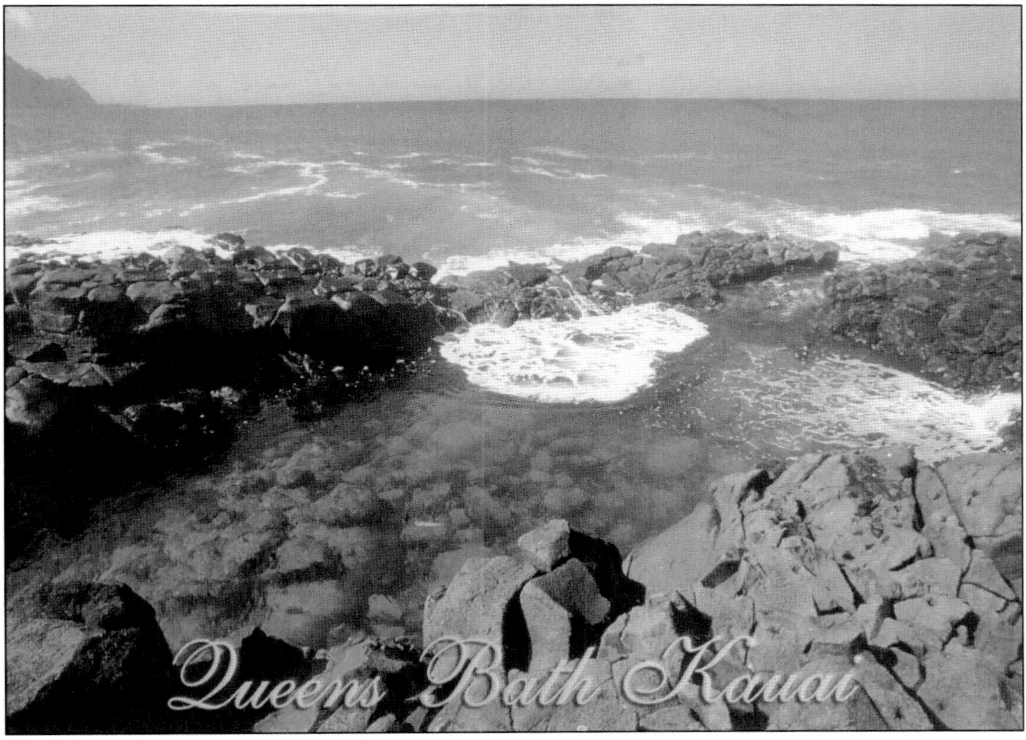

Queens Bath is an idyllic, natural lava rock pool in summer on Kauai's North Shore; however, it is extremely dangerous in winter when the surf is high. (37, U.)

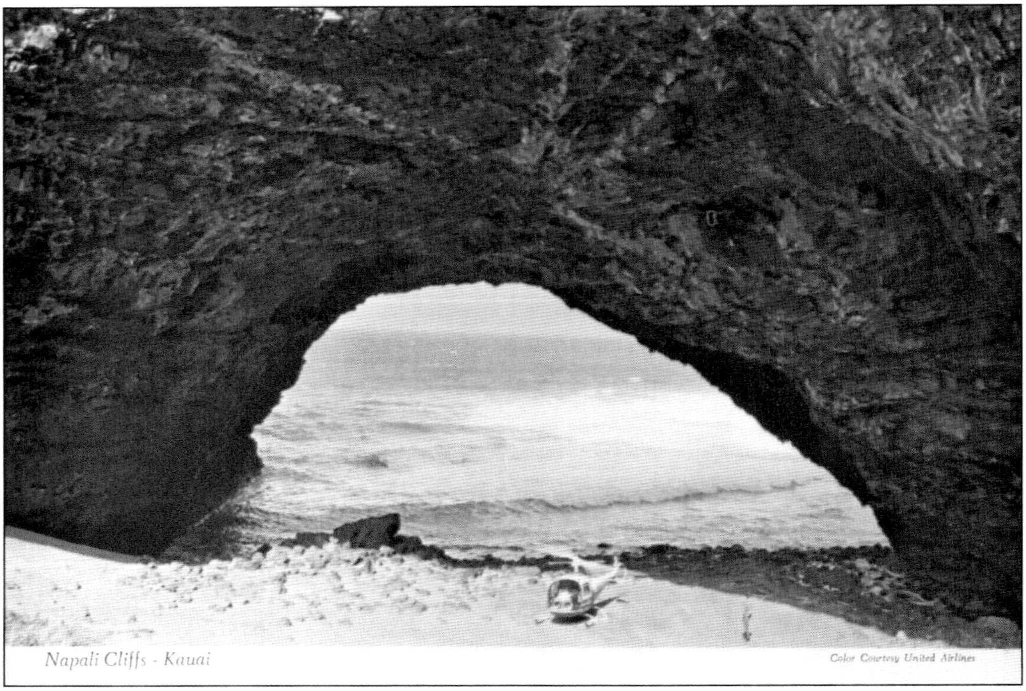

Shown above, the Honopu Arch along the Na Pali Coast is a famous natural landmark. The volcanic rock formation dwarfs the helicopter, revealing its massive size. ***Honopu*** means "conch bay." The arch connects two beaches that would otherwise be separated. In the early days of helicopter tours on Kauai, landings near the arch were allowed. With more and more companies giving tours and as people became more environmentally aware, the landings were stopped. During the whaling days of Kauai's history, Honopu was a populated Hawaiian community that was known for olona ropes that were stronger and lasted longer than the hemp ones that were made in New England. (Above, 17; below, 12, T.)

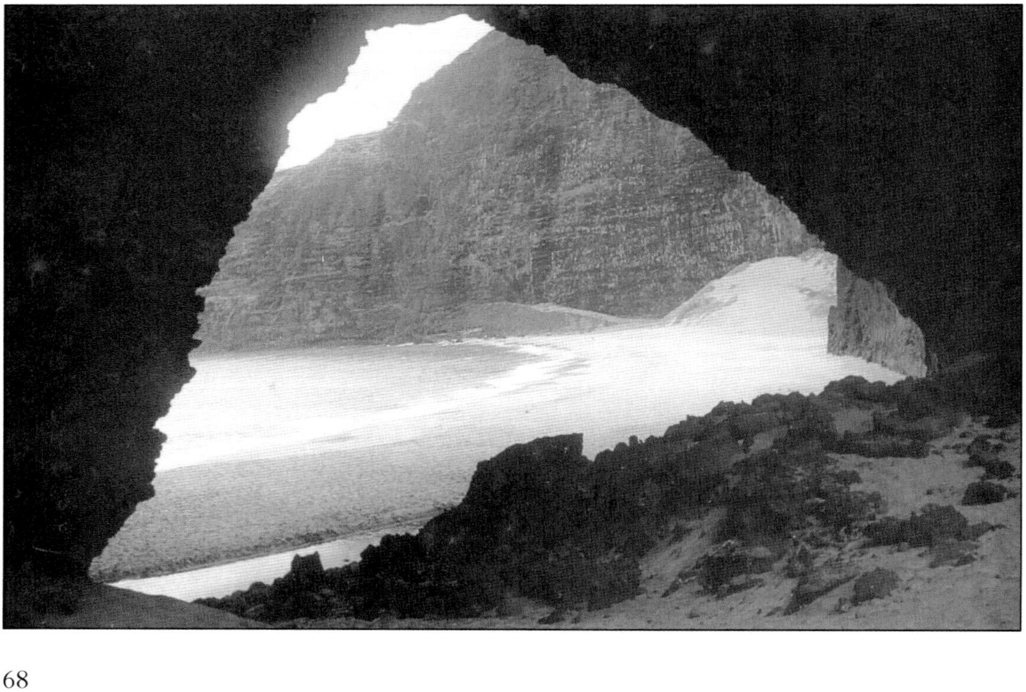

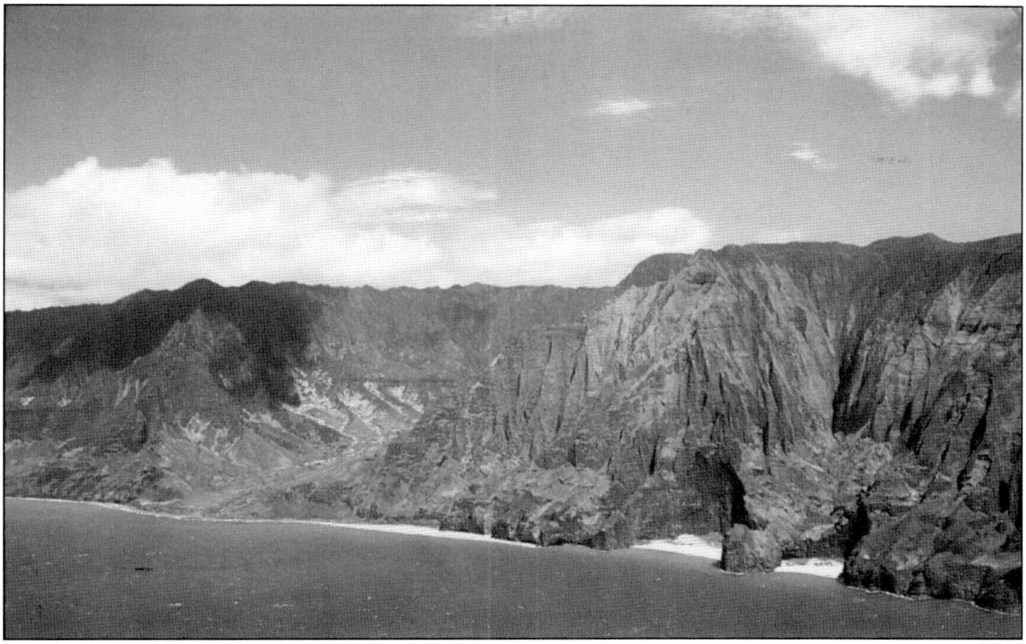

This1964 aerial postcard (above) of the Na Pali coastline seen in many movies shows the green Kalalau Valley on the left and the rocky Honopu Valley on the right. The arch is located in the paw-like area between the two beaches at right. Below, the Captain Zodiac tour is heading out of one of the more spectacular caves along the Na Pali Coast known as Koamano, named after the Shark God and supposedly one of his homes. The wide entrance leads to an inner chamber that is exposed to the sky. There is another story about the cave in which Pele had carved it out for her home while on Kauai. An enemy found Pele and tried to drown her, and she destroyed the roof hoping to crush him. The Captain Zodiac tours began in 1974 on Kauai. The company is now in Kona on the Big Island. (Above, 36, N; below, 12.)

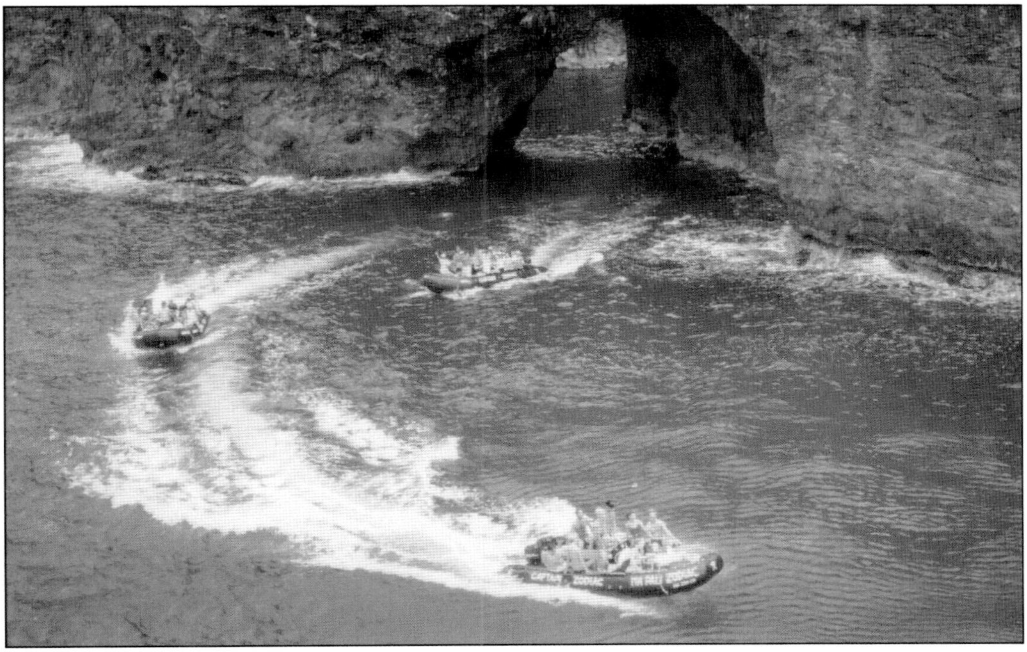

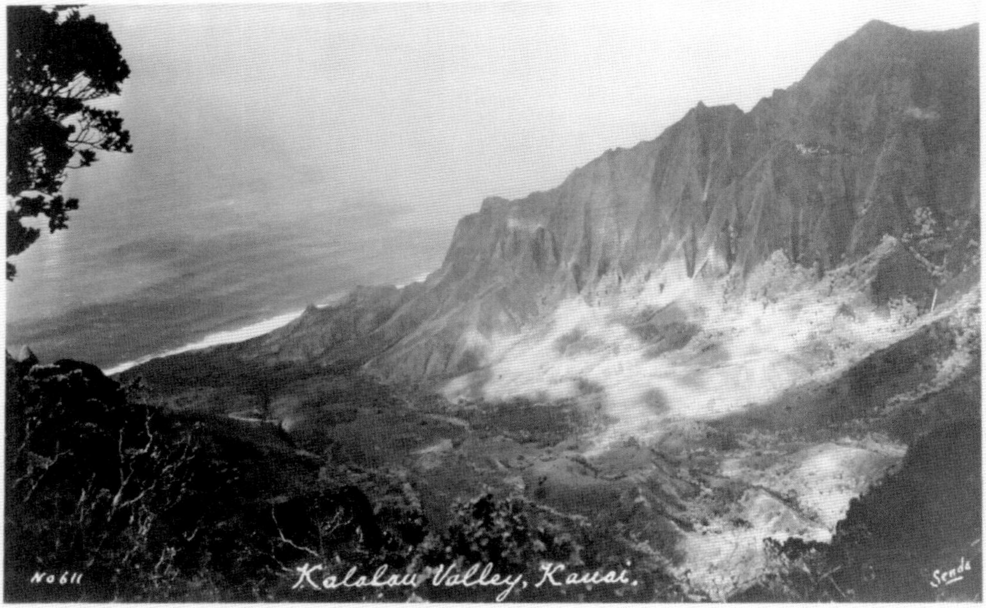

Kalalau Valley (above) was a favorite of W.J. Senda to photograph. It is quite possibly one of the most dramatic views on Kauai. On a sunny day, one can enjoy a panoramic vista from 4,000 feet down to the beach at Kalalau below. The valley is two miles across. In ancient times, it was a highly populated place. If one hikes into the valley, stonework and terraced areas can be found everywhere. Below, this view of Kalalau Valley was taken from a helicopter. At the right side of the photograph, the lookout and visitors are visible. On a clear day, the view is awesome; but just as quickly, the weather can change, clouds sweep in, and nothing is visible. (Above, 0, A; below, 11.)

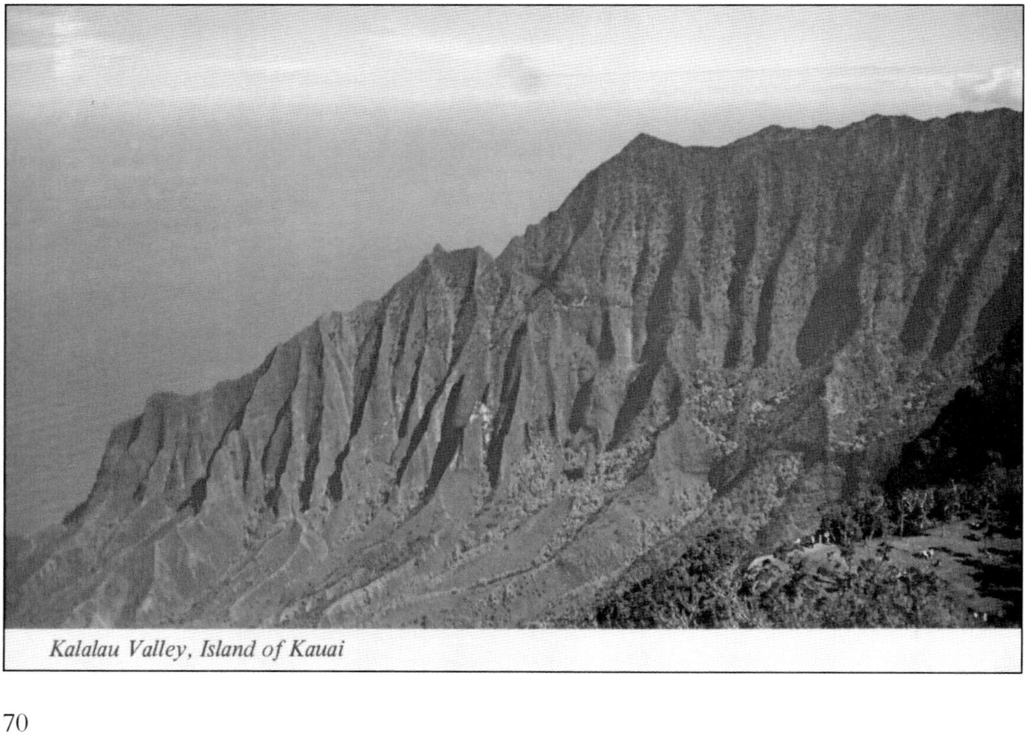

Kalalau Valley, Island of Kauai

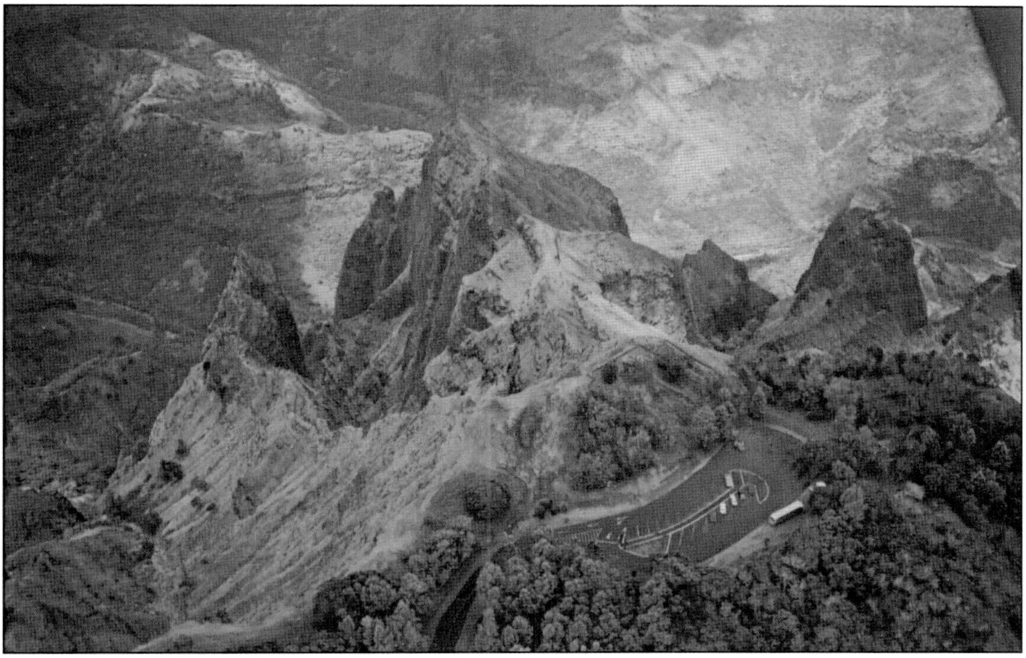

This view above, taken from a helicopter, shows the Waimea Canyon Lookout. At 3,400 feet above sea level, it has spectacular views from two vantage points. The postcard below taken in the 1930s from the same lookout shows multiple horizontal layers of lava flows that were built up over time. These flows have been dated at about 4 million years ago. Though it appears to be sedimentary rock, it is volcanic. Two interesting things to note are that the observer is standing above the Waimea Canyon looking northeast into the Poomau Canyon with its distinctive pinnacles, and lava flows on the west side of the canyon, the side the photographer was standing on, are about a million years older than the east side, which is different from most canyons that have similarly aged rocks on both sides. (Above, 22, R; below, 0, A.)

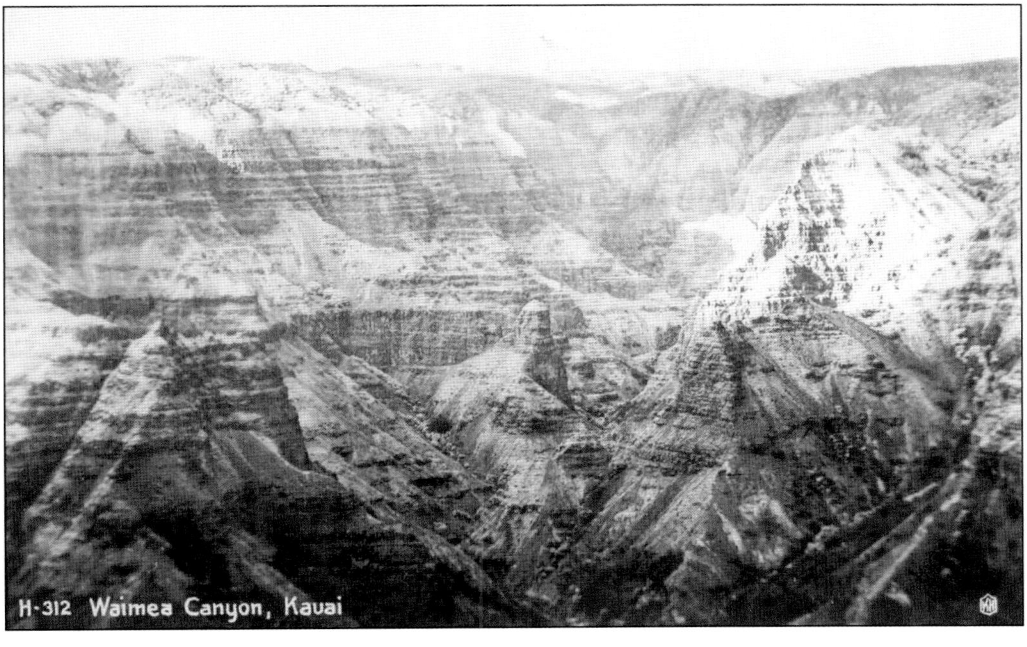

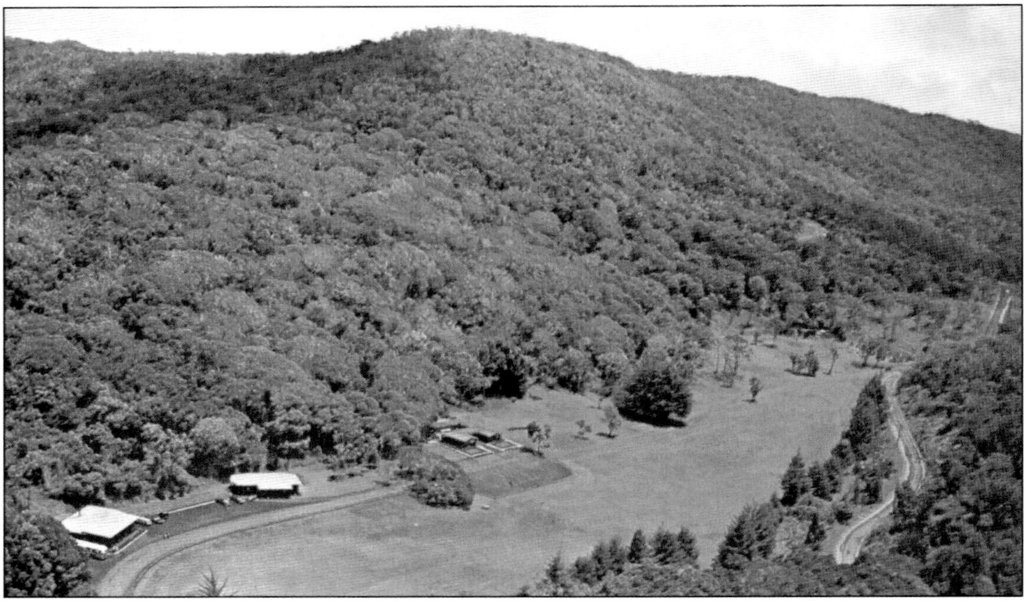

Kokee State Park (above) has been a state facility since 1953 and covers 4,345 acres. This aerial view shows the Kokee Lodge (bottom left) and, further up, the Kokee Natural History Museum. These are two recycled World War II–era buildings that were relocated to the site in Kanaloahuluhulu Meadow. From these humble beginnings, the museum sees roughly 110,000 visitors a year. The card below boasts that Waimea Canyon is a "scenic masterpiece" and "likens it to the Grand Canyon of Colorado, though only a mile or so in width. With its wonderful castled crags, peaks, precipices, and branching gorges, running back into the heart of the island where probably a vast crater used to be, all marveolusly colored. The "Canyon" covers some 25 square miles in area and offers a bounteous reward of health and inspiration to those who thoroughly explore it." (Above, 34; below, 7.)

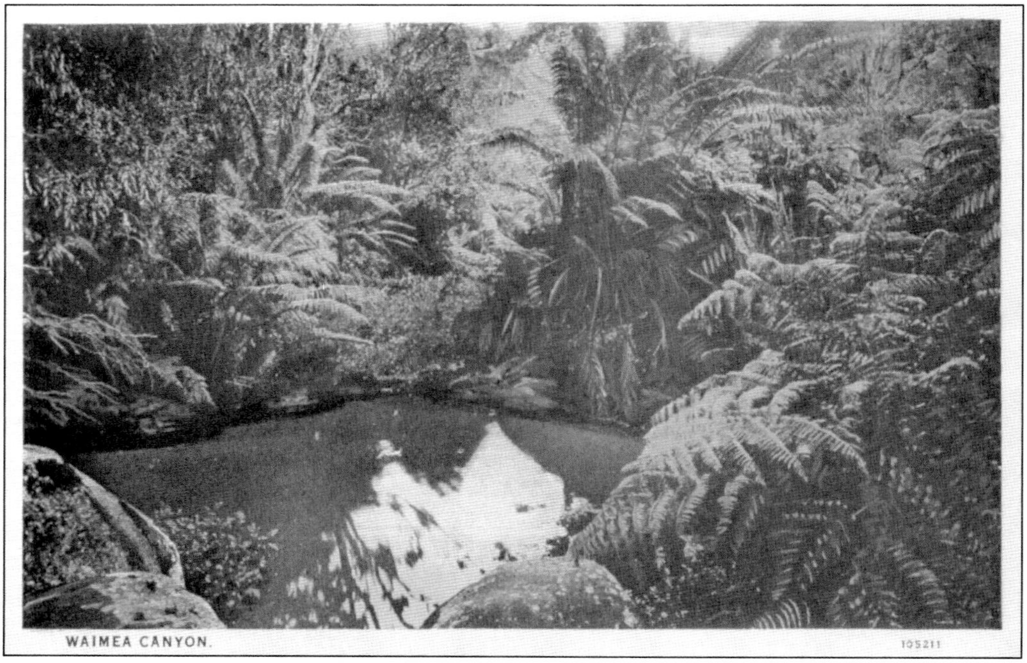

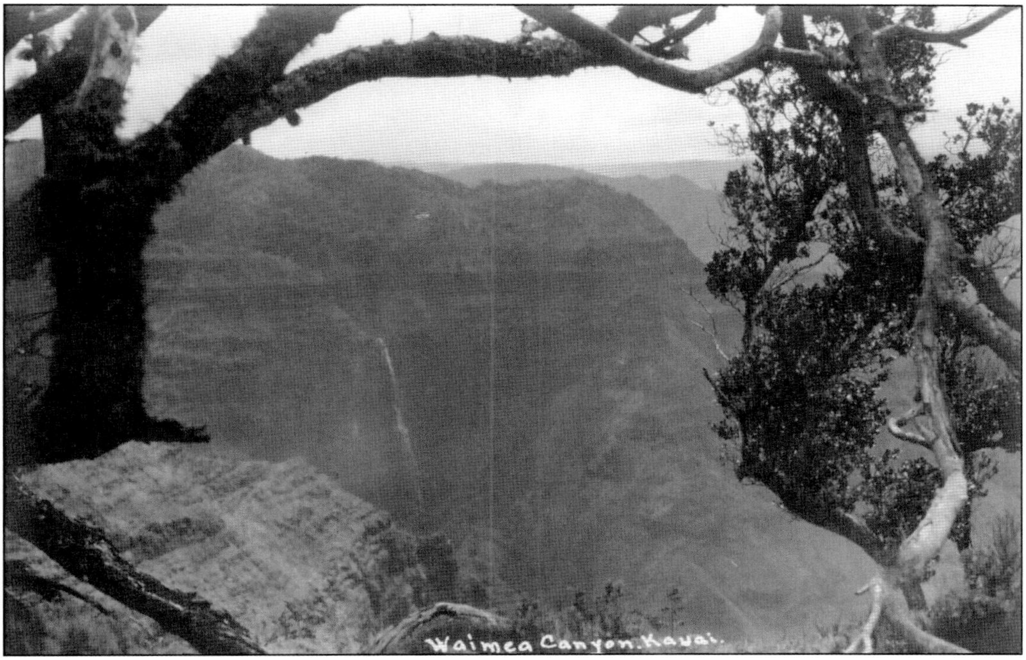

The image of Waipoo Falls on the card above was taken in the 1920s; the one below was made much later. This waterfall is directly opposite Waimea Canyon Lookout, so the visibility of the falls depends upon the amount of rainfall that has fallen recently. Many times during the year, it is not detectable. (Above, 0, A; below, 22.)

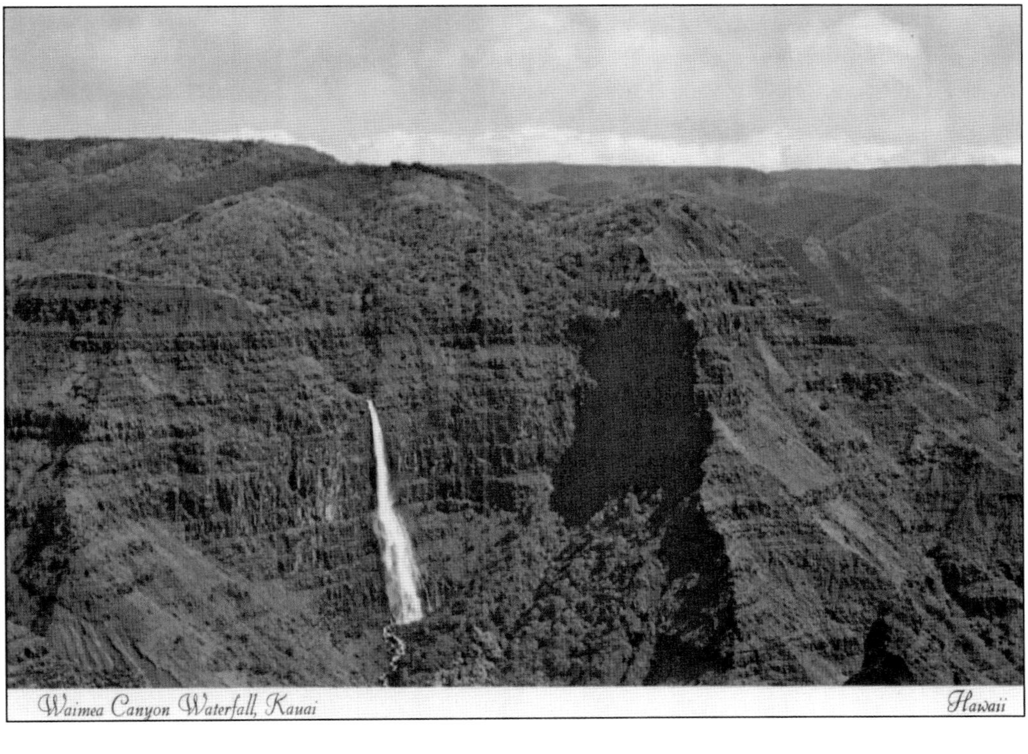

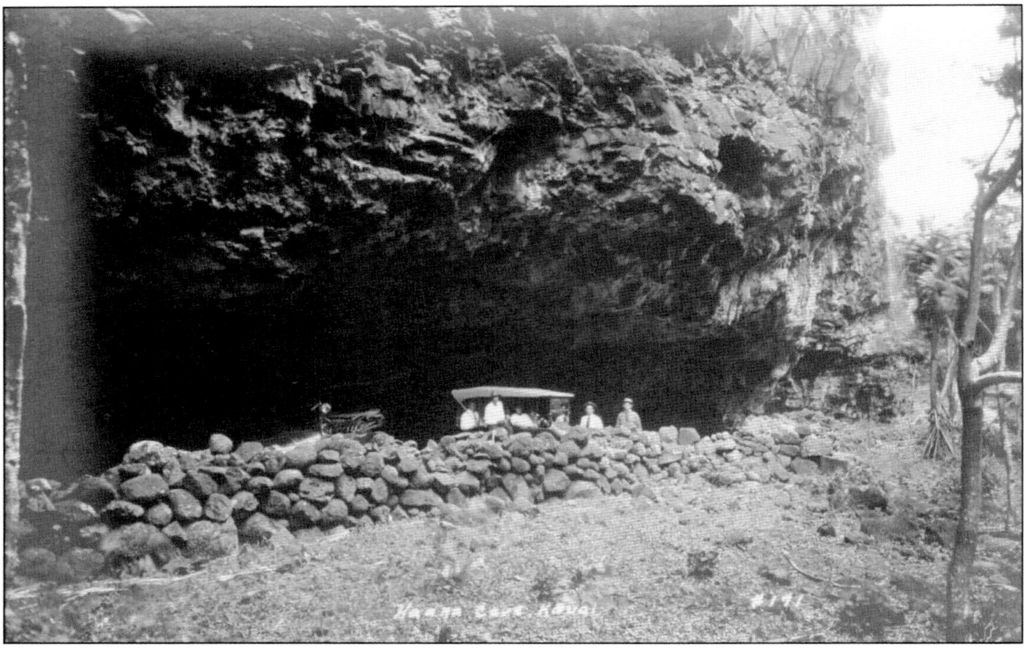

The cave in this 1930s postcard (above), labeled "Haena Cave, Kauai," is known better as the Dry Cave for its lack of water. Its Hawaiian name is Manini-holo. The cave was named after a legend about the head fishermen of the Menehune, named Manini-holo. The straight translation of *maniniholo* is "traveling reef surgeonfish." Below is an early 1960s postcard of the Haena Dry Cave showing the pink Jeeps that were a popular rental car on the island at the time. (Above, 0, A; below, 34, Q.)

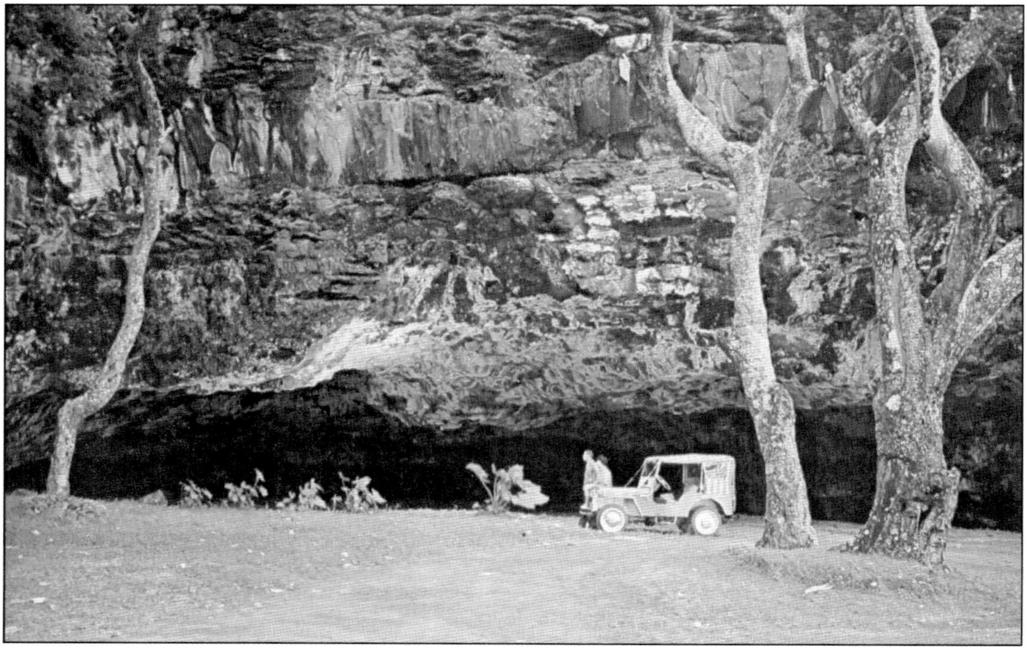

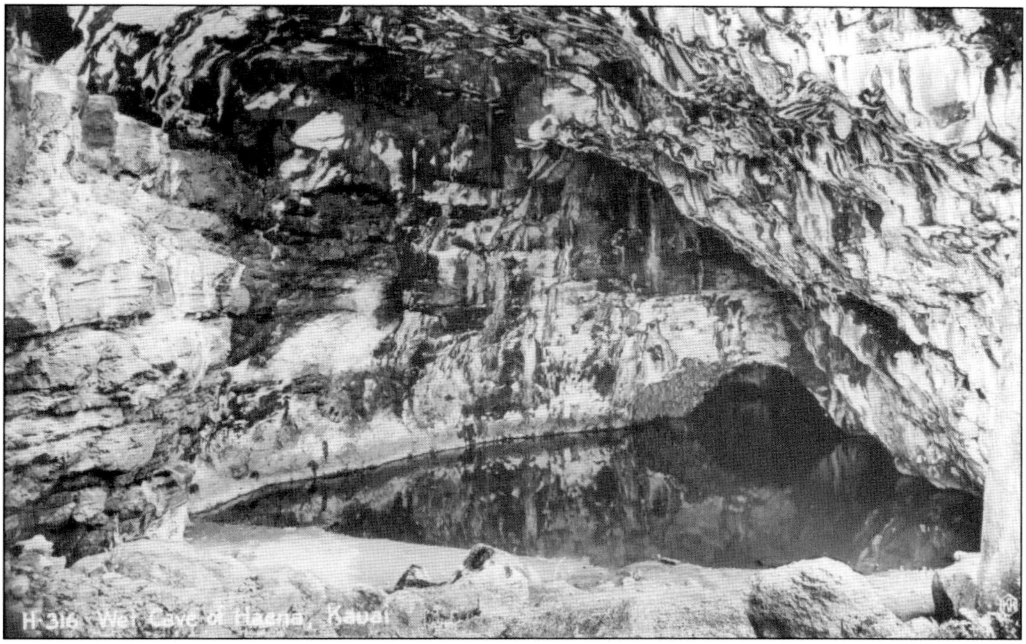

The image of the Wet Cave in Haena above was taken in the 1940s. The postcard below is from the early 1960s. Haena Wet Cave is also known as Waiakanaloa, translated as "Kanaloa's water." This cave also has a grotto known as the Blue Room because in sunny weather, blue light is reflected in the water. Visitors do not hear about this spot much any more due to many reasons: water levels have been lower and inconsistent, people have drowned by getting caught in the grotto when it is filled, and the water is not as sanitary as it once was. (Above, 0, A; below, 34.)

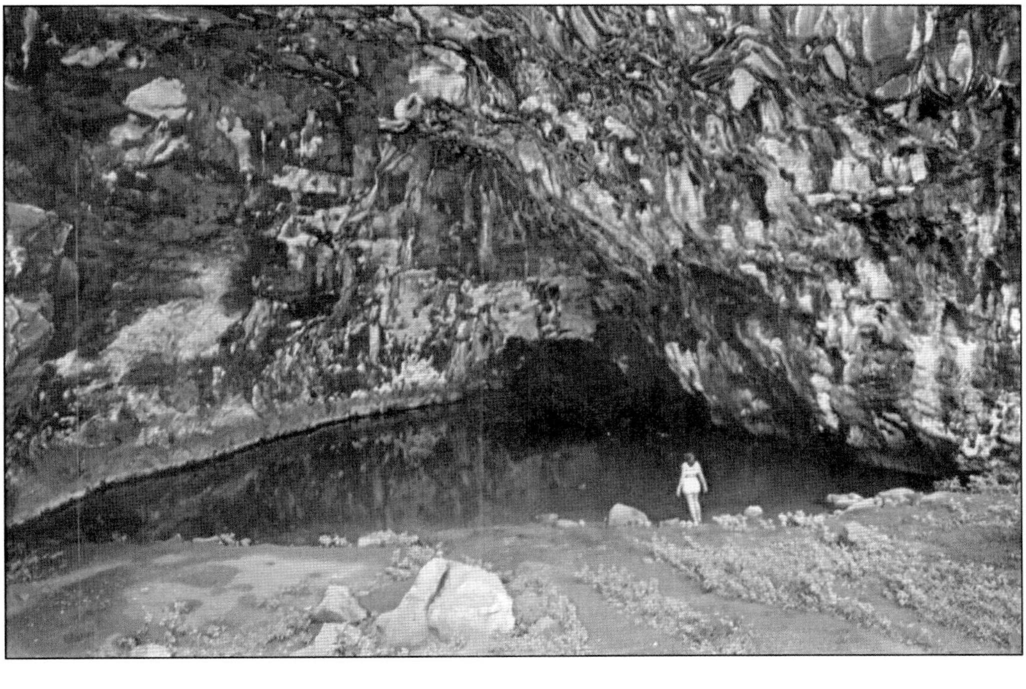

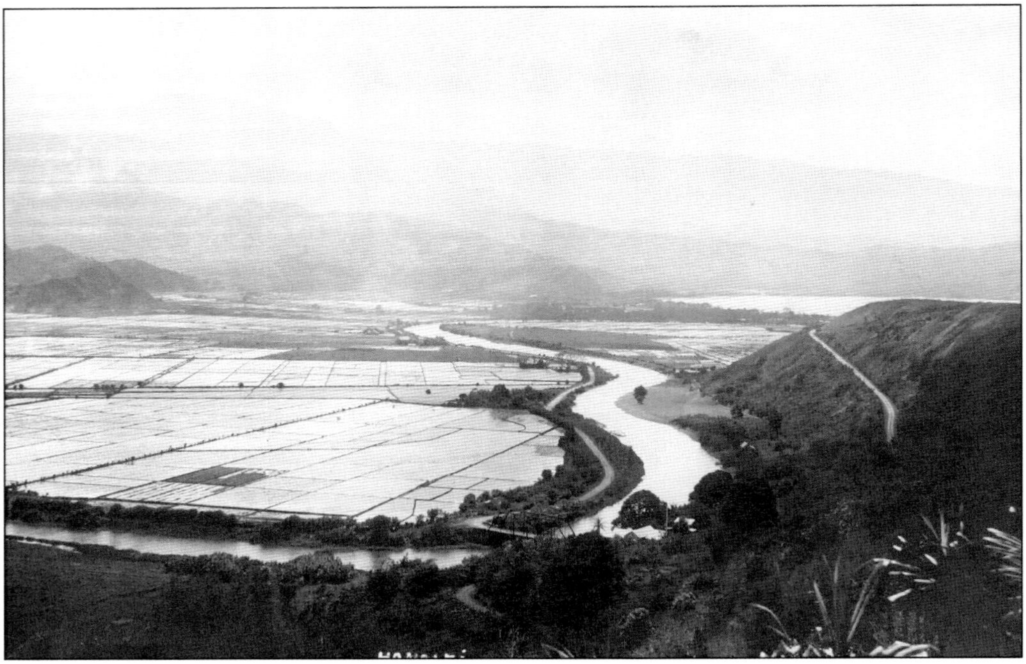

This wonderful view of Hanalei Valley (above) looking toward Hanalei Bay was taken in the 1930s. From the early 1900s, the valley was planted in rice. By the 1930s, Hanalei supported four rice mills and was producing much of the state's rice crop. Nearly 60 years later, this double rainbow celebrates the valley's return to raising taro as the ancient Hawaiians had done for centuries. Hanalei's marshy lowlands provide the perfect environment for either rice or taro. This welcome resurgence back to taro has required the building of a poi mill in Hanalei Town. Hanalei produces more taro than any other area in Hawaii. (Above, 0, A; below, 38, V.)

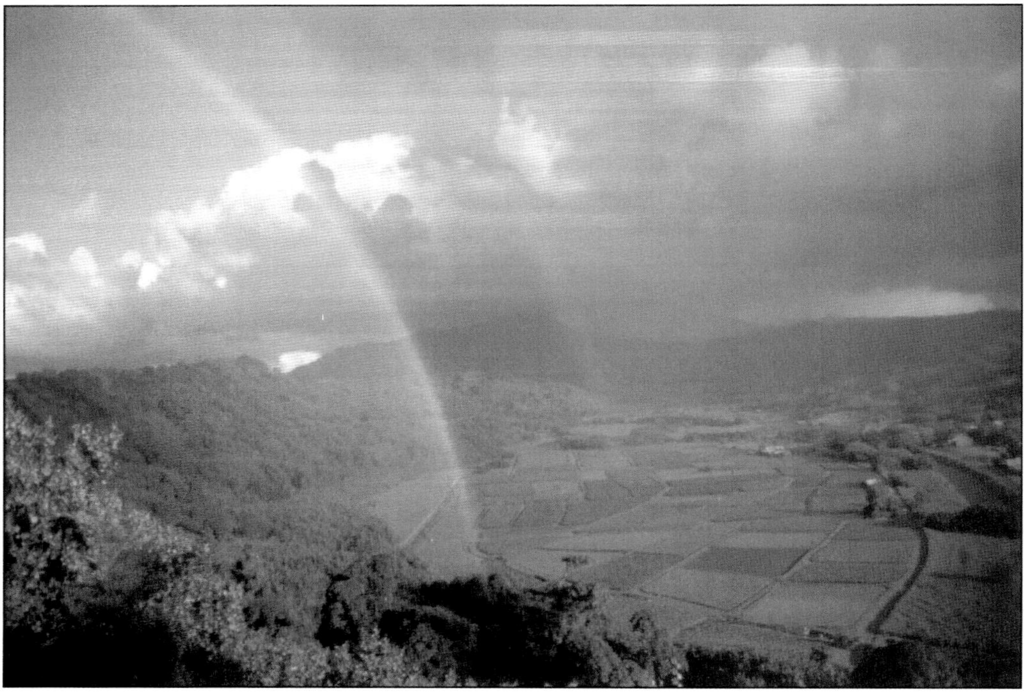

Spouting Horn has been a visitor must-see from the very beginning. This early postcard shows how spectacular it is. During strong storm surges in the winter months, salt spray could reach the nearby sugarcane crops and damage the cane, so a story persists that a local sugarcane company dynamited the area. (0, A.)

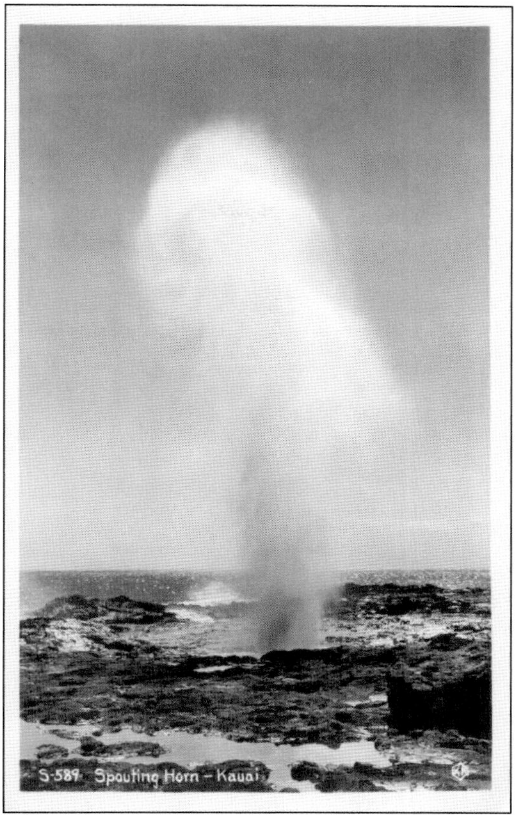

Spouting Horn is a volcanic lava tube that creates a geyser-like explosion of seawater as the wave action forces the water up through the tube and into the air. This 1969 postcard shows curious visitors standing much too close to the action. One rogue wave would have them swept out to sea. (14, G.)

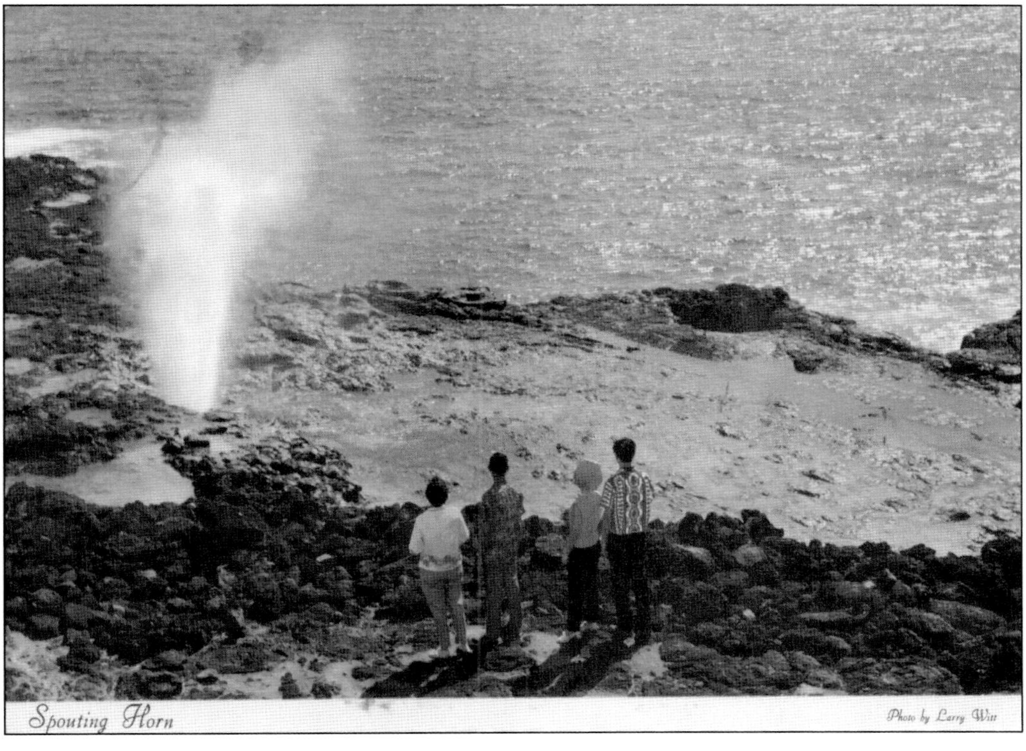

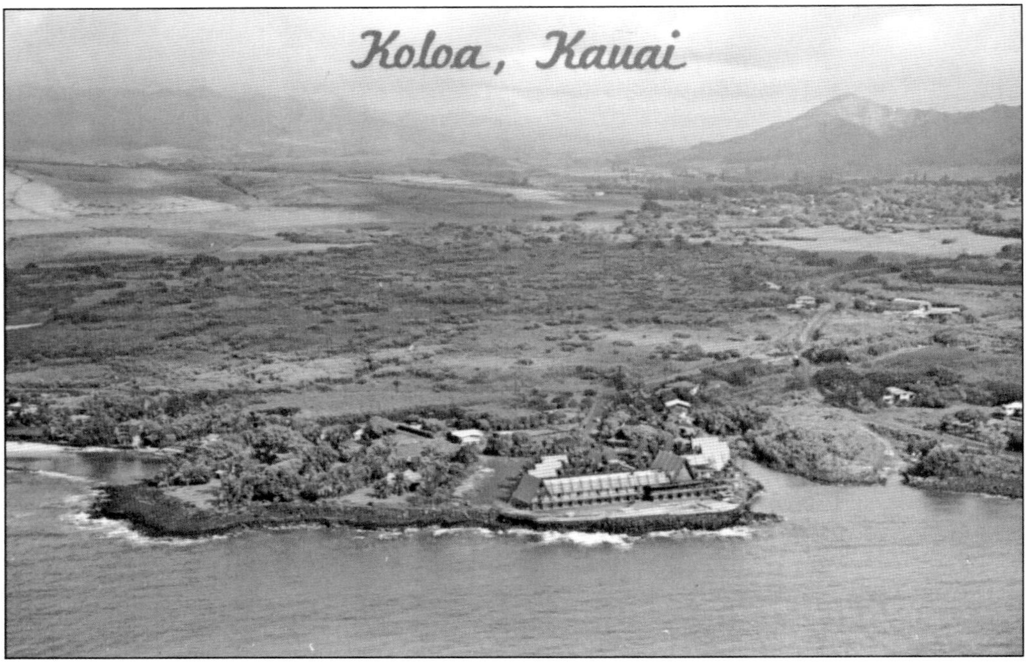

Koloa Landing, just right of center, was once a busy port packed with many ships from whaling and the sandalwood trade. The hotel visible just to the left is the original Whaler's Cove. (17, G.)

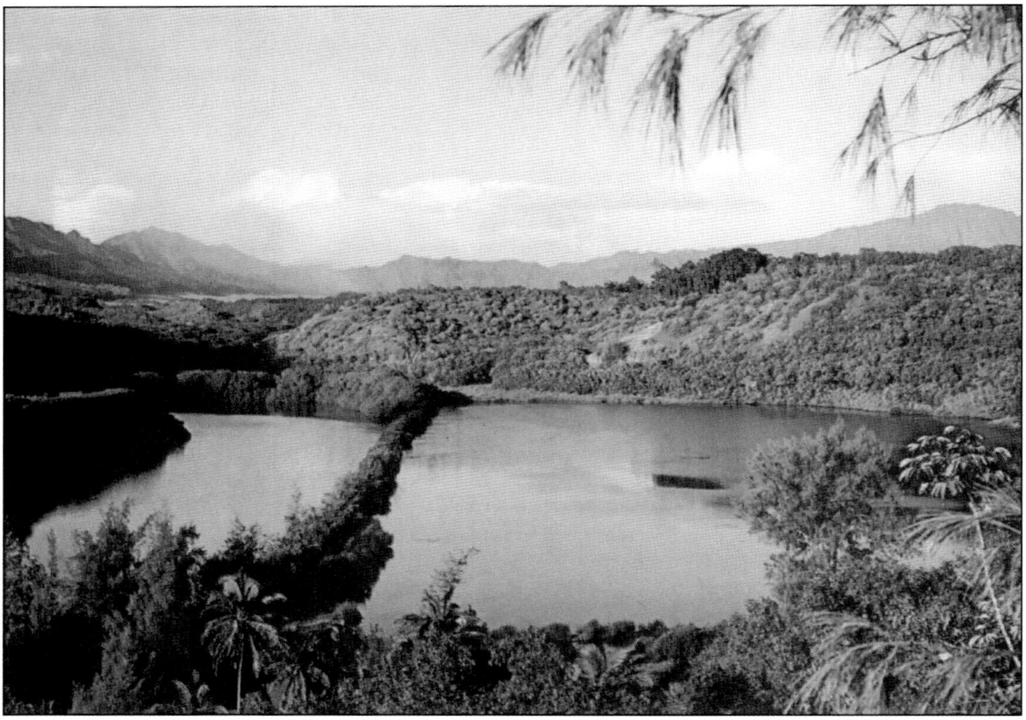
This more current photograph of Alekoko still mentions "the dwarfs, known as Menehune, finishing Herculean projects in one night." The mystique is alive and well; the fishpond, however, is not. Now overrun by massive mangrove root systems, the wall is visually lost to the trees. It will take another Herculean effort to restore the wall to its former glory. (15, S.)

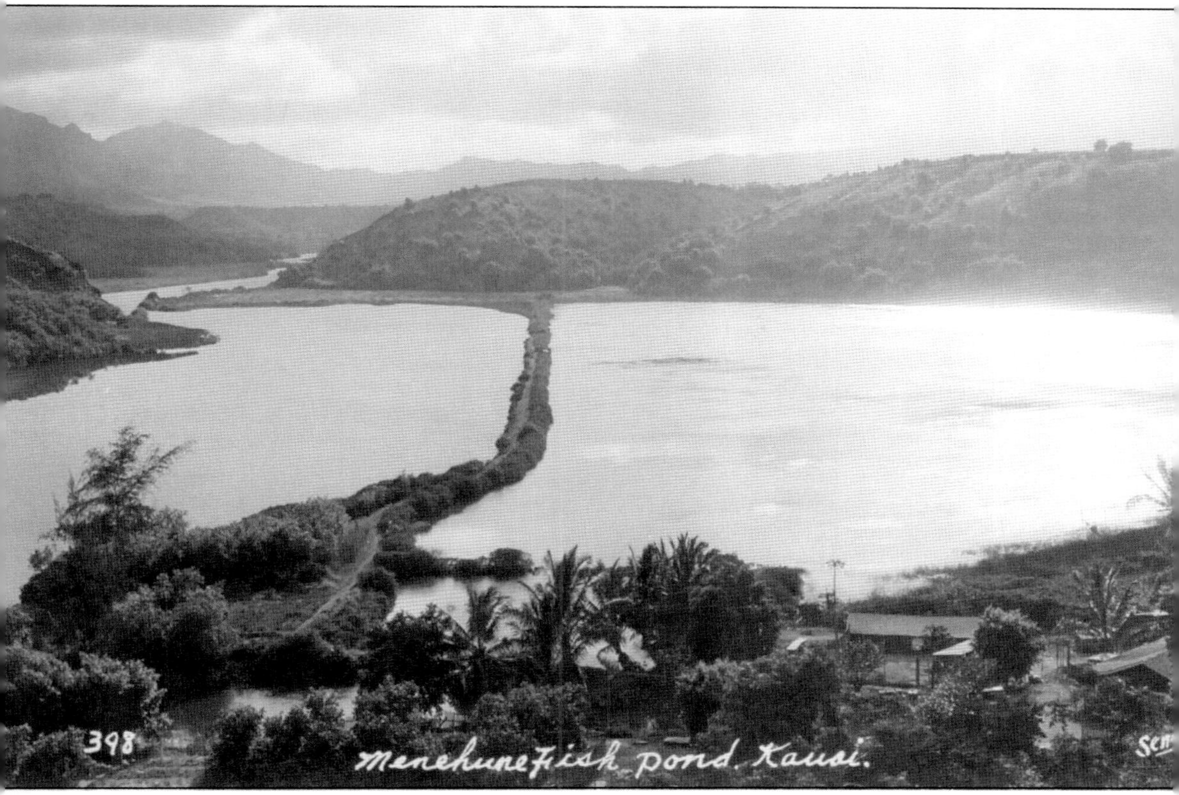

This older view of the Menehune Fishpond looks quite different from the one on the previous page. At one time, the area was well maintained, and people lived there. There is a home in the lower right corner. (0, A.)

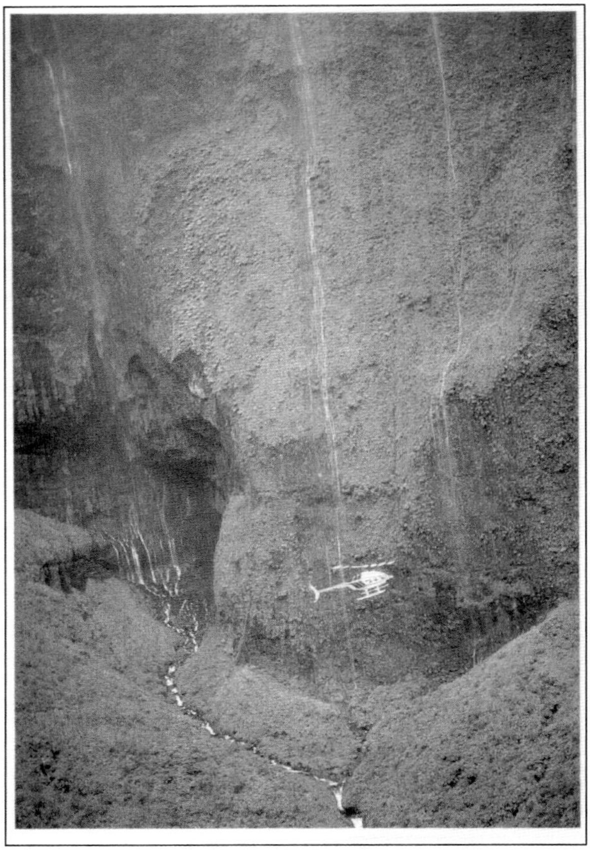

Waialeale Crater is what is left of a shield volcano that formed much of the island of Kauai. It is the island's second highest point and promoted as "the wettest spot on Earth." While disputed, that claim is far from a complete exaggeration. The summit is often shrouded in clouds and has averaged more than 430 inches of rain per year since 1912, when record keeping began. With a total of 683 inches, 1982 was a record year for precipitation. Helicopter tours that include a visit to the inside of the crater are a favorite. This day shows little rainfall, but the area can look like a white curtain of water on a rainy day. (12, T.)

The Kilauea Lighthouse, once the westernmost lighthouse in the United States, is only a historic building today. Kilauea Point is now part of a wildlife refuge for many birds. Visitors enjoy watching the nesting habits of seabirds such as the Laysan albatross, red-footed booby, and red-tailed or white-tailed tropic bird. (40, W.)

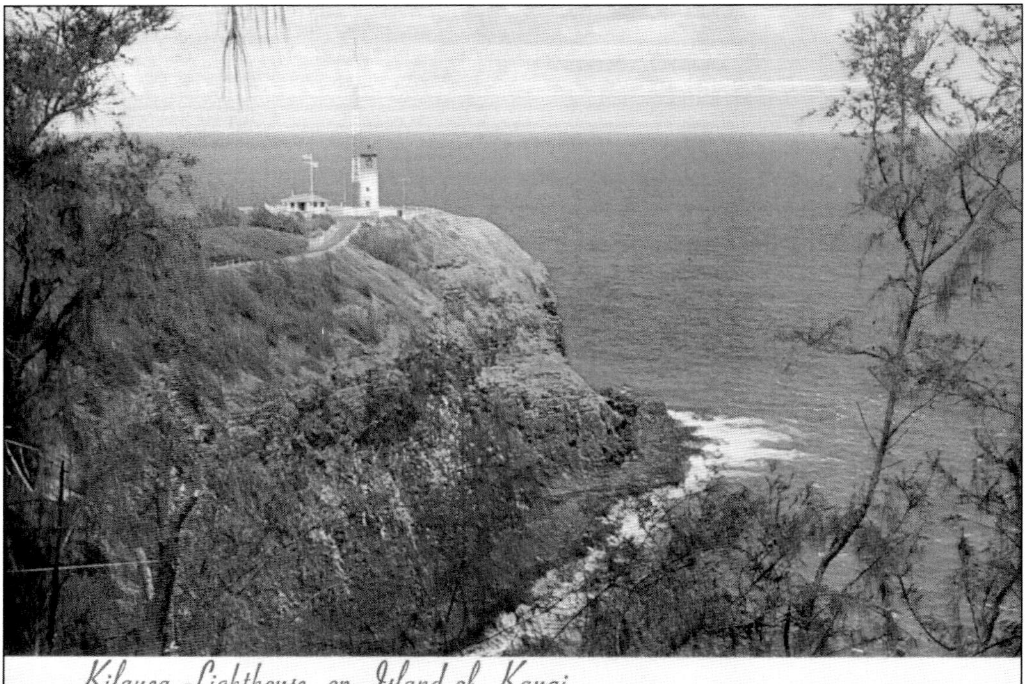

Kilauea Lighthouse on Island of Kauai

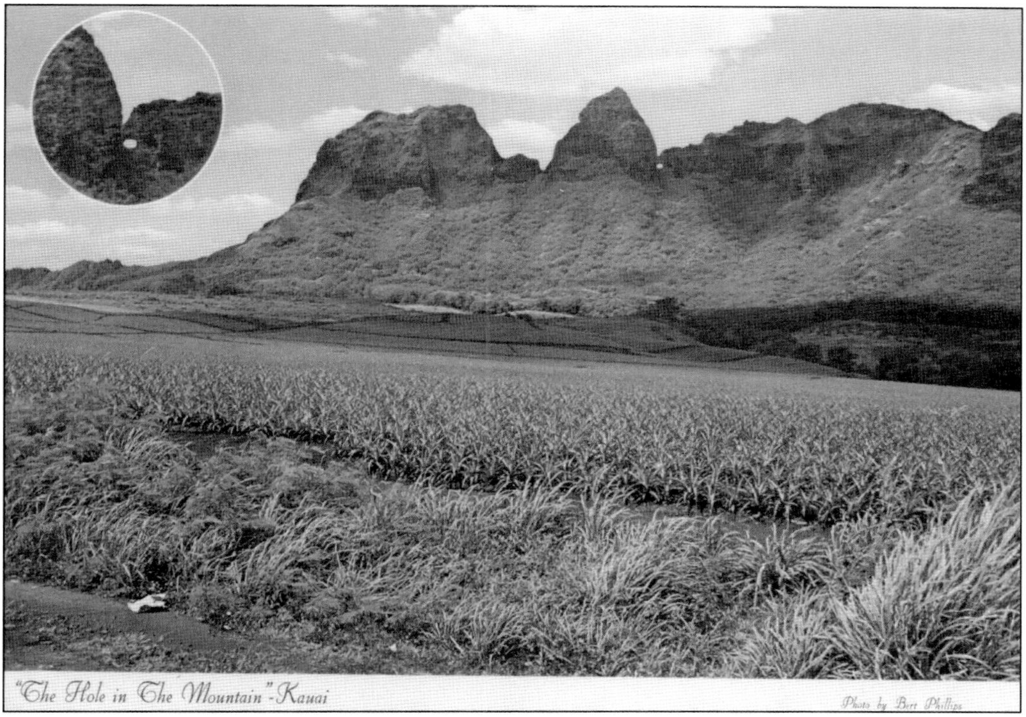

Another favorite attraction was the Hole in the Mountain, in the Kalalea mountain ridge. Around April 15, 1981, however, a massive rock slab about five feet thick and 10 feet high came tumbling down and blocked the hole. Until a Hawaii Visitors Bureau sign suggesting a stop was removed, tourists left wondering where the hole was. Not to be discouraged, today's visitors stop to look at the King Kong Profile. (22, E.)

Kauai was a primary filming location for Steven Spielberg's *Jurassic Park*. The crew built the set of the Jurassic Park Visitor Center (upper left) where Valley House once stood. The pond in front is unchanged from when Zephaniah Spalding, of the Makee Sugar Company, owned it. The gate was built near the end of Kuamoo Road near the arboretum. (39.)

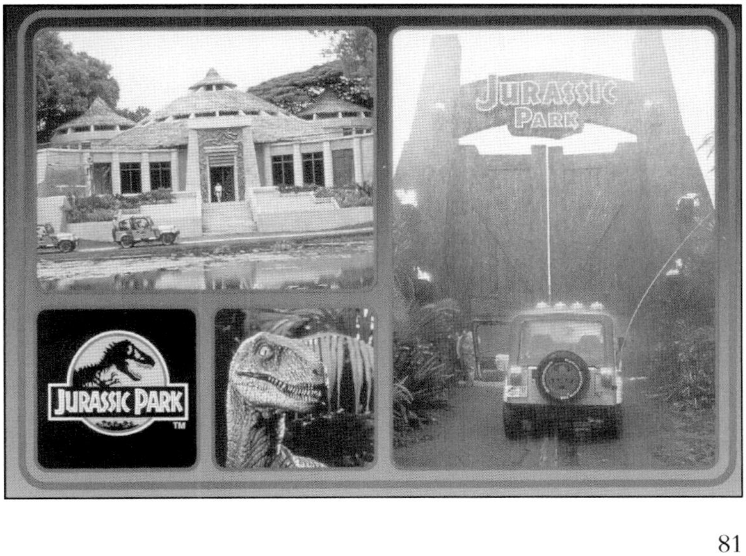

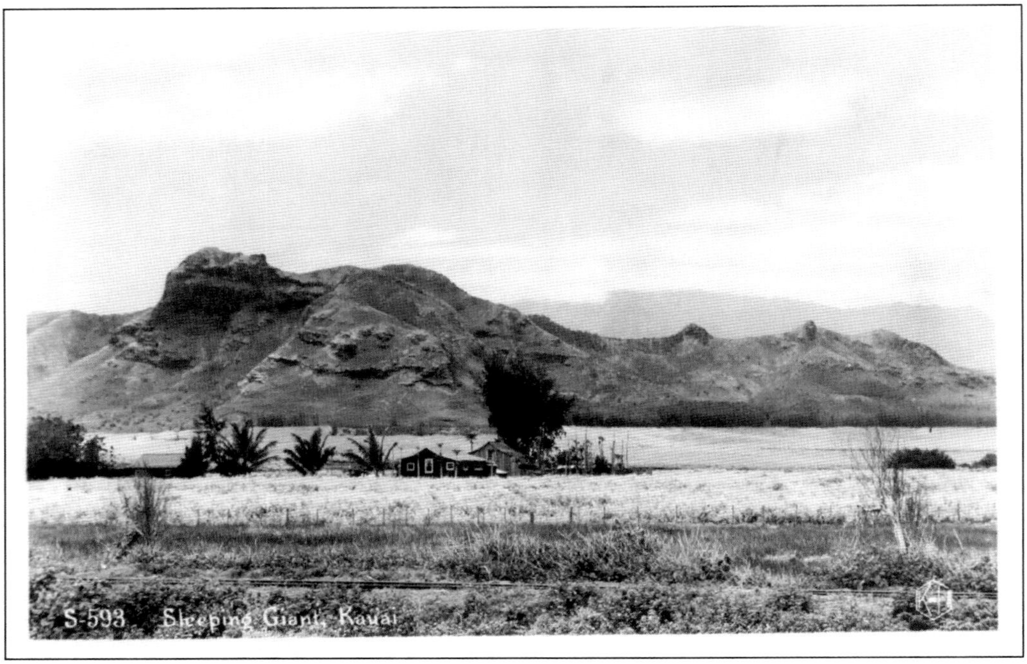

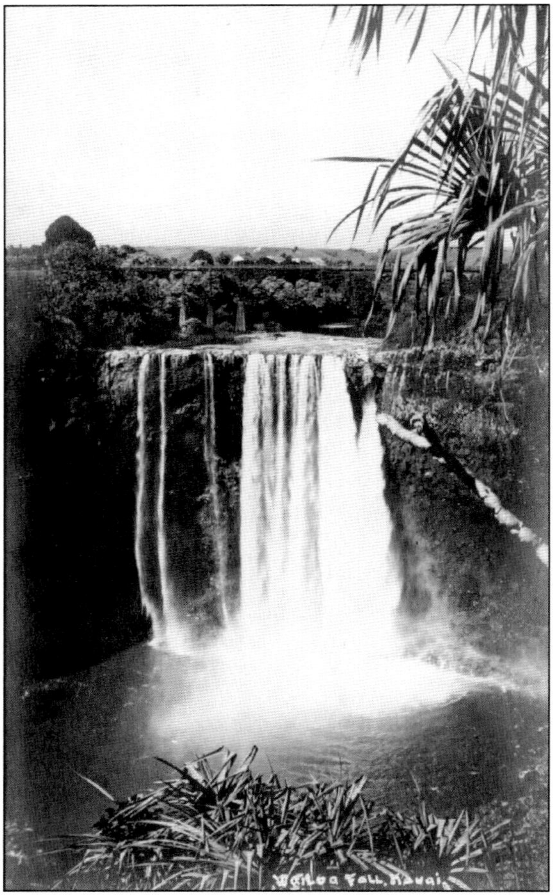

Mount Nounou, affectionately referred to as the Sleeping Giant, has been a longtime visitor must-see. There have been many legends regarding this name and how the "giant" came to be there. (0, A.)

This is a beautiful view of Wailua Falls in the 1920s. Today, visitors cannot view the falls from this angle unless they are in a helicopter. Wailua Falls is near Lihue, but it is hidden. The 80-foot drop into the pool below feeds into the Wailua River. (0, A.)

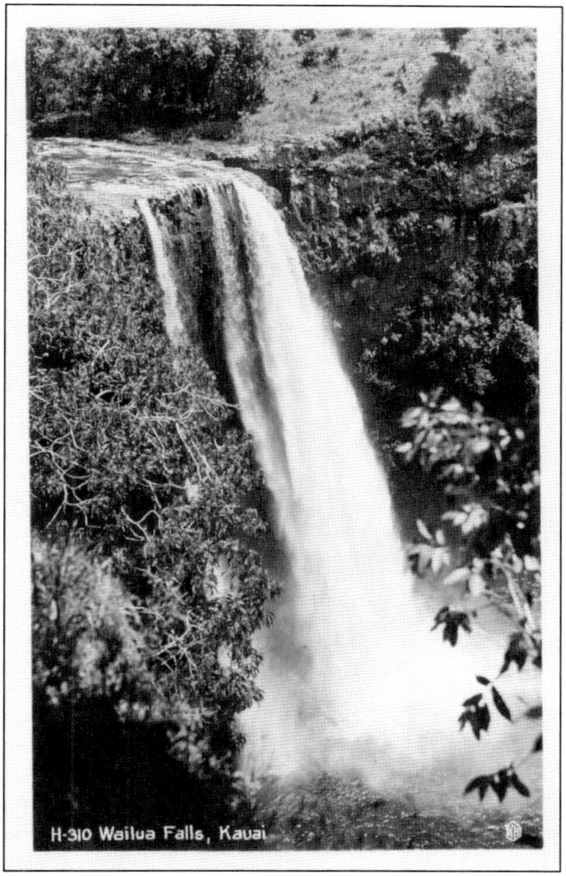

Both these views of Wailua Falls are from the lookout from which visitors can view the falls today. In the card at right, taken in the 1930s, there has been good rainfall and the falls are running well; in the postcard below, it has obviously been a dry year and the waterfall barely resembles the one made famous in the opening scenes of the television show *Fantasy Island*. (Right, 0, A; below, 15.)

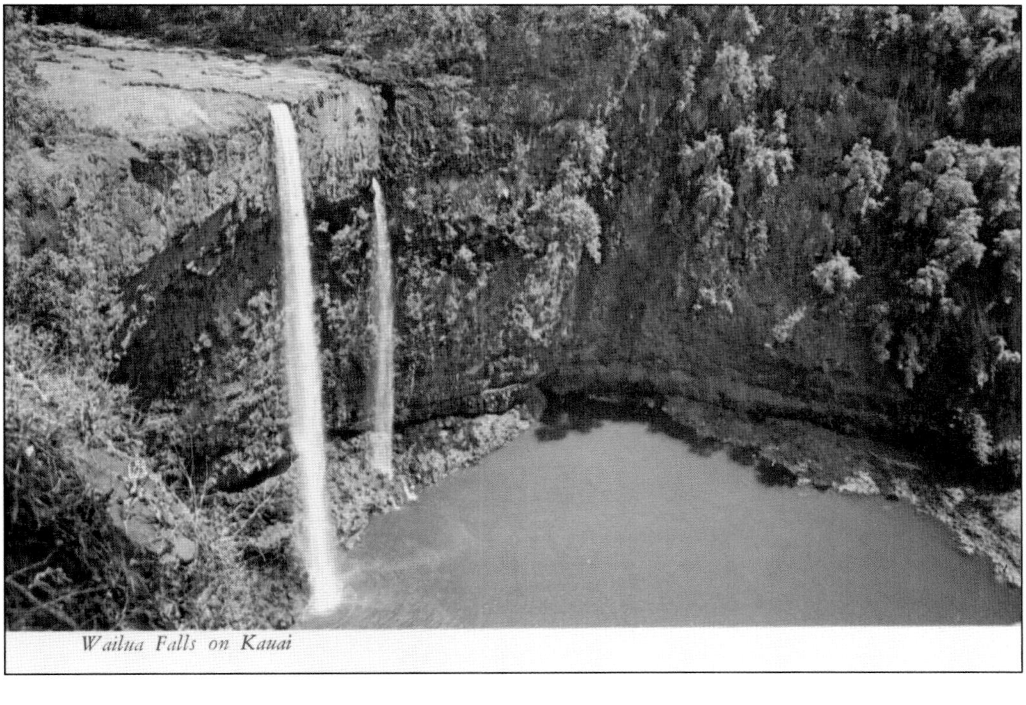

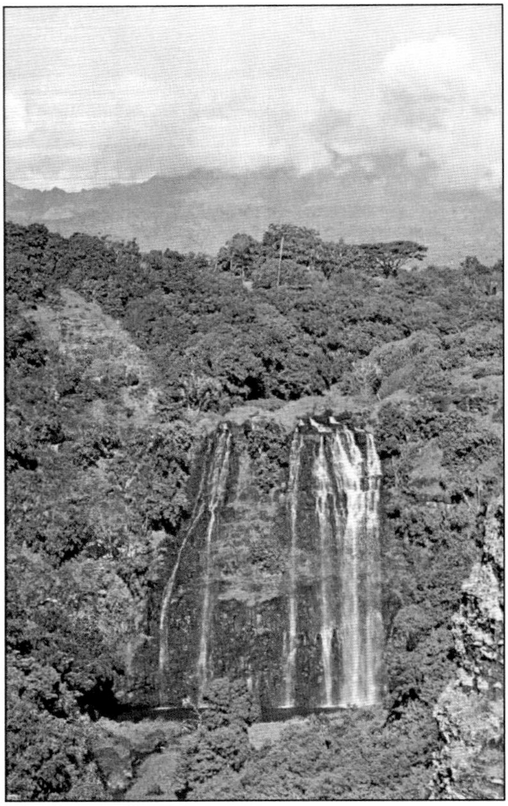

Opaekaa Falls, easily visible from Kuamoo Road, has a 150-foot drop. The falls is named for the amount of shrimp that once was easily harvested from its base. The literal translation of *opaekaa* means "roiling shrimp." (34.)

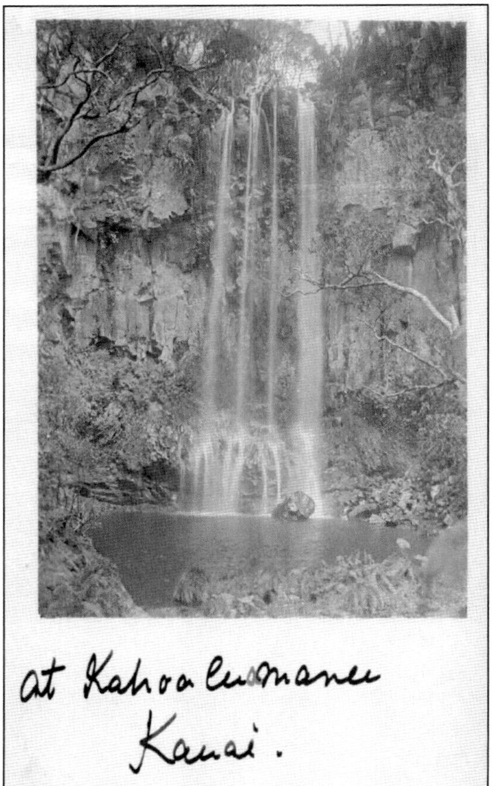

There is a place known as Kaholuamanu in the Waimea Canyon area. There was a trail that riders took to the area, but time and inaccessibility make some things whispers of the past—except through postcards such as this. Whatever the name of this waterfall, it is beautiful. (0, A.)

Kauai is known for its secluded waterfalls, and Kalihiwai Falls is one of them. With a 60-foot drop that feeds into the Kalihiwai River, it is a difficult waterfall to visit. (26, Z.)

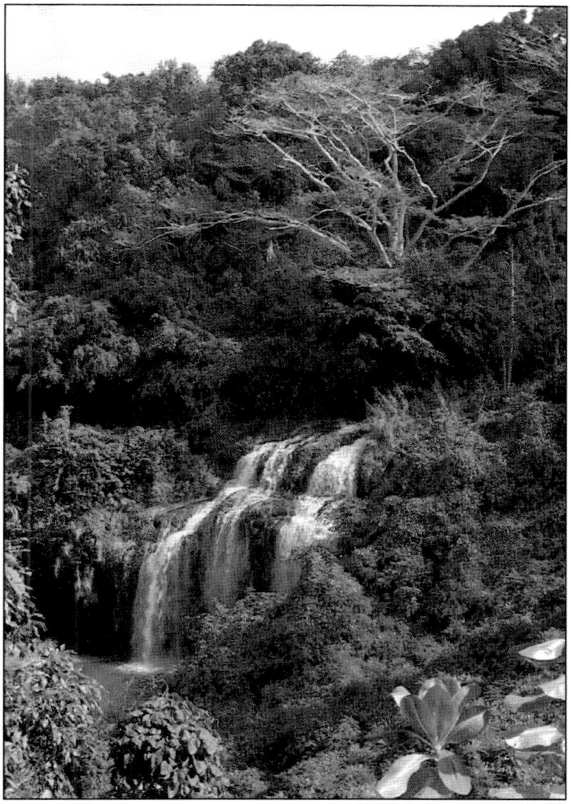

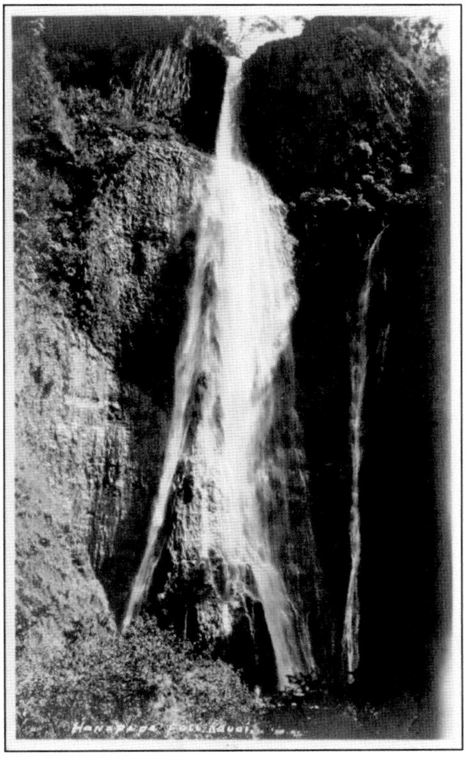

On this postcard mailed from Lihue in 1929, the writer says, "I arrived by interisland boat last night." This card shows Maniwaiopuna in the back of the Hanapepe Valley. The waterfall can now be visited for short ground stops by Island Helicopters to visit this once inaccessible cataract that was used in the movie *Jurassic Park*. (0, A.)

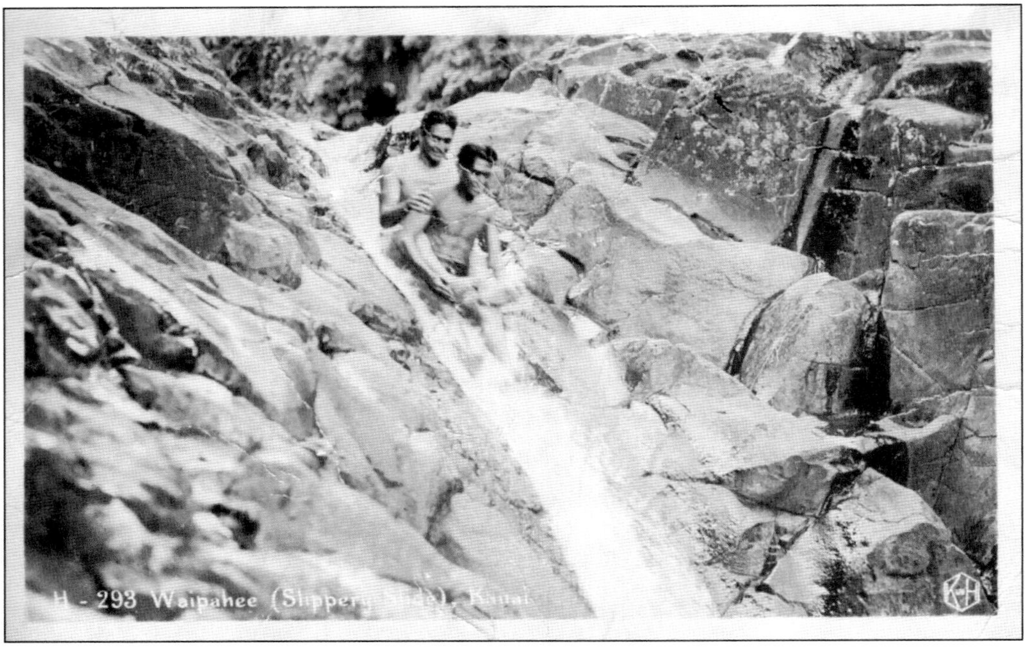

Mailed for free on August 5, 1942, and passing Army censors to Hopkins, Minnesota, the postcard above says, "We're getting in some swell hiking and mountain climbing in our spare time. We are up in the hills a long way from civilization and boy do I like it. Wish we had a place like this close to home." Waipahee, meaning "water slide," is a natural slide in the Anahola area. It was popular on hot summer days because of the cold mountain stream that feeds it. It is no longer open to the public. Slippery Slide (below) in Kilauea was a man-made slide used in the "Happy Talk" scene in *South Pacific.* When the water is not too fast, a crude cement plaque with the words "South Pacific" can be seen. Due to worry over liability, it is no longer open to the public. (Above, 0; below, 22.)

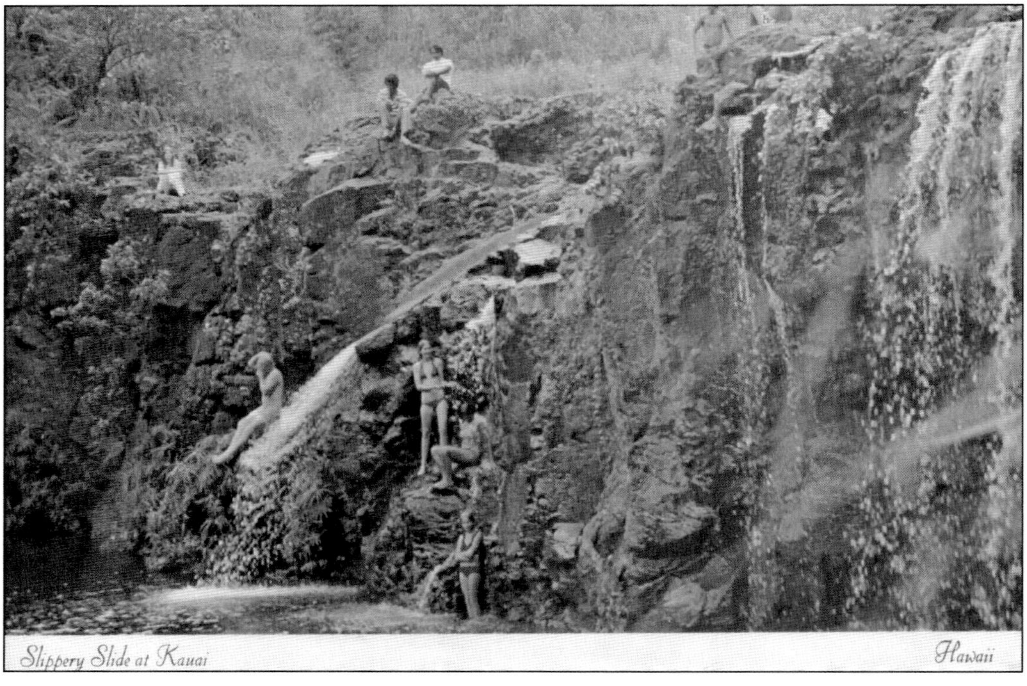

This waterfall is not labeled. Looking at the foliage, it is no doubt another falls tucked away within the Waimea Canyon area. The beauty is there, so a lack of identification really does not matter. Kauai has so many waterfalls that another hidden, unnamed one just adds to the island's charm. (0, A.)

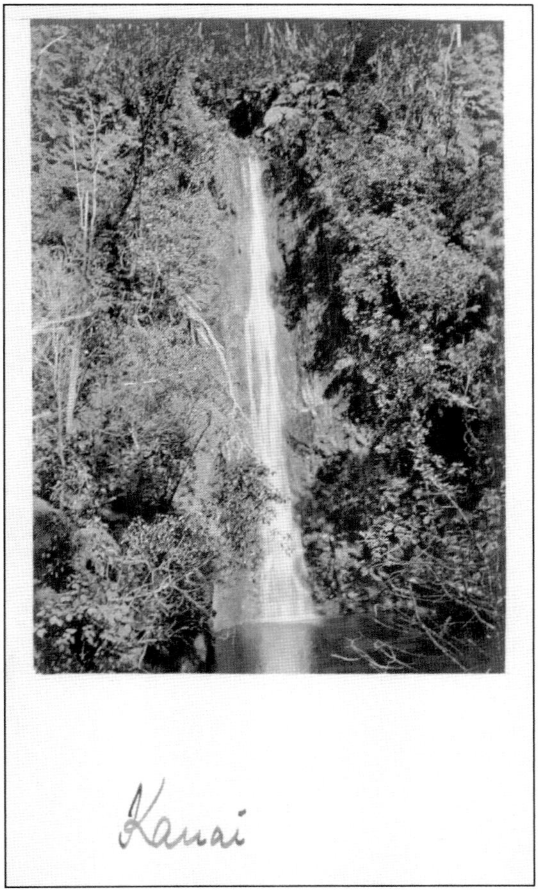

Smith's Boats began in 1946. Walter Smith Sr. and his wife, Emily, started out with one rowboat and a borrowed outboard motor. It is now a four-generation family business. This shows the early days of Smith's Boats, when it was accessed from Kuamoo Road. (34, Q.)

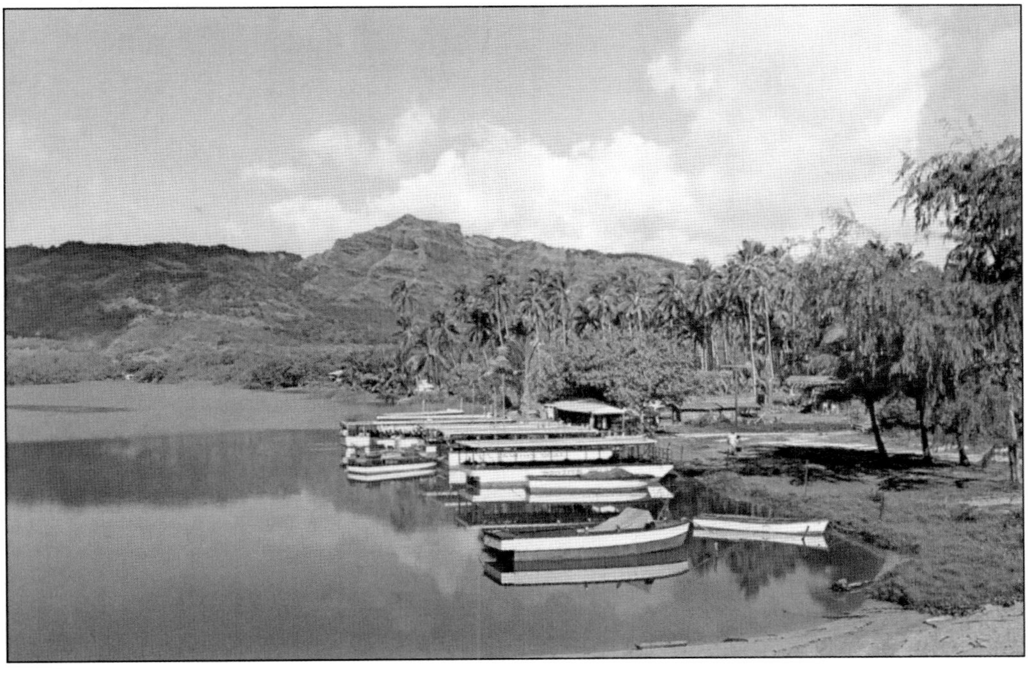

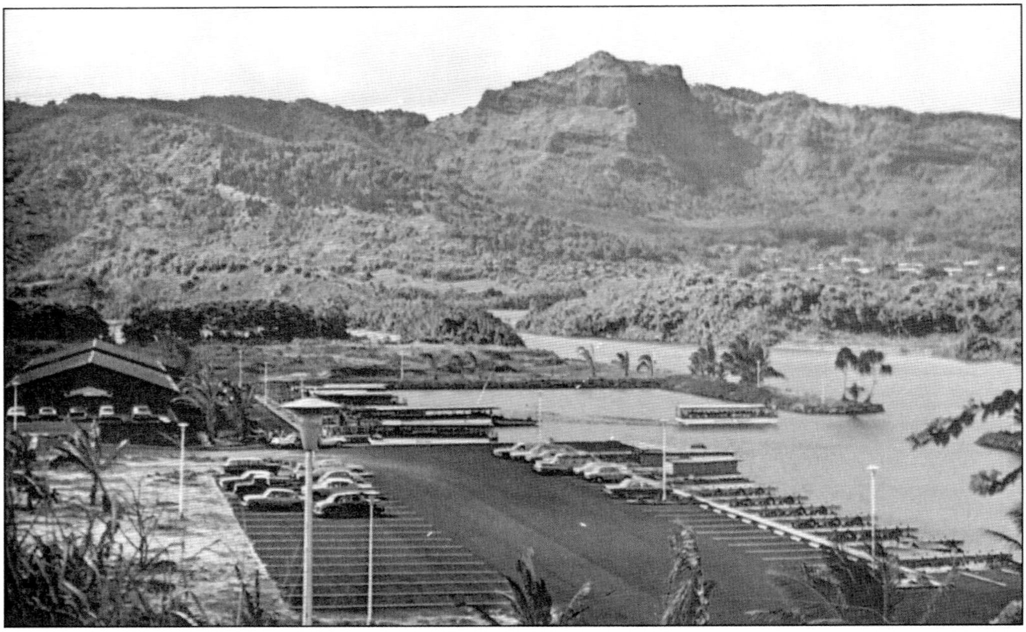

In the 1960s, the new Wailua River State Park Marina (above) was built, and the Smiths' boat operation moved from the Kuamoo Road side to its own entrance on the Lihue side of the river. The Sleeping Giant is visible as a boat leaves for a visit to Fern Grotto. From this aerial view (below), one can see a boat just returning from a visit to the grotto. The place known as Paradise Pacifica and later Smith's Tropical Paradise is yet to be constructed. (Above, 10, X; below, 27.)

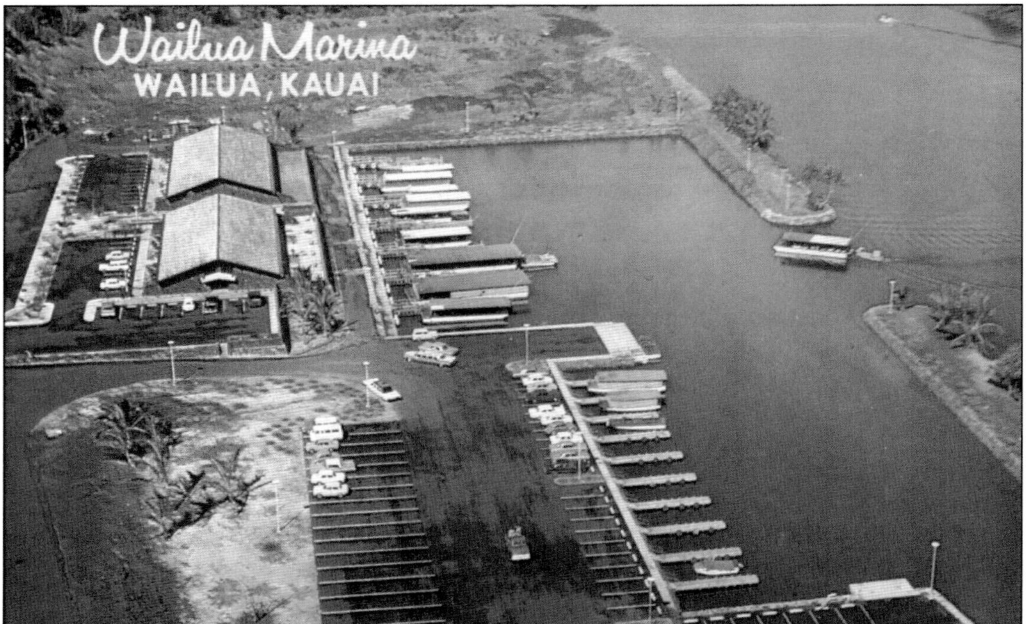

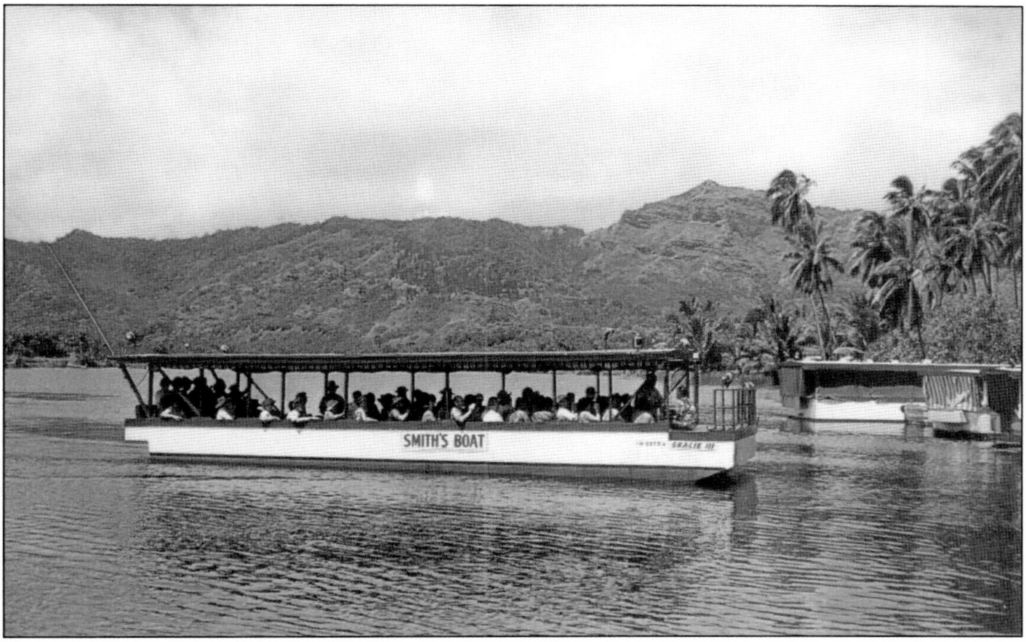

In the postcard above, the *Gracie III* looks to be docking on the right side of the river before the marina was finished. The Wailua River is Hawaii's only truly navigable waterway. Tour boats are designed to make sure everyone has wonderful views of the river no matter if one is going upstream or downstream. The card below shows the river excursion from the visitor's viewpoint. The trip takes an hour and a half round-trip, complete with stories of the area, singing, and, of course, the hula. (Above, 27, A; below, 22, E.)

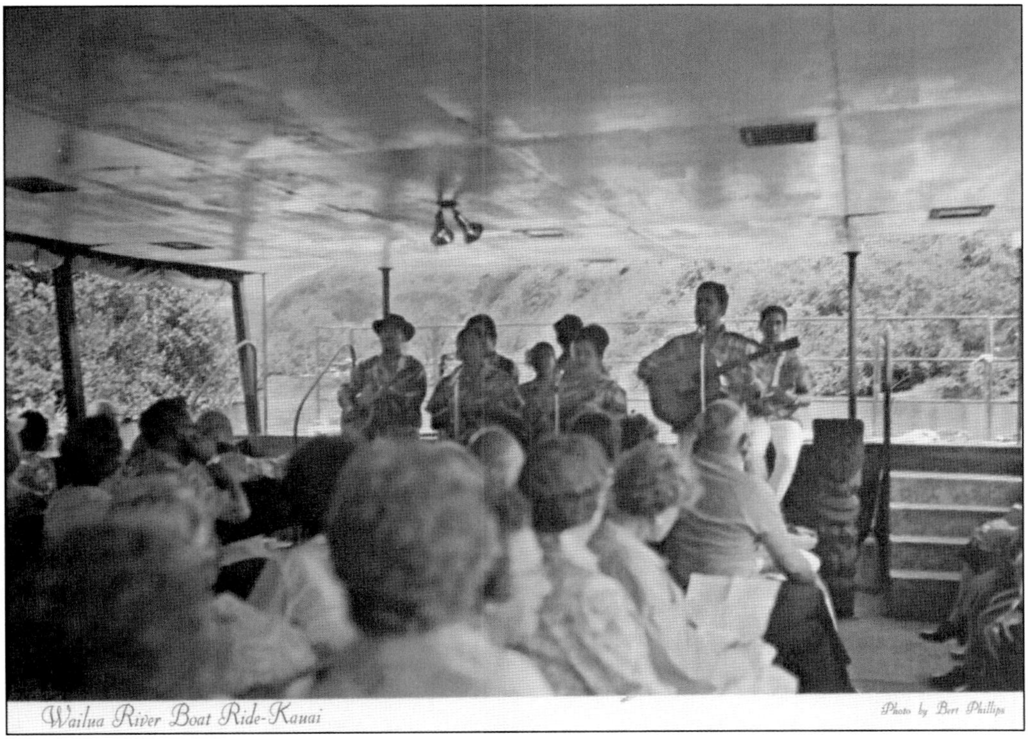

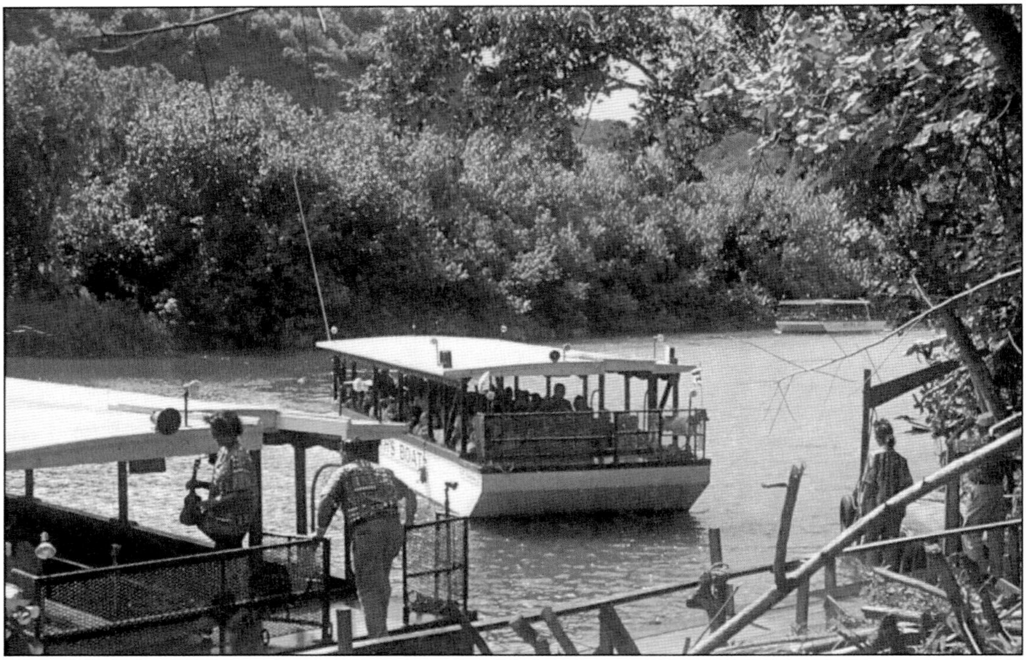

The tour boats travel a distance of two miles upriver against the current. Here, a boat is docking for the short walk to the grotto just as another one leaves. The author of this 1966 postcard writes, "We have had mostly cloudy weather, but here even the rain is beautiful." Thankfully, the Hawaiian aura continues with each card like this one that is written. (31.)

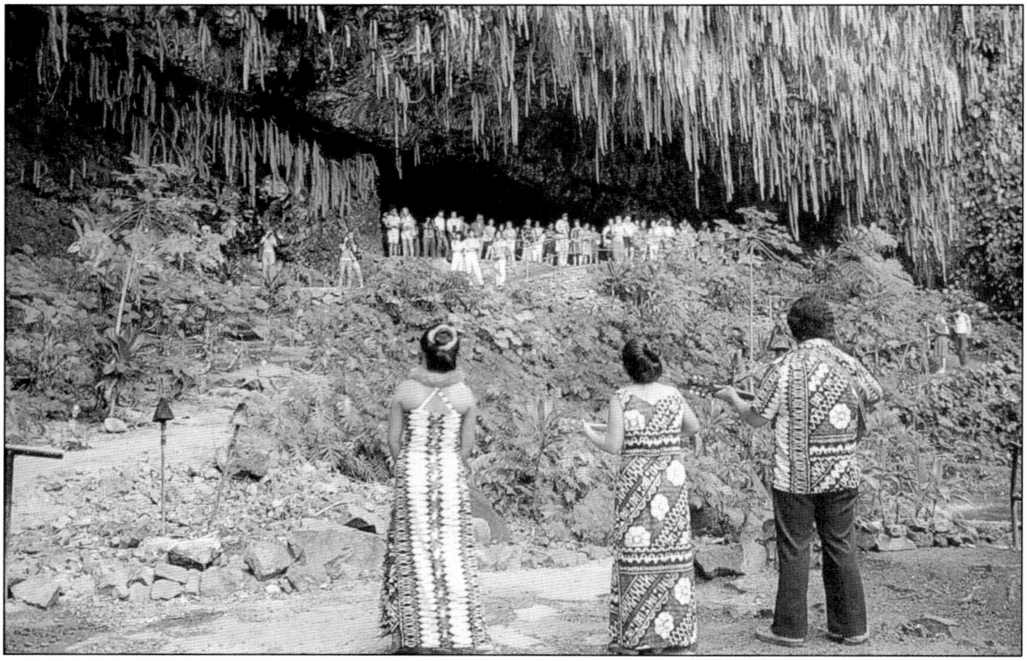

The Fern Grotto is a lava formation that created a giant natural amphitheater with Boston ferns growing upside down. Since ferns are delicate and prefer filtered sunlight, the loss of the tree canopy during times of hurricanes has been a setback for the plants. Many say the highlight of the visit is when musicians and singers perform the haunting "Hawaiian Wedding Song." (30, K.)

In 1971, the Princeville course designed by Robert Trent Jones Jr. was the newest golfing area in the state. It is the Princeville Golf Course, 27 holes—the 18-hole Makai Course and the nine-hole Woods Course—known as the "Woods, Lake, and Ocean." Jones went on to design the Prince Golf Course, with the first nine holes opened in 1987 and its official full-course opening in August 1990. It is touted as a world-class course that is both spectacular and challenging. (22.)

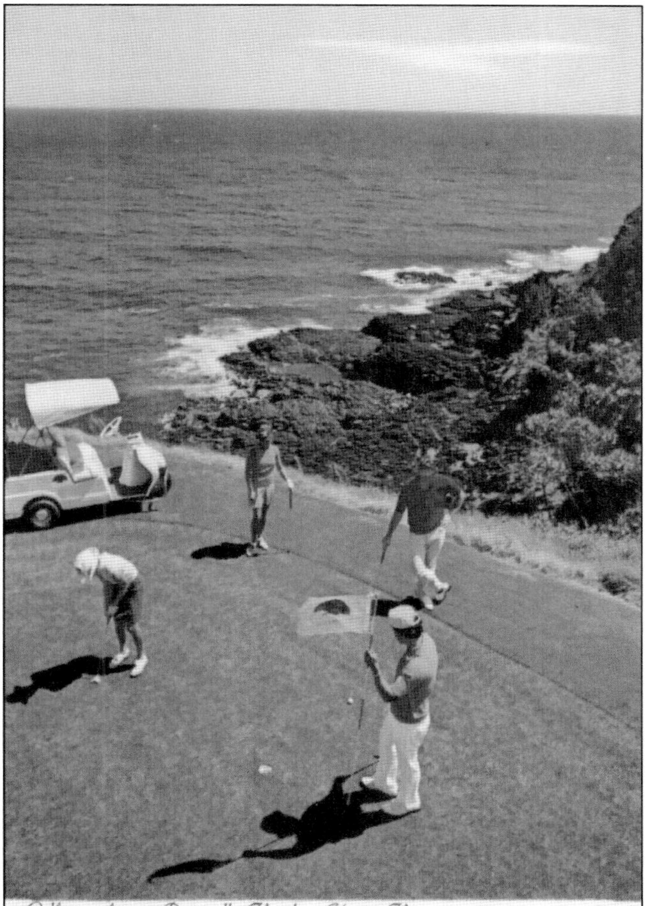
Golfing at famous Princeville, Hanalei - Kauai, Hawaii

The Wailua Golf Course began as a nine-hole course in the 1930s. An additional nine holes were added in 1961. The course designer for the seaside front nine was Toyo Shirai. This public course has hosted three USGA Amateur Public Links Championships and been voted one of Hawaii's best golf courses as well as one of the best municipal courses in the United States. (27.)

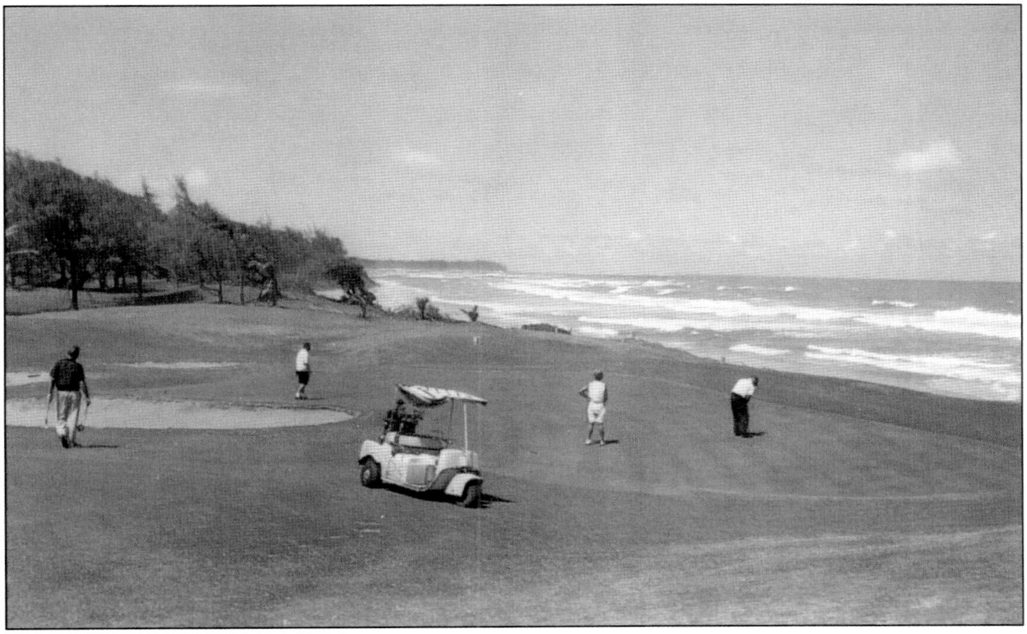

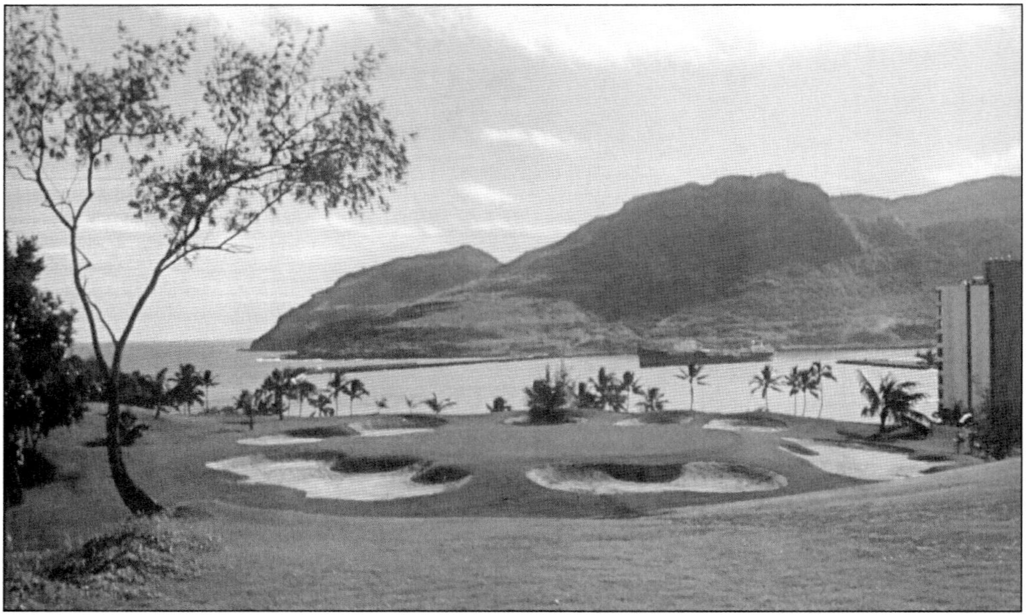

This postcard (above) is labeled as the Kauai Surf Golf and Country Club's new nine-hole course. It has always been known for its spectacular views of Nawiliwili Bay, which golfers consider one of its best features. This view is of the seventh green. The postcard below is of the same course years later. Shown here is the 13th hole overlooking scenic Nawiliwili Harbor. The white-roofed building in the background is the Inn on the Cliffs. The restaurant was destroyed in Hurricane Iniki and never rebuilt. Both names, the Kauai Surf and the Westin Kauai, have now gone. The new managing entity is Marriott. Jack Nicklaus redesigned the simple Kauai Surf golf course and oversaw its redesign in 2010–2011. The Kiele is the more challenging of the two 18-hole championship courses Nicklaus designed. (Above, 31; below, 30, P.)

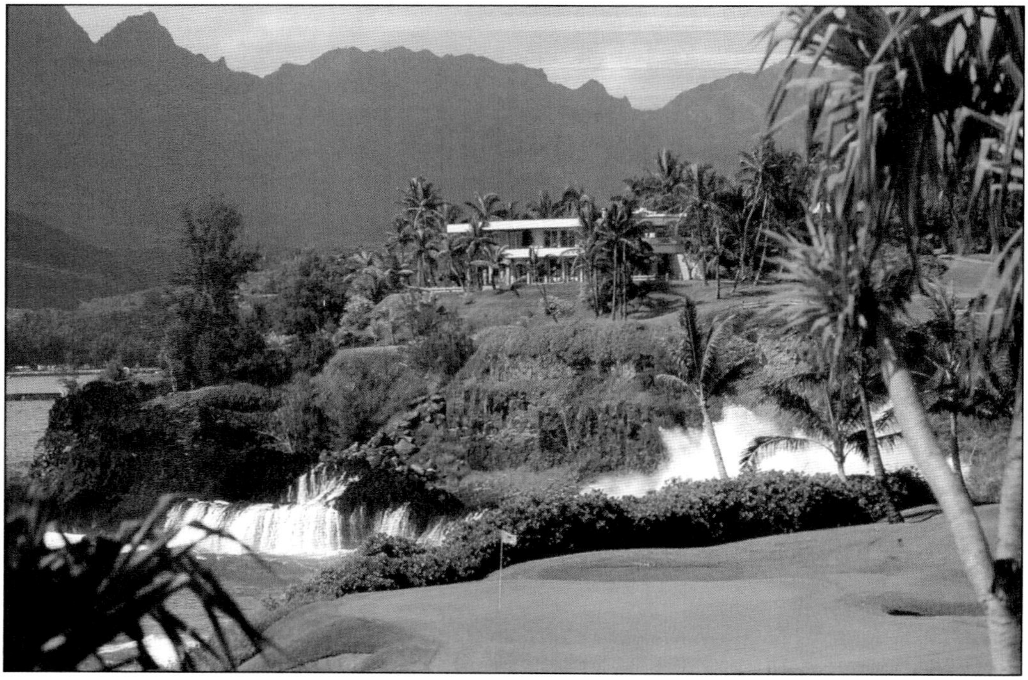

Six

Hotels

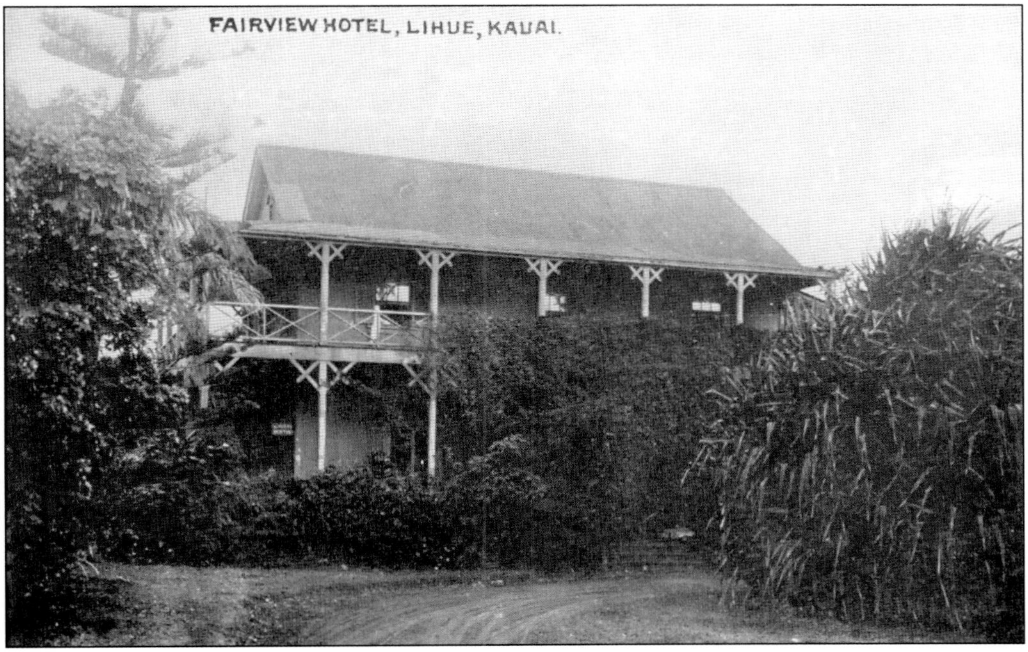

Most early visitors stayed in homes of prominent families on the island. In those days, it was rare to see a traveler seek out this distant island that boasted no active volcano. The very first lodging on the island was the Fairview Hotel in Lihue. It was located on Rice Street where Kalapaki Villas is today. (29.)

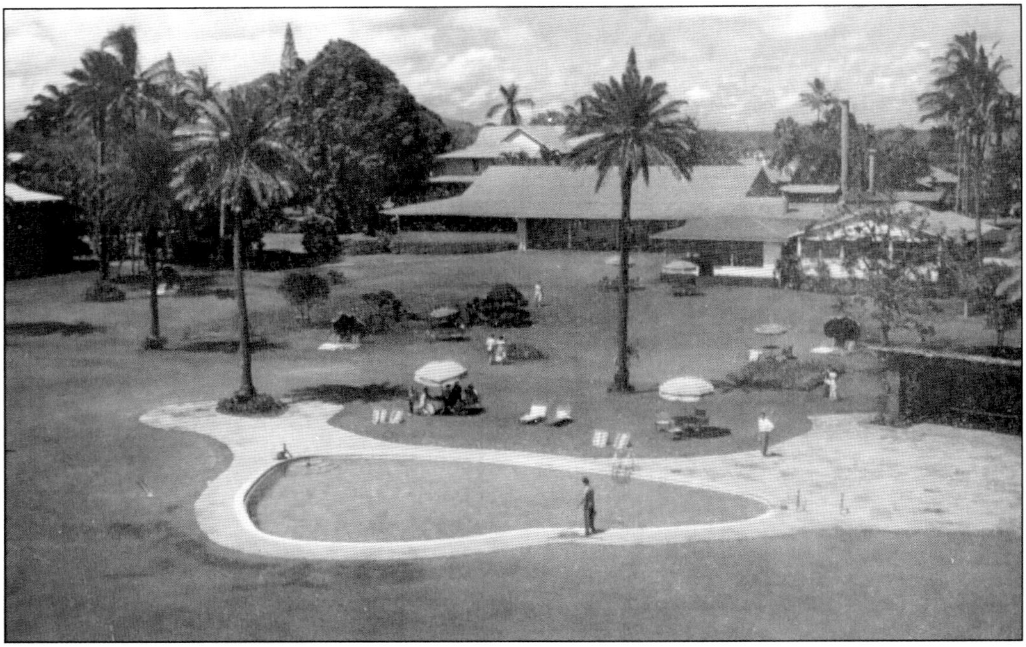

This aerial view of the Kauai Inn looks back toward Rice Street and the lanai. The tall two-story house belonging to the Moragne family is just visible in the background. (27.)

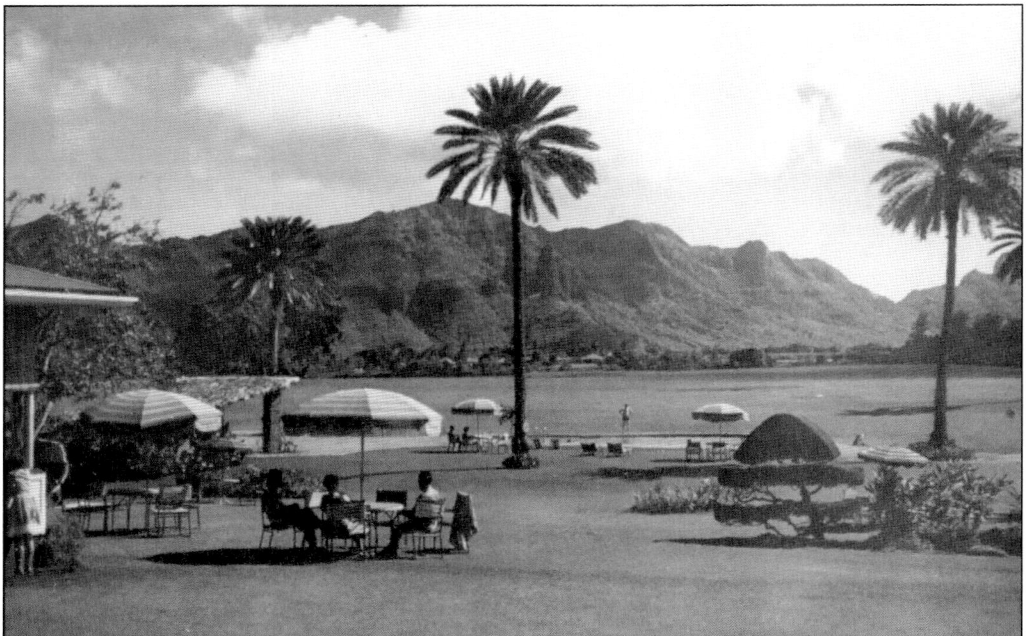

After World War II, the Kauai Inn became a favorite place for tourists to stay on the island. It stood in the same place where the Fairview Hotel had once been. From the lanai, it boasted uninterrupted views of the mountains above the Alekoko Fishpond. (27.)

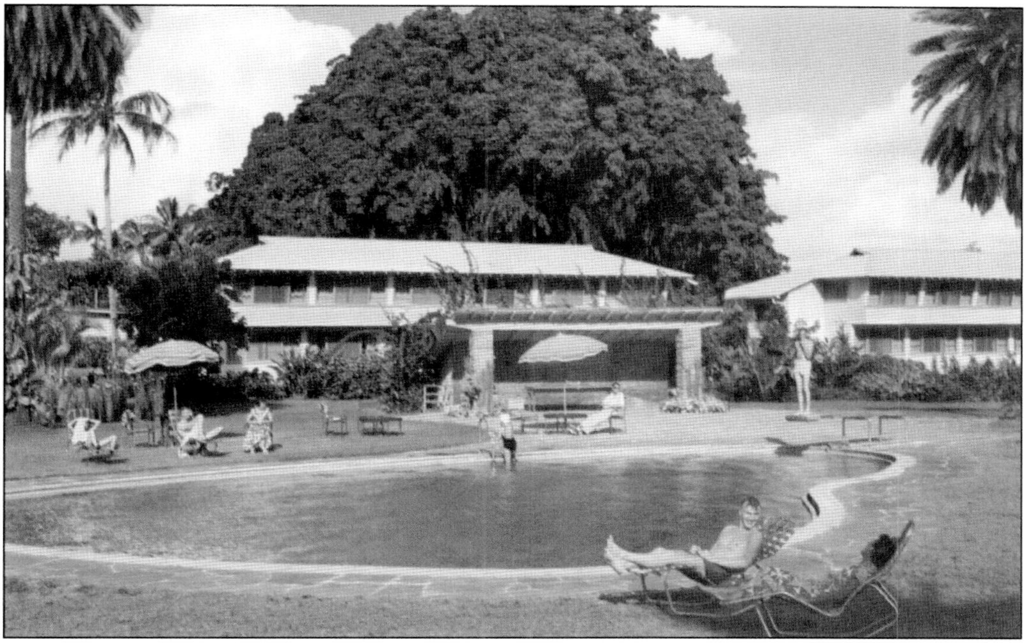

The Kauai Inn pool gave the impression of having all the space in the world. With a lake-like look, it had plenty of room for swimmers and sunbathers to lounge without feeling crowded. The buildings shown were later moved to the grounds of the Kauai Surf; both lodgings were run by Interisland Resorts. Again known as the Kauai Inn, these structures now stand in Niumalu. (31.)

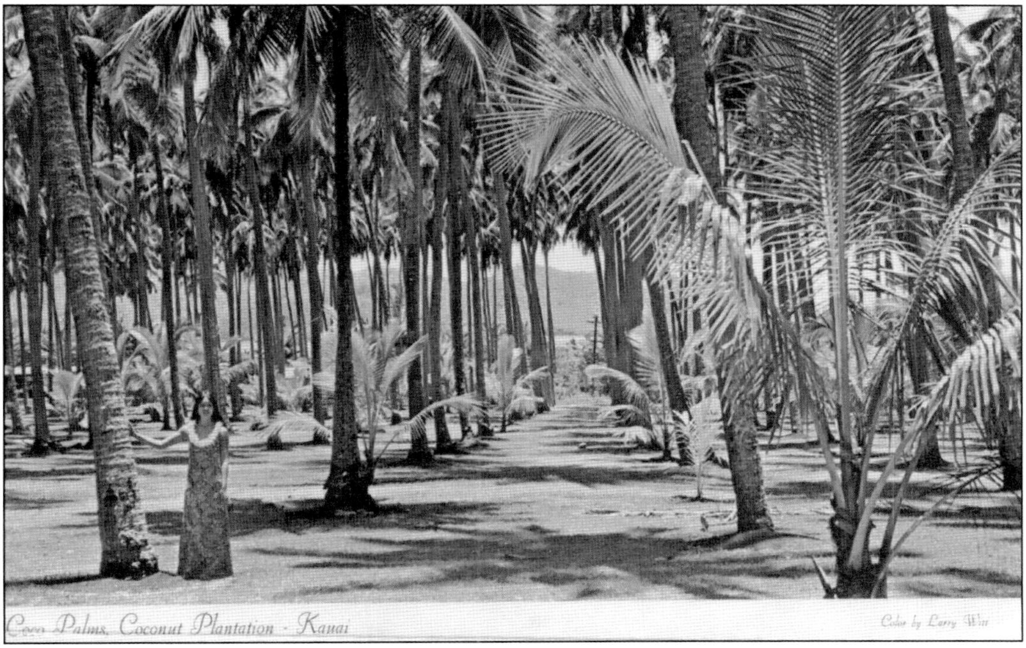

The Coco Palms tree-planting ceremony was inaugurated at the hotel May 10, 1955. It was Grace Guslander's intent to honor people who were important to Kauai, Hawaii, or the world. Some people who were thusly honored are Duke Kahanamoku, James A. Michener, Kathryn K. Hulme, Princesses Liliuokalani Kawananakoa and Kapiolani Kawananakoa, Daniel K. Inouye, John Gregg Allerton, Prince and Princess Hitachi of Japan, Neal S. Blaisdell, and John A. Burns. (22.)

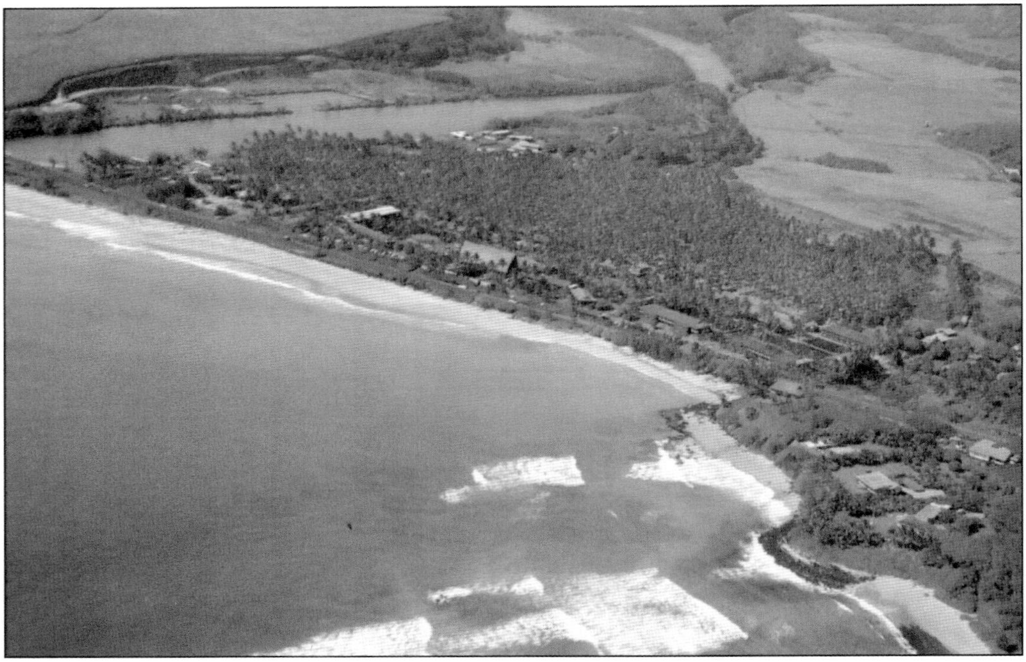

Set in the midst of this large coconut palm grove, Coco Palms is near both the blue Pacific Ocean and the Wailua River. Just the barest outline of the new Wailua Marina can be seen in the upper-left corner. The land behind the marina became Paradise Pacifica. When that business closed in the early 1980s, Freckles Smith, owner of Smith's Boats, assumed the lease, made improvements, and reopened it at Smith's Tropical Paradise. (27.)

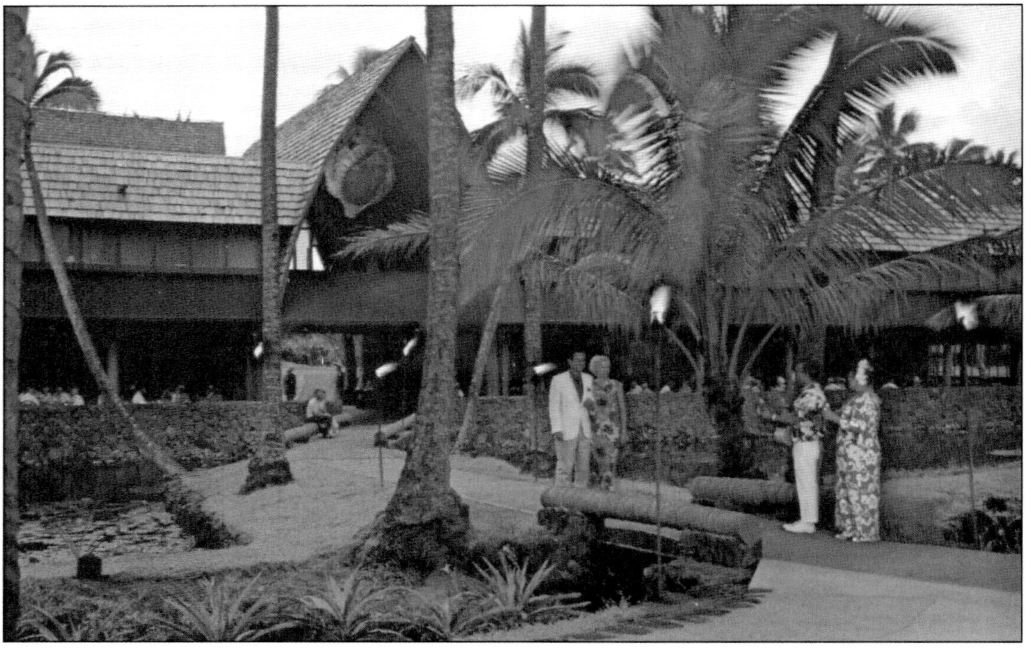

The lagoon side of the Coco Palms Resort shows the entrance to the Lagoon Dining Room. Local entertainers Larry Rivera and Emily Kealoha are serenading California couple Marilyn and Phil Jaffe. (27.)

Guy Matsunaga built the new Coco Palms Resort lobby that opened on January 25, 1965. The floor of the lobby was made of coral, and glass triangular windows reminded more than a few visitors of a church rather than a reception area. (27.)

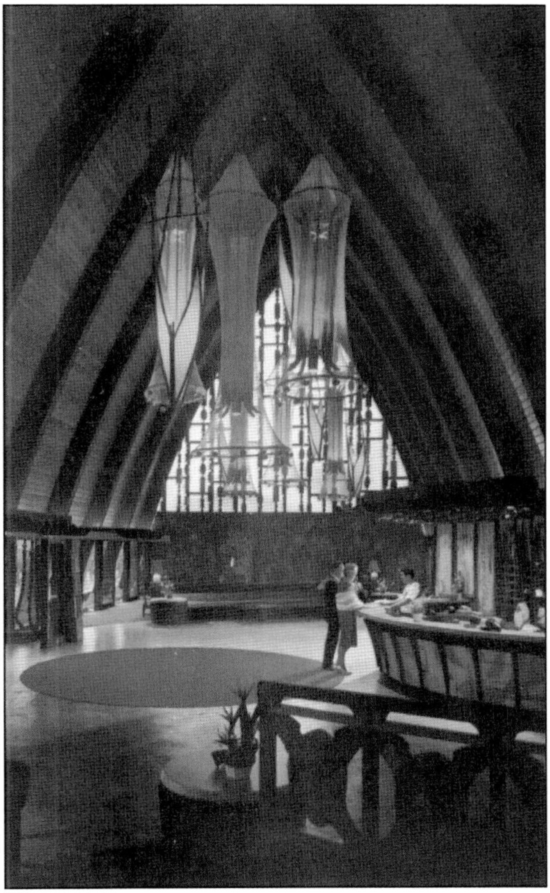

The new exterior entrance to Coco Palms Reception shows off the Oracle Tower in the foreground. It is a replica of what would have been found near every *heiau* (Hawaiian temple). The reason why it is at a hotel had nothing to do with the Hawaiian culture. No such towers exist today at heiau sites, so this one shows visitors what one would have looked like. (27.)

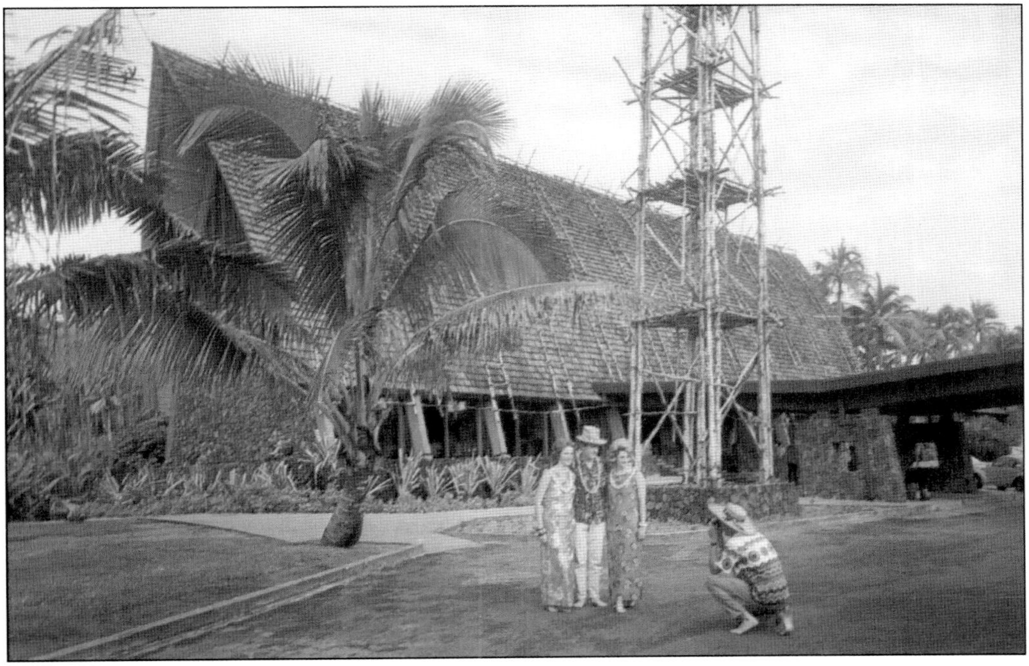

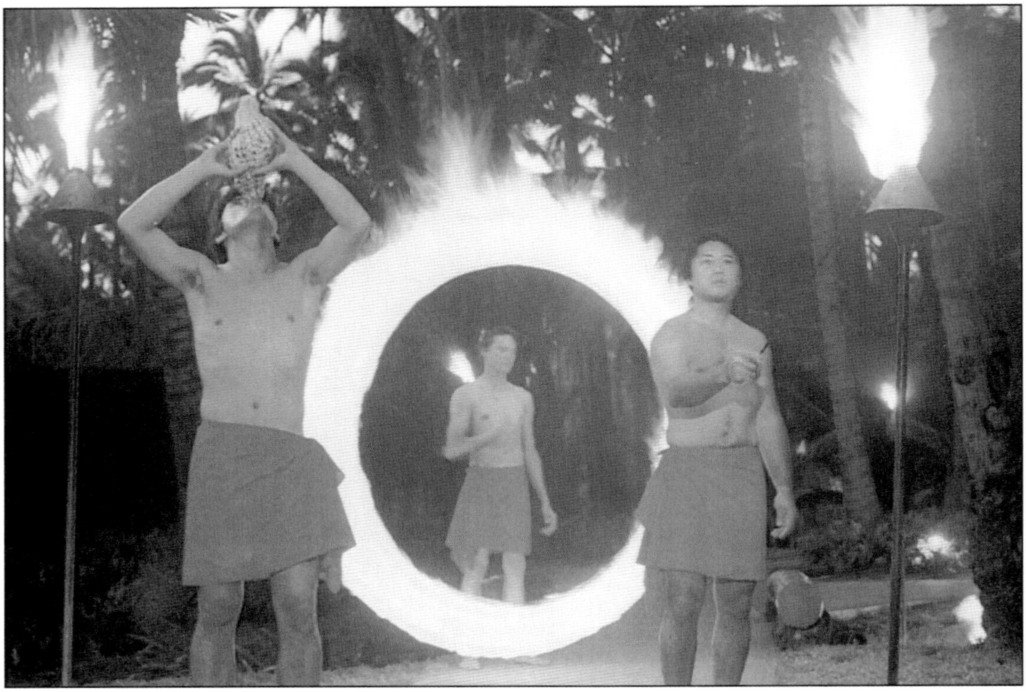

The torch-lighting ceremony (above) became synonymous with the Coco Palms. Contrary to myth, it was not a real Hawaiian ceremony. It was, however, a very dramatic way to call visitors to dinner. It was also a time to share bits of Hawaiian culture as the guests listened to the conch being blown and heard a bit of the history narrated as the torches were lit. The conch shell blower (left) is unidentified, Onio Punzal is in the center, and Wayne Kinoshita is at right. Below, at this Torch Lighting Ceremony, local boy Sebastian Alalem is blowing the conch, Willie Carrillo is holding the stick, and John Kaleohi is lighting the torch. (Above, 0; below, 31.)

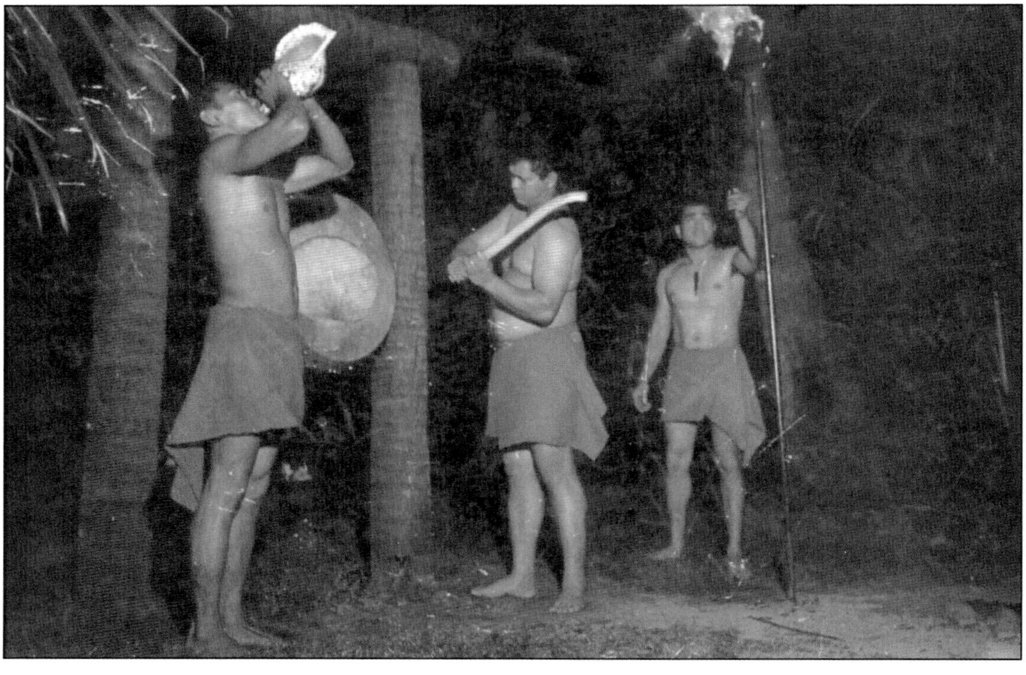

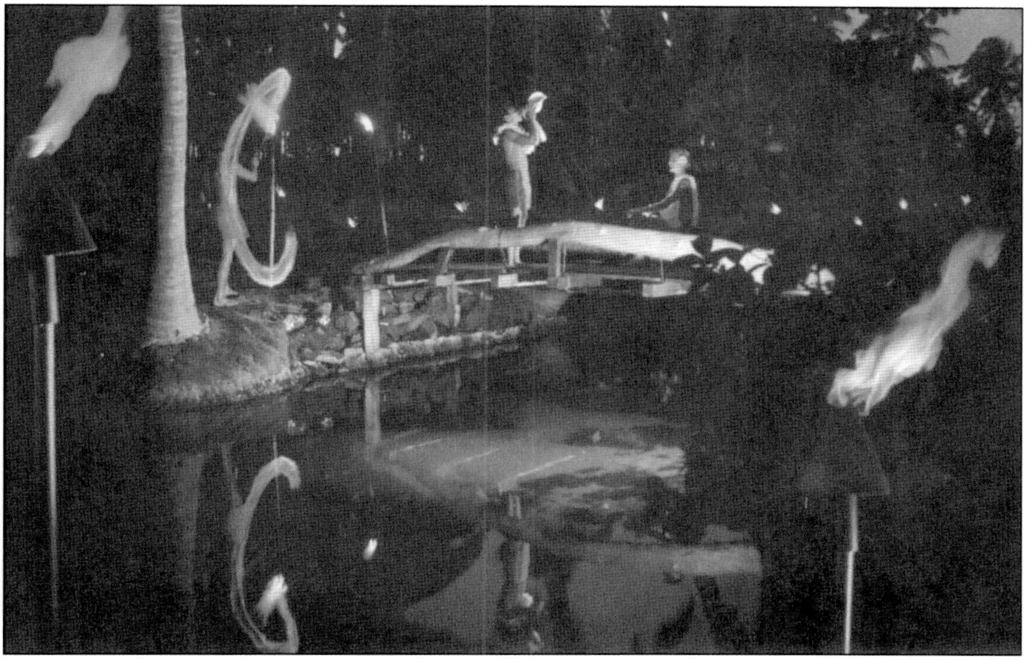

The Coco Palms Hotel made an effort to hire local people in all areas of the facility. Shown above, local boy Onio Punzal sounds "The Call to Dinner" with the blowing of the conch shell. The beating of drums and the lighting of torches made dinner at the Coco Palms an unforgettable experience. Even residents enjoyed visiting the hotel's restaurant for its splendid ambience. Twilight at Coco Palms was always a special time, as this additional view below shows. These are the same lagoons made famous in the wedding scene in *Blue Hawaii*. Visitors from all over the world came to see the ceremony. In the front of the canoe is Larry Kahunaele; paddling is Donald "Hawk" Kawaihalau. (Above, 27; below, 27.)

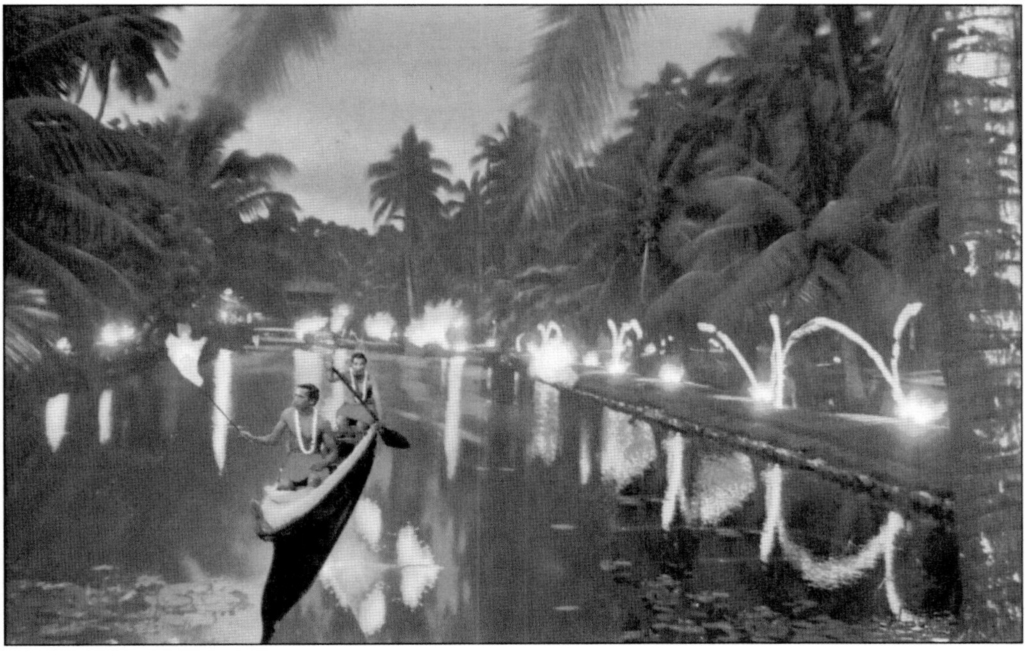

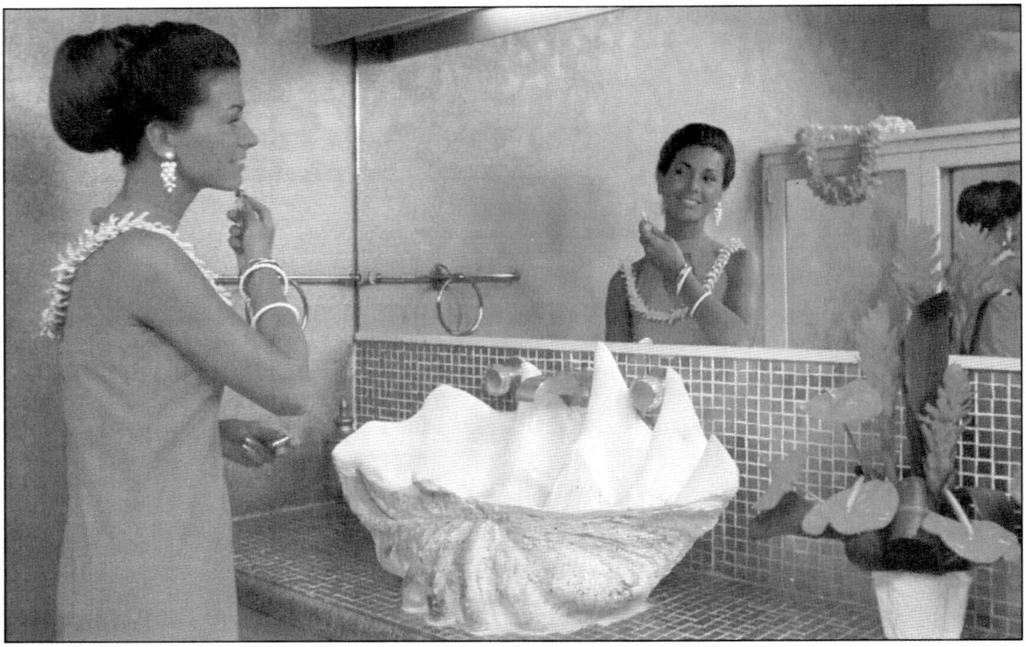

Kings Cottage's giant clamshell basins were an attention-grabber to visitors who stayed at the Coco Palms. Giant clams are not native to the Hawaiian Islands, but the shells added to the tropical mystique that this hotel wove around its guests. (27.)

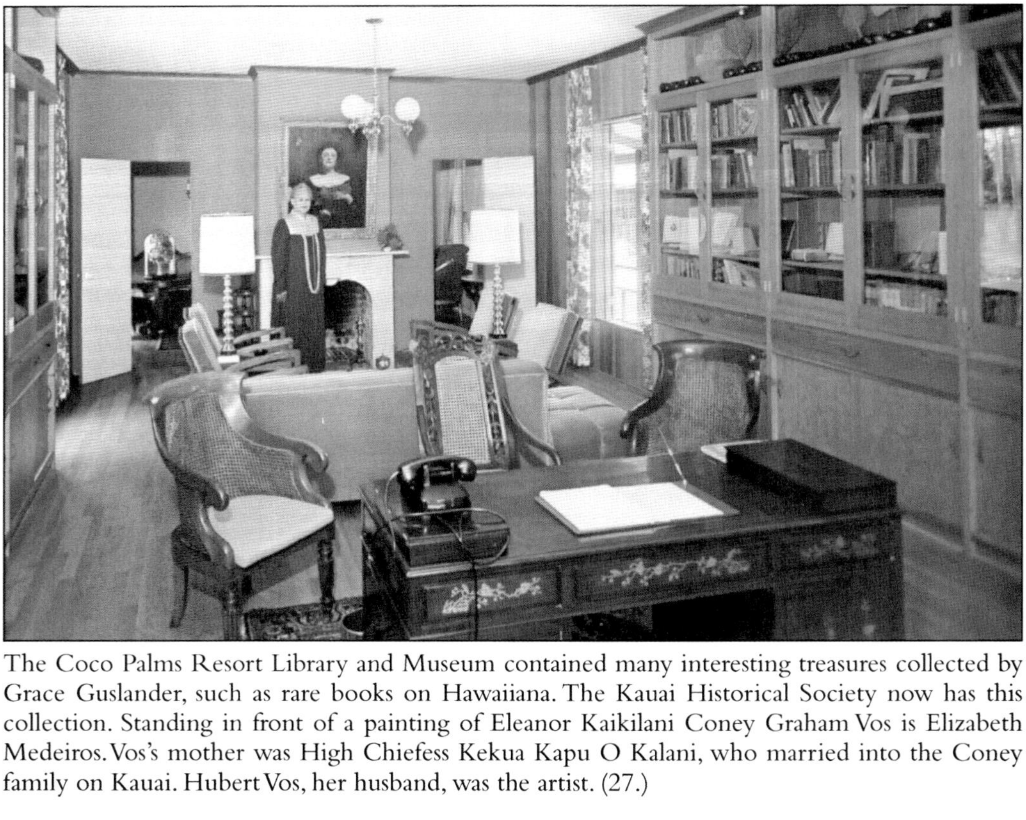

The Coco Palms Resort Library and Museum contained many interesting treasures collected by Grace Guslander, such as rare books on Hawaiiana. The Kauai Historical Society now has this collection. Standing in front of a painting of Eleanor Kaikilani Coney Graham Vos is Elizabeth Medeiros. Vos's mother was High Chiefess Kekua Kapu O Kalani, who married into the Coney family on Kauai. Hubert Vos, her husband, was the artist. (27.)

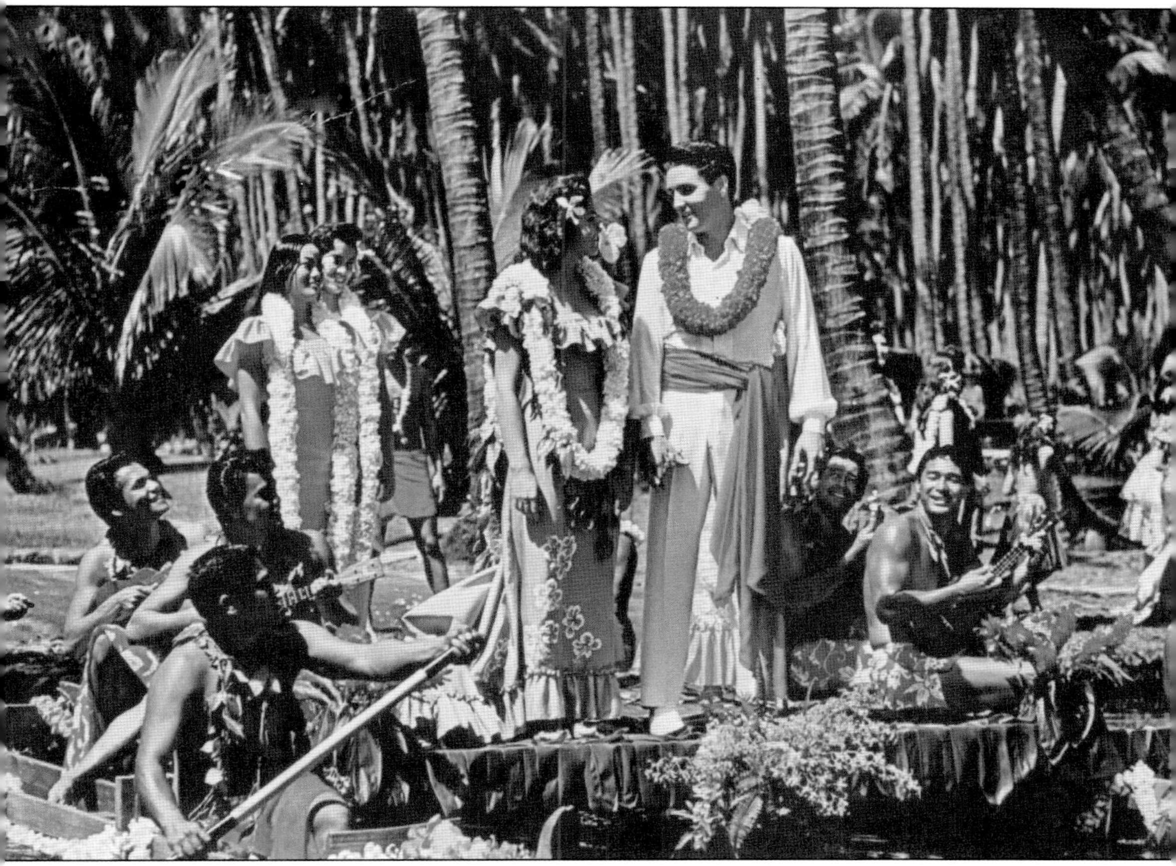

In 1961, *Blue Hawaii* was filmed in Hawaii, much of it at the Coco Palms Resort. This famous wedding scene shows Chad Gates (Elvis Presley) and his bride, Maile Duval (Joan Blackman), being paddled down the lagoon that once had been an ancient Hawaiian fishpond. The girl directly behind Blackman is Kauai resident Janet Largusa. (0.)

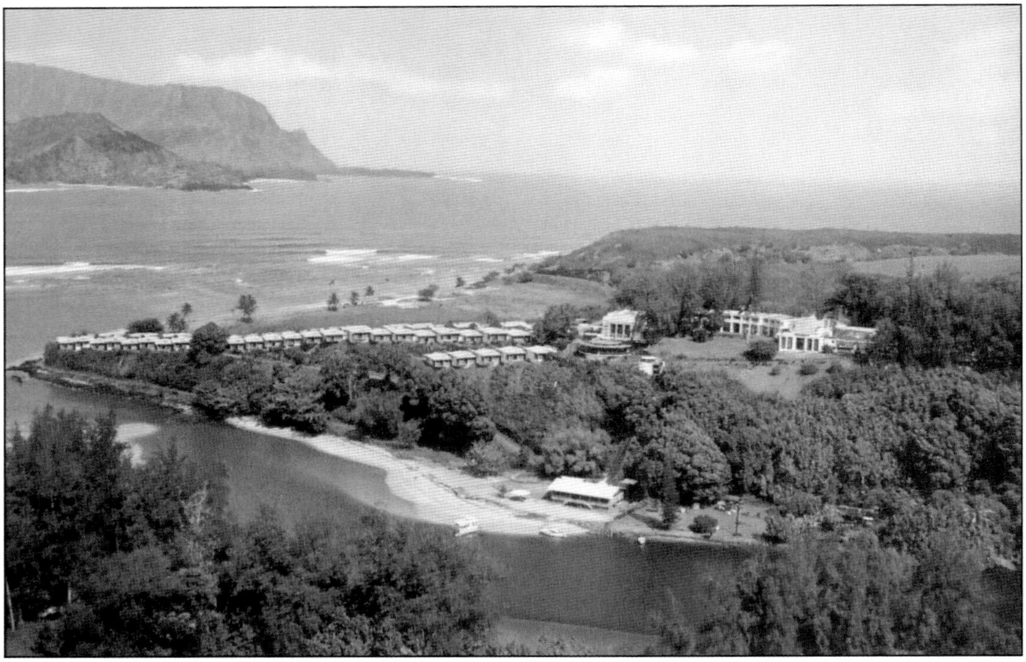

This aerial postcard shows the Hanalei Plantation hotel and its cottages in relation to the river and reflects the hotel's low impact on the property. From this vantage point, one can see, from center left going right, the Reception building, the Crystal Room dining facility off the pool area, and just in front of it, the House of Happy Talk bar. The white rectangle to the left of the bar is the funicular tram that took guests down to the beach. The large white-roofed building shown center bottom was part of the property used for private parties. (27.)

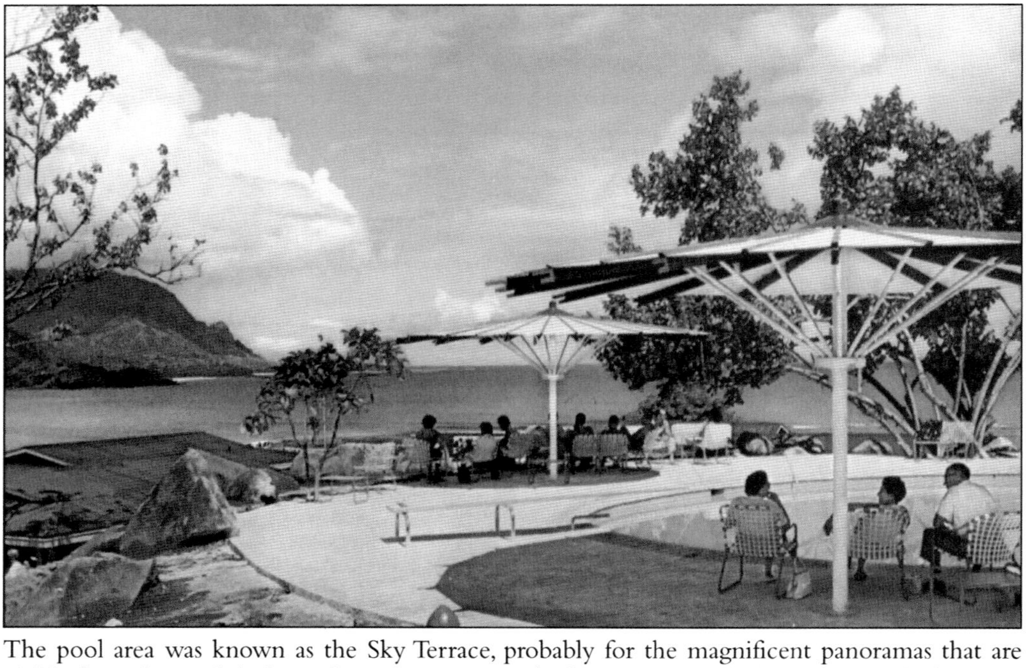

The pool area was known as the Sky Terrace, probably for the magnificent panoramas that are visible from the pool deck. In the early 1960s, pools always came with diving boards, before they came to be considered a liability beginning in the 1970s. (10.)

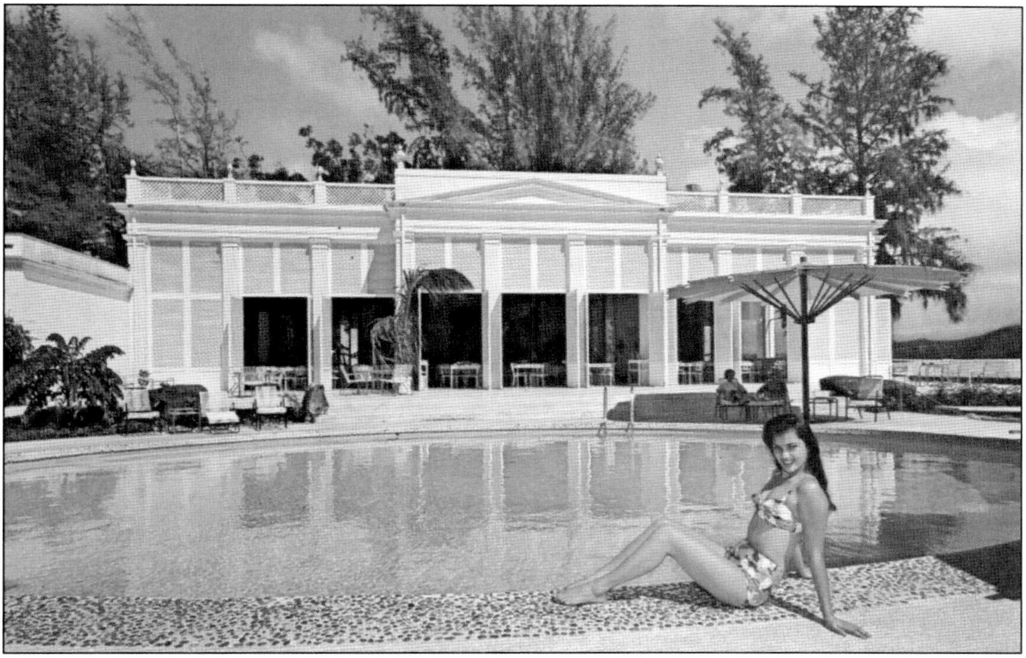

This view of the Sky Terrace (above) shows that it is just a few steps from the plantation dining room, known as the Crystal Room. A later view (below) of the Sky Terrace taken from a higher angle includes guest cottages that provide an extra feeling of privacy. A *Time* article from 1963 mentions that these units were "designed for couples who will shell out $50.00 a day and be satisfied at night with entertainment no more boisterous than a book." After all, it is in a setting made famous by the film *South Pacific*. To put the cost into perspective, a double at Coco Palms was only $28 a day. (Above, 34, Q; below, 27.)

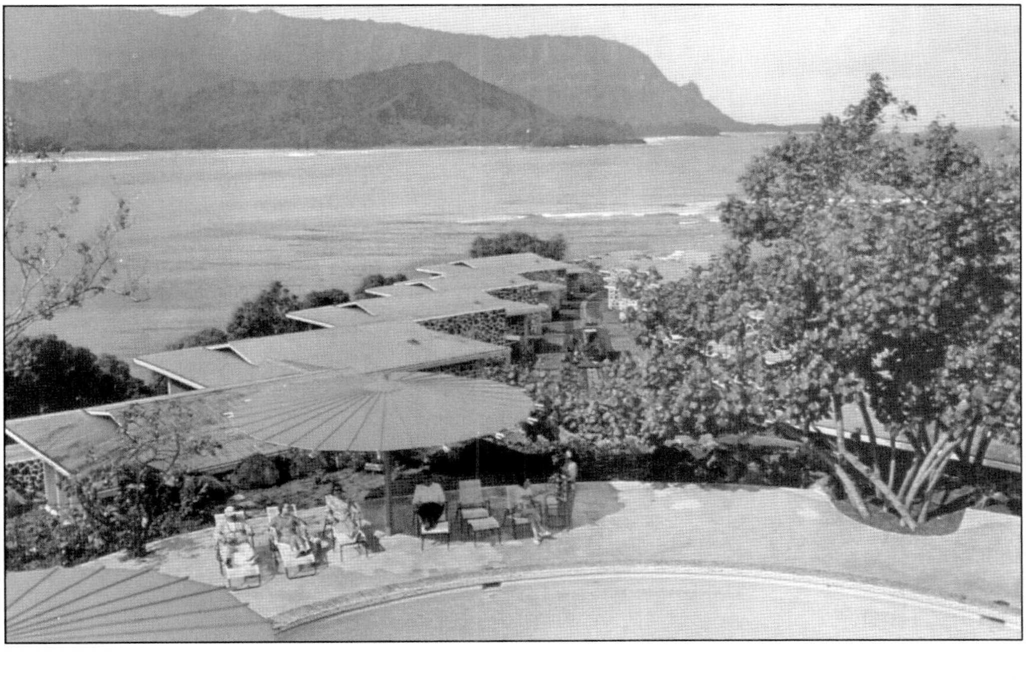

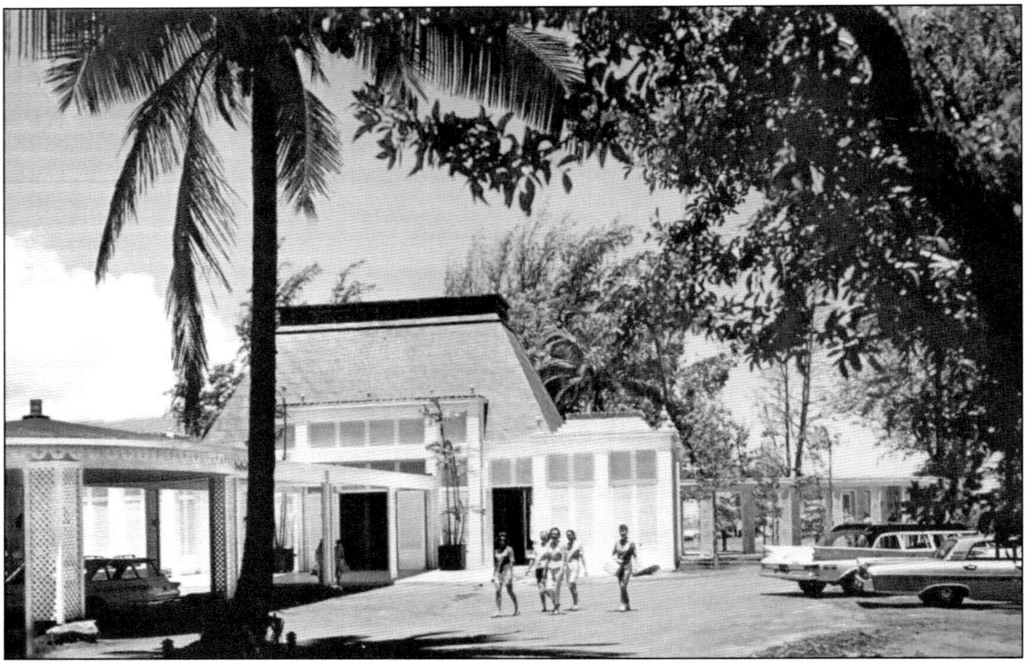

The Hanalei Plantation opened in 1961 with David Penhallow as its manager. This view (above) shows the entrance to the hotel with its signature green copper roof. This elegant resort occupies a breathtaking promontory just above the Hanalei River. Although this was the location of the actual filming of *South Pacific,* the hotel was not there at the time. This was the site of the private residence of Miranda Birkmyre. At the conclusion of filming, the home was sold so the land could be developed into a hotel and resort. The view below shows a breezeway and gazebo that connect the Reception Building in the background with the dining room and bar, the House of Happy Talk. A putting green is in the foreground. (Above, 10; below, 27.)

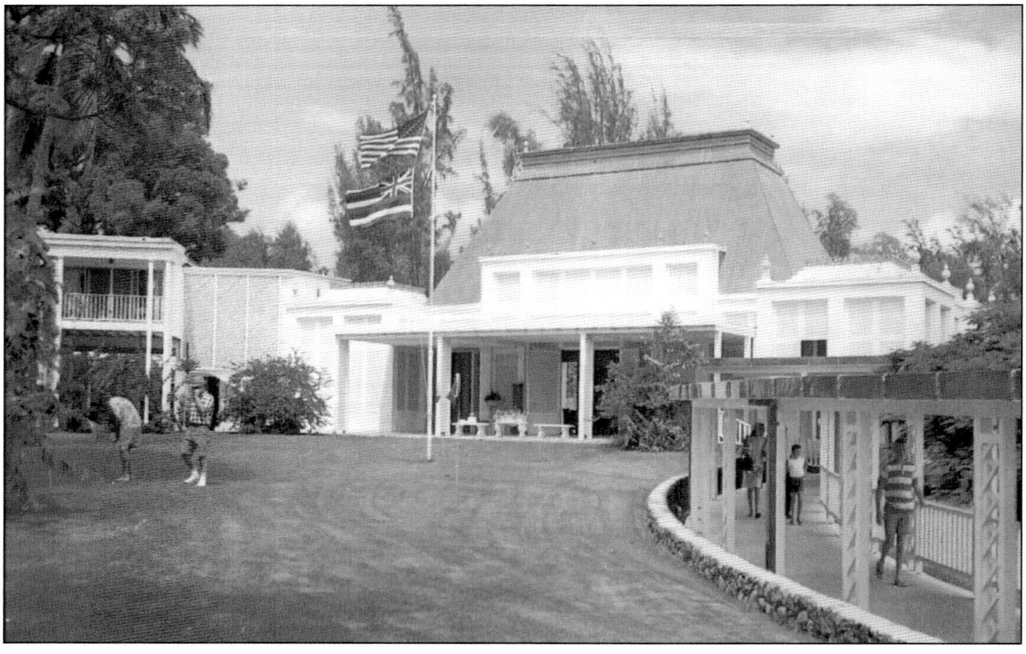

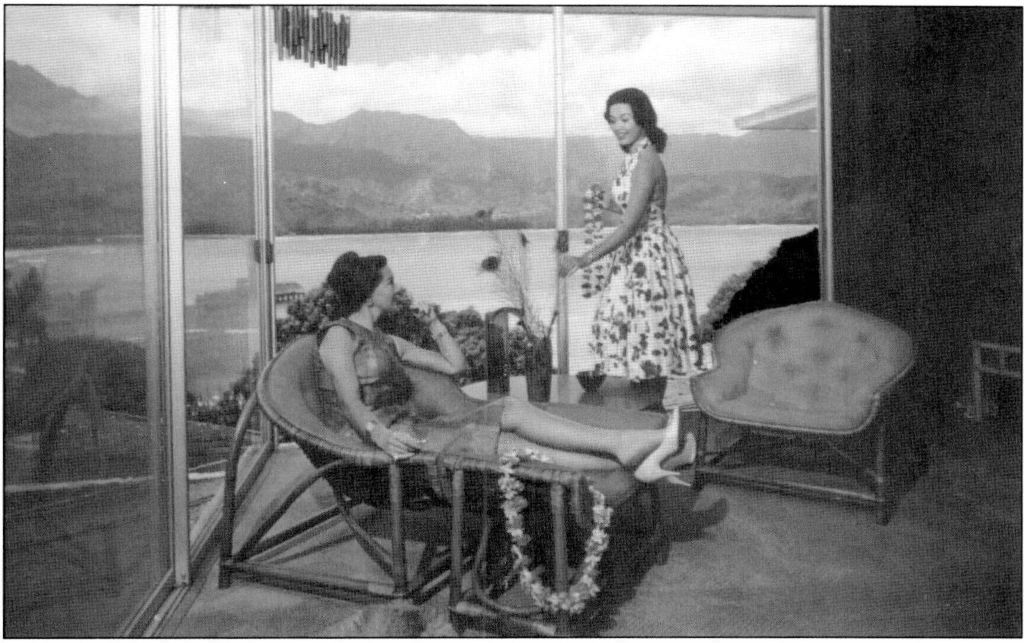

These two interior shots of the Hanalei Plantation show much of the character of 1960s Polynesian décor. In the view above, bamboo and rattan are the standout features. Even the wind chime would add ambience next to the open screen door. The rooms in the main part of the hotel would have spectacular views of Hanalei Bay. Note the famous Hanalei pier behind the unidentified, seated lady. Below, the view shows an interior of one of the private cottages that cost $50 a night in 1961. These cottages had views overlooking the river as well as the distant mountains and the ocean below. (Above and below, 27.)

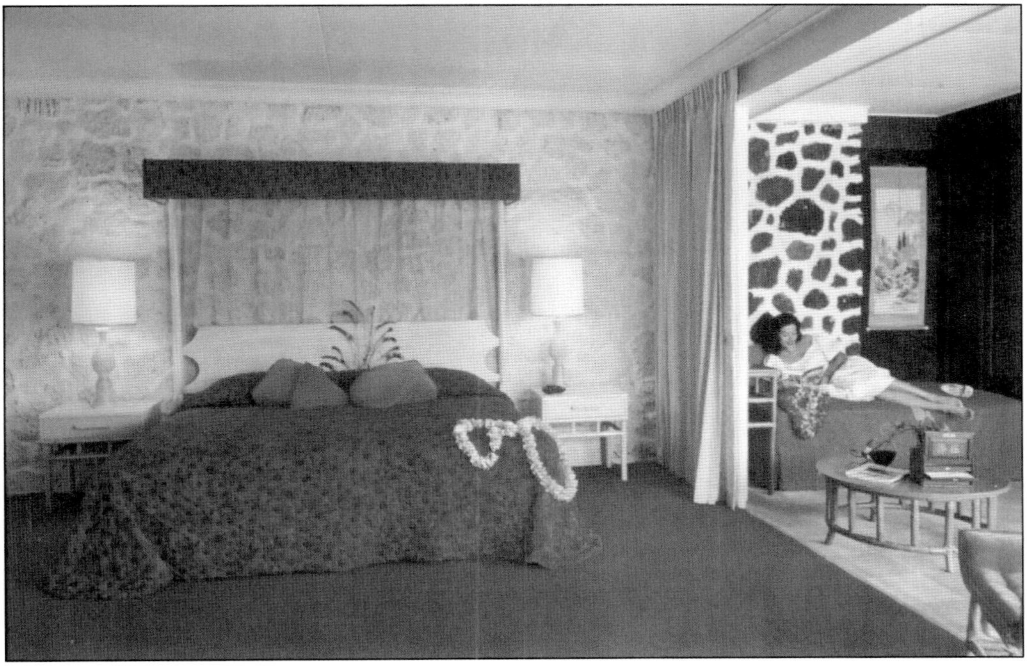

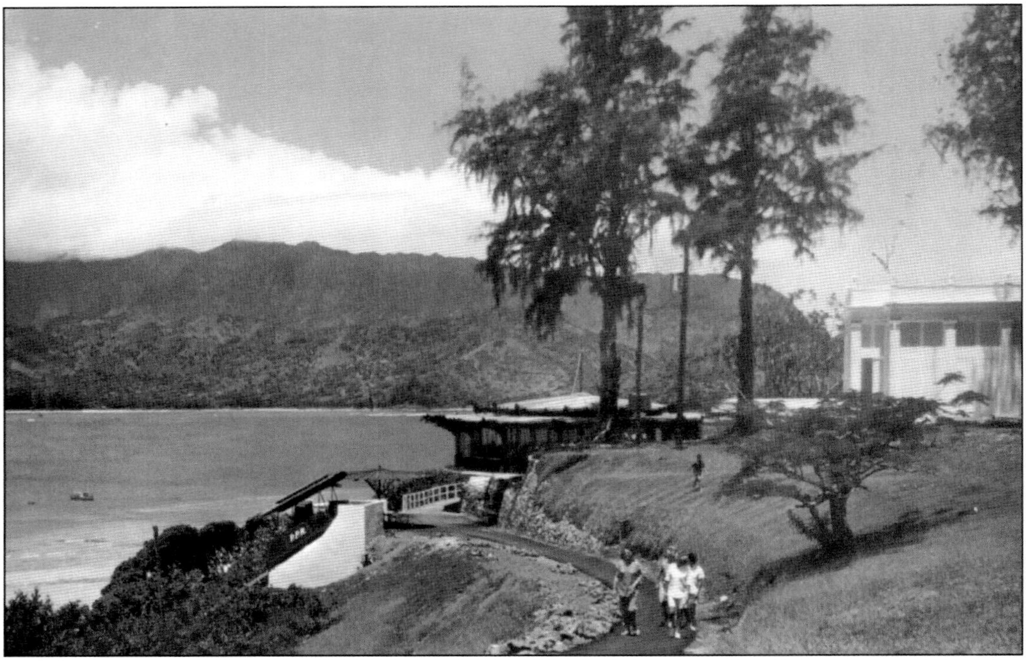

Guests at the Hanalei are seen strolling back up the path. The have either been to House of Happy Talk bar, the round building at the bottom, or have just returned from the beach using the funicular tram, labeled PPR, shown near the white cement building at the left. (27.)

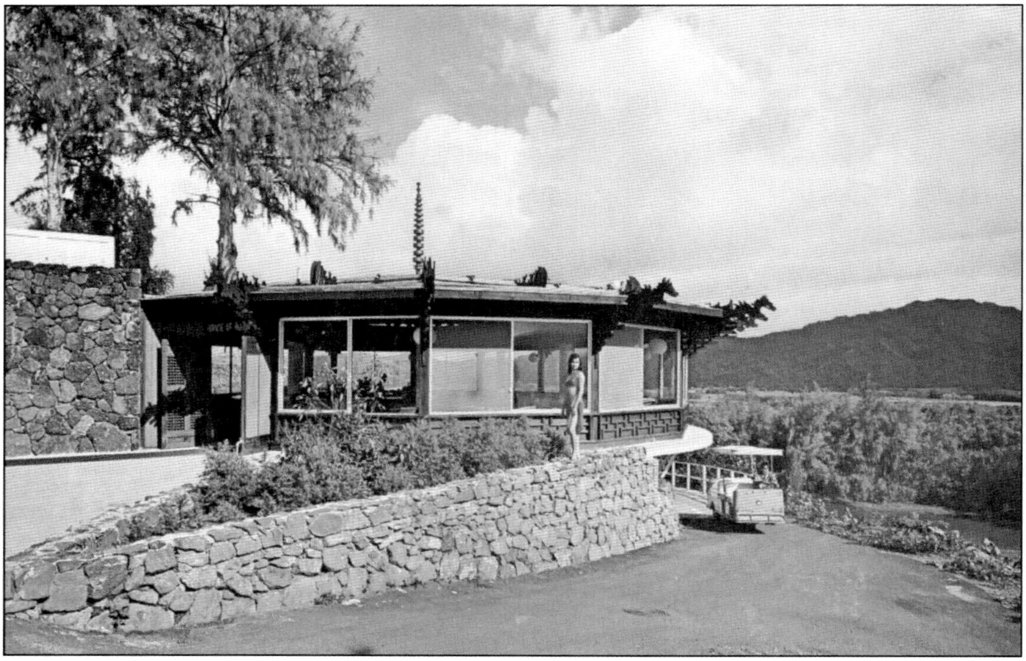

The bar at the Hanalei Plantation, part of Island Resorts, was named after a scene from the movie *South Pacific.* The Asian theme is carried out with the carved dragons that circle the roof. Many local entertainers, such as Barry Yap and Bobby Rumion, performed here. (34, Q.)

This shows the Hanalei Plantation from the river. The land was originally owned by Henry Birkmyre and was still in the Birkmyre family when the movie *South Pacific* was filmed. The next year, it was sold to build the Hanalei Plantation. The round building was named the House of Happy Talk bar after a scene from the movie. It is in roughly the same location as the original Birkmyre home. Also visible is the white poolside dining room, and at right is the entrance to the resort. (27.)

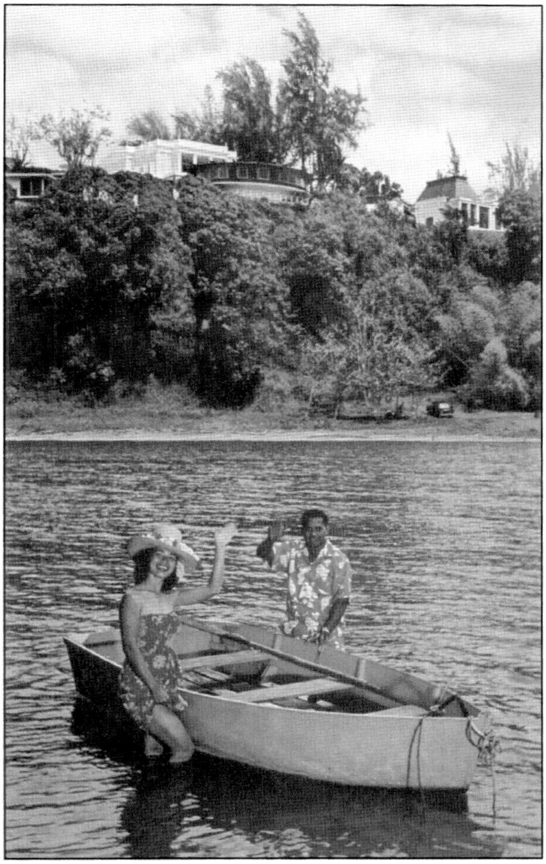

Nothing has changed but the name and proprietors of the Club Méditerranée, better known as Club Med (office shown here). Name replacements at many properties happen from time to time with the transfers of ownership. It can be confusing and is a source of frustration for local residents. (41, Q.)

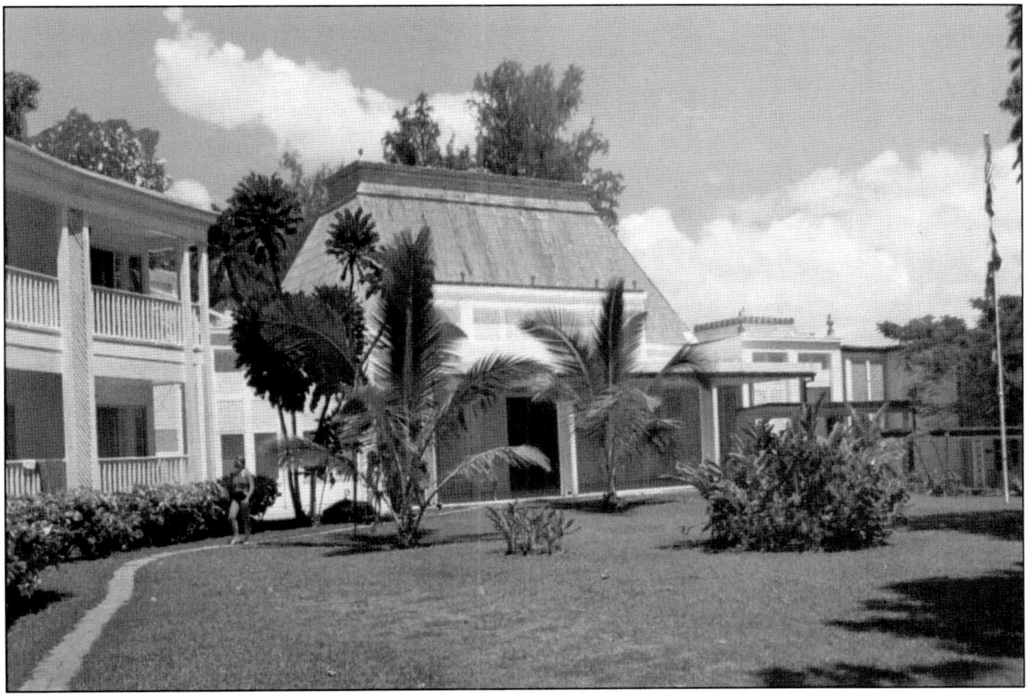

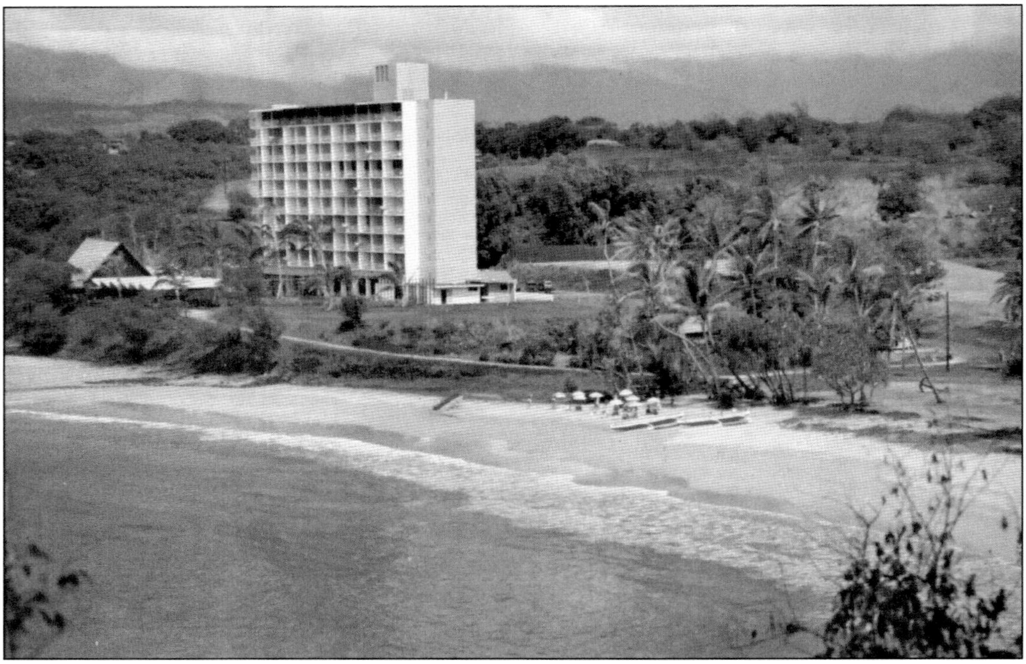

The Kauai Surf was build by Interisland Resorts in 1959 and fronting Kalapaki Beach. It was Kauai's first multistory hotel. Kauai later enacted a rule that no hotel could be taller than a palm tree, which roughly translates to not higher than four stories. This early card shows at left the Planters Bar and the Outrigger Lanai. (31.)

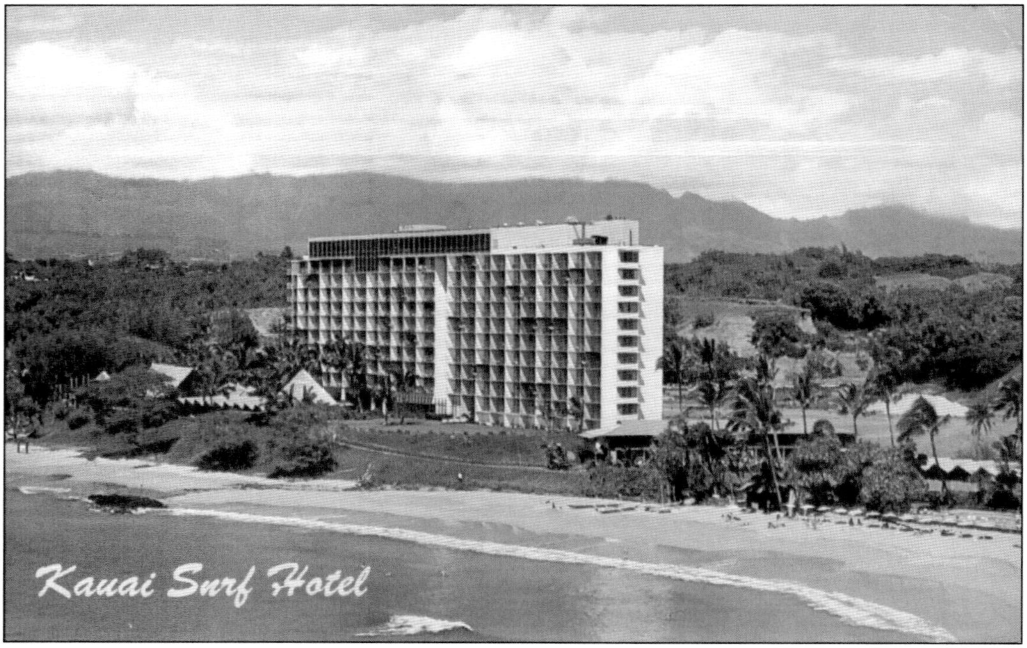

Soon, Kalapaki Phase Two was added to the original section of the Kauai Surf as was the Golden Cape restaurant on the top floor. Bungalows from the old Kauai Inn were moved to the beach at right. A coffee shop and pool by the beach were also added, at right. At left, the roofs of the Planters Bar, the Outrigger Lanai, and the Surf and Sirloin are visible. (27.)

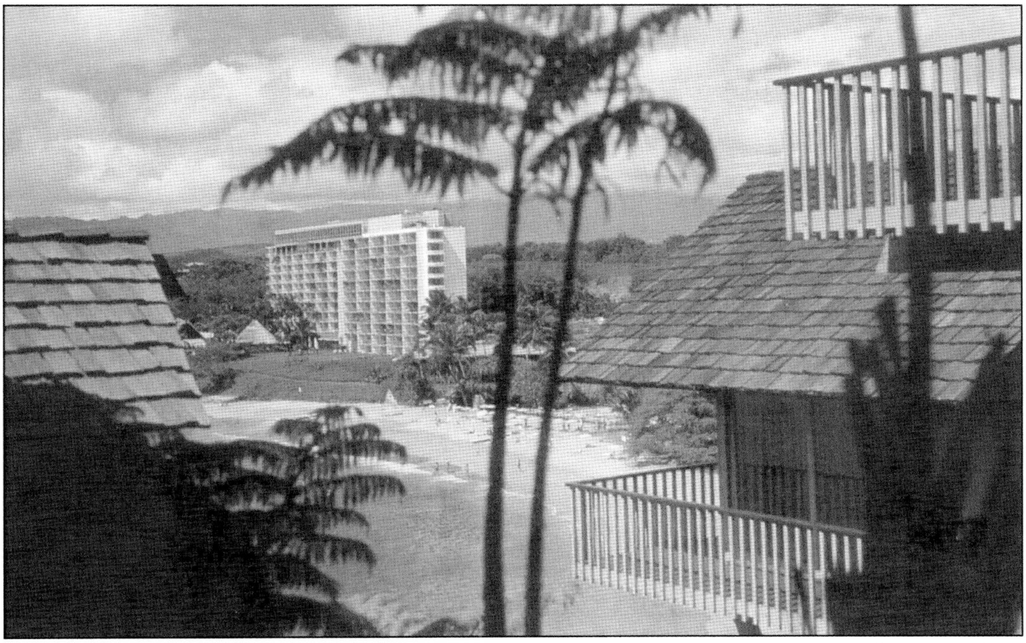

The Pali Kai Cottages that hang from the cliff above Kalapaki Bay were originally part of the Kauai Surf and run by Interisland Resorts. Now they are privately owned. (31.)

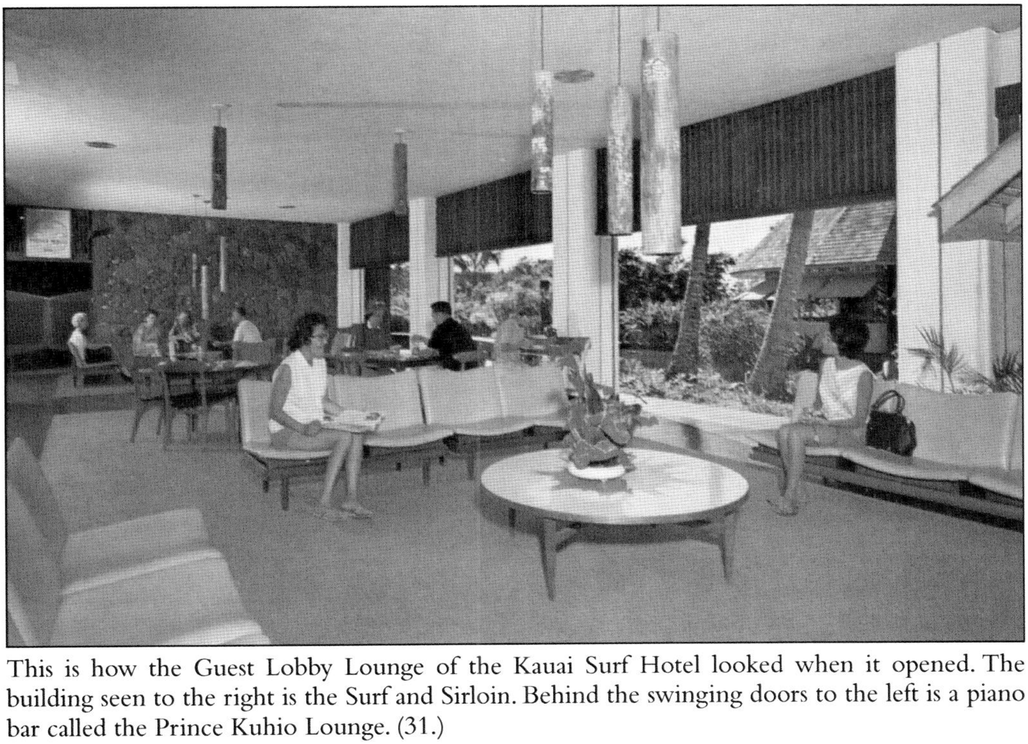

This is how the Guest Lobby Lounge of the Kauai Surf Hotel looked when it opened. The building seen to the right is the Surf and Sirloin. Behind the swinging doors to the left is a piano bar called the Prince Kuhio Lounge. (31.)

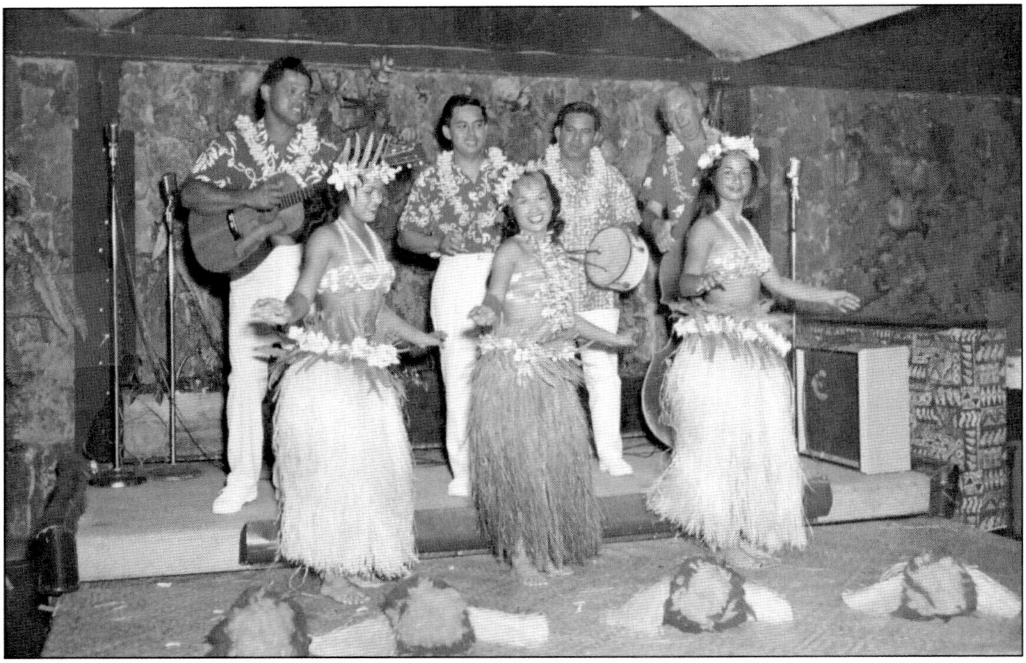

The Planter's Bar at the Kauai Surf had a nightly Polynesian show. Performers include, from left to right, (dancers) Doreen Sanchez, Kuulei Punua, and Bernie Bettencourt; (musicians) Percy Kinimaka, Victor Punua, Jimmy Watson, and Bill Lucidarme. (31.)

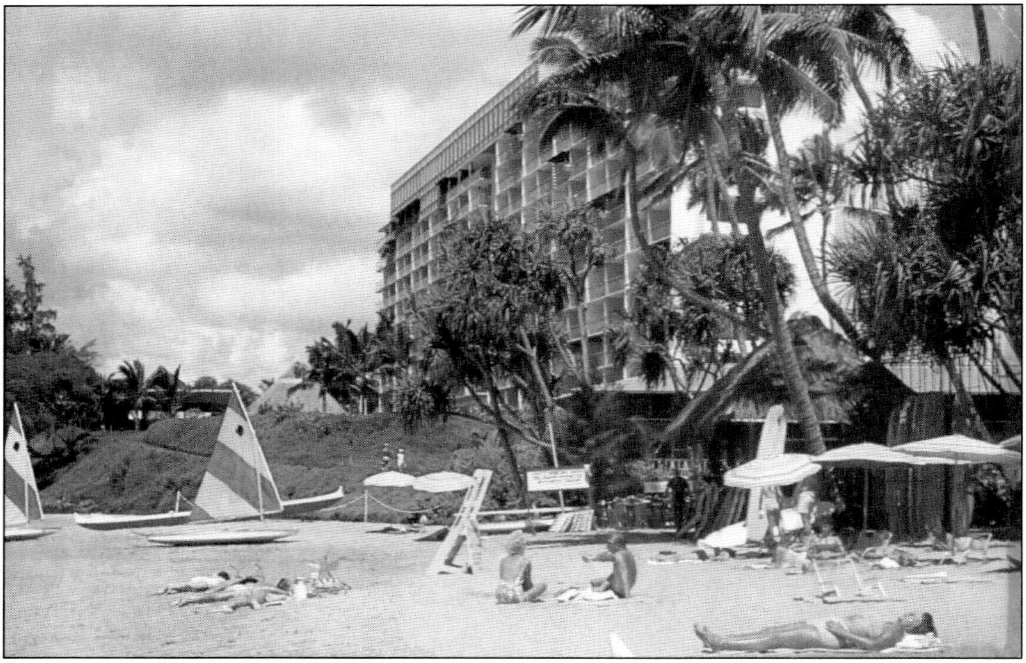

Shown from beach level are the Kauai Surf Hotel, Kalapaki Phase One and Two along with a beach shack that rented surfboards and taught lessons. (31.)

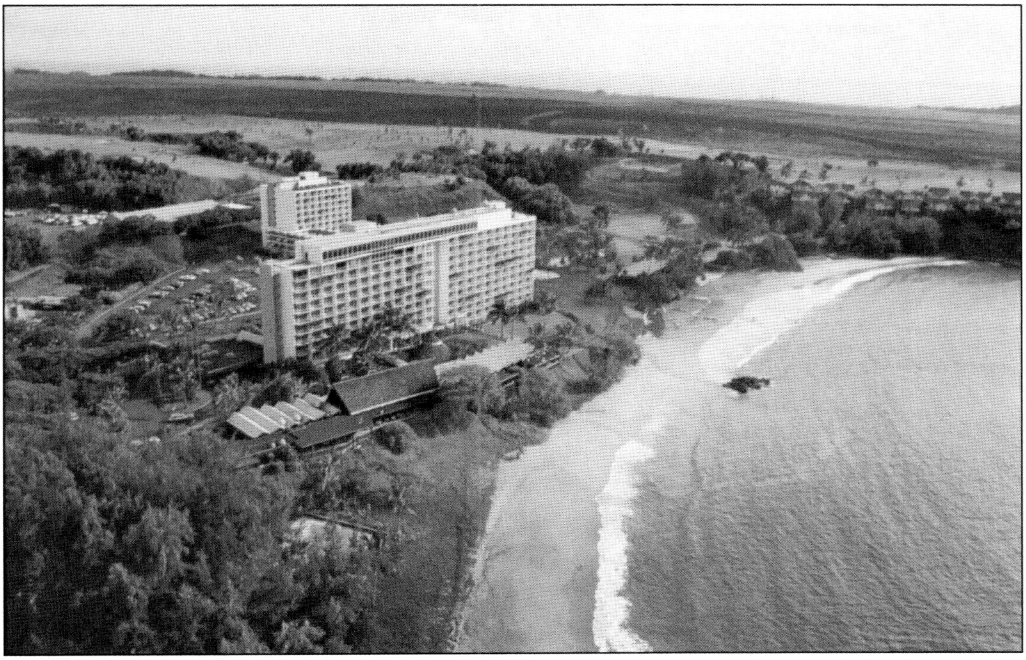

This view of the Kauai Surf looks eastward and shows the Lagoon Building and the first Garden Building addition. The background includes the golf course and, beyond that, the newly harvested sugarcane fields of Lihue Plantation. The Pali Kai Cottages are just visible at right. The pool at lower left is at the future location of the Fisherman Restaurant. (0.)

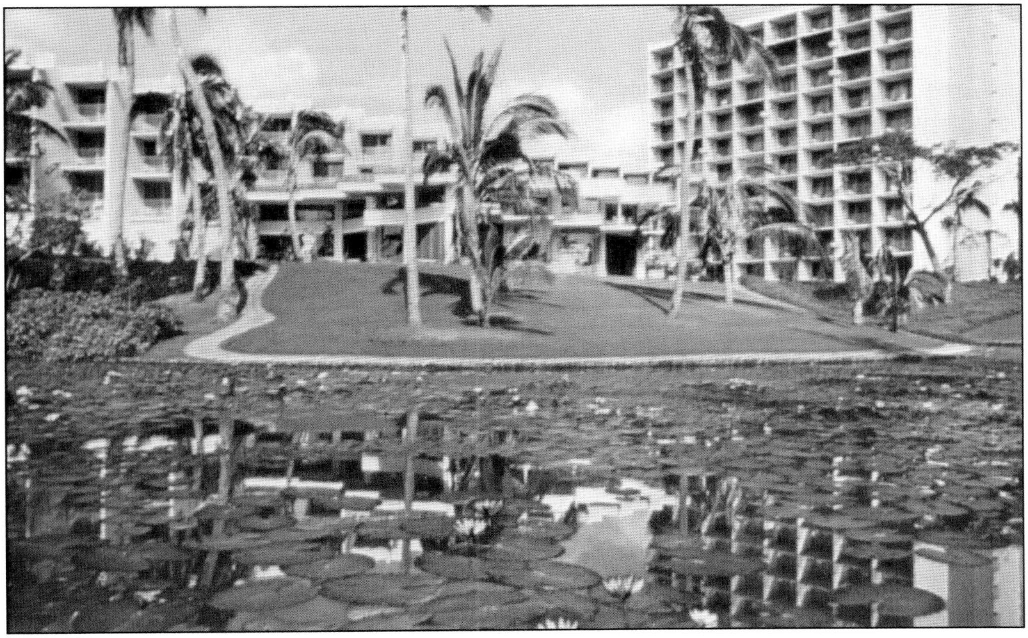

In this 1971 postcard, a mother writes, "Daddy played golf this morning while I swam in this lovely bay." When leaving the lobby and going east leads to the outside and a very large lily pond filled with ducks and swans. The Lagoon's rooms are above the new lobby that is visible at center, and the Garden Building Phase One is visible at right. (28.)

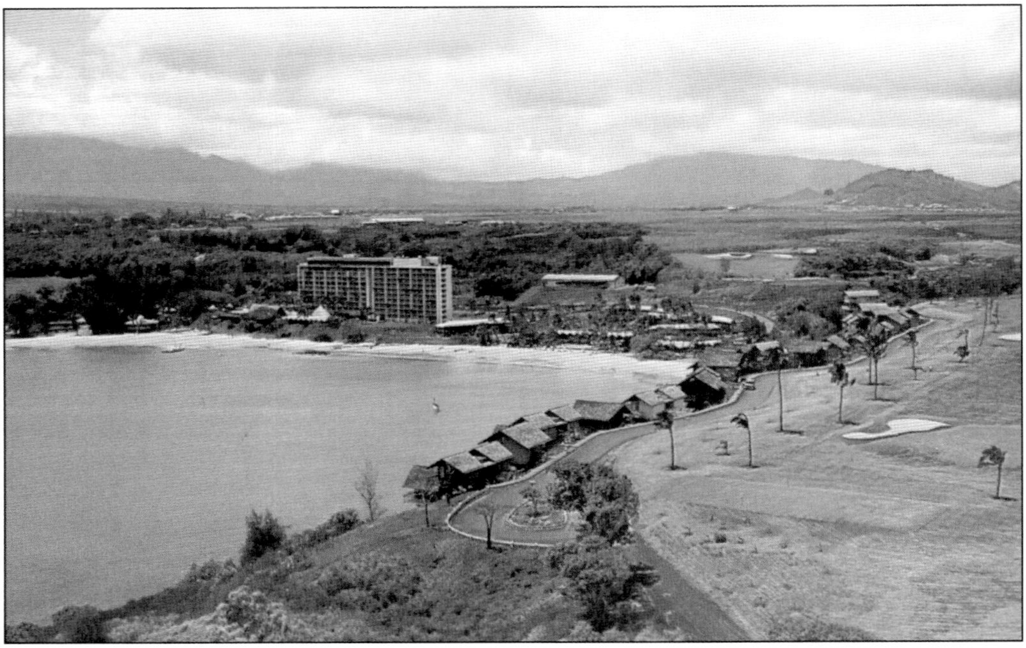

This Kauai Surf Hotel aerial view shows the first nine of the golf course at right. The roof visible at left near the beach is the Fisherman Restaurant. Today, Duke's and Café Portofino occupy that location. The tops of the Pali Kai Cottages are visible, hugging the cliff near the golf course (27, A.)

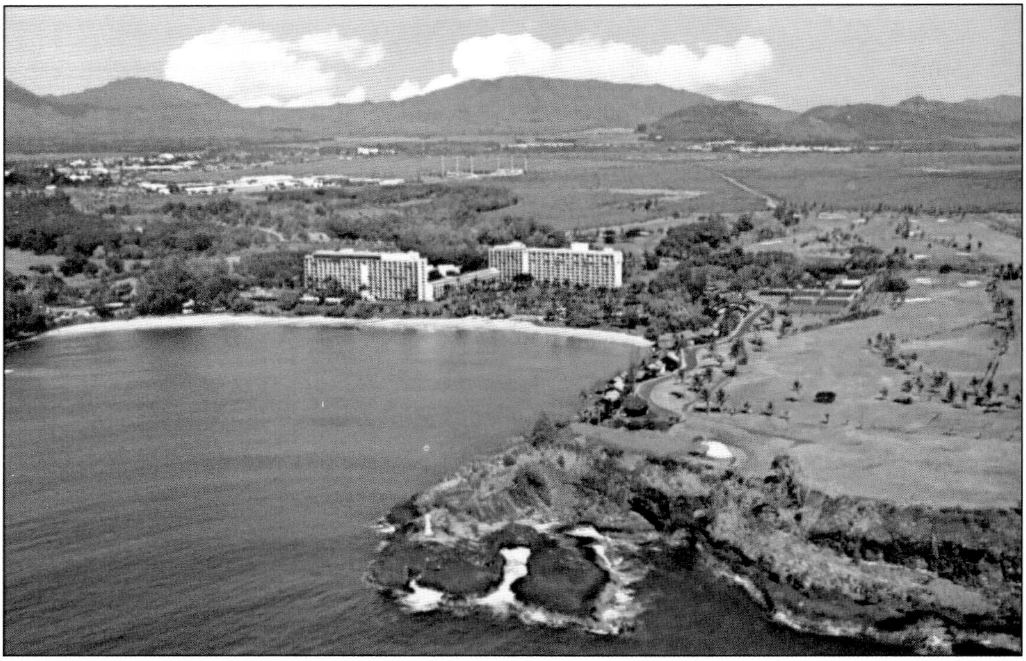

The aerial of the Kauai Surf from the 1970s shows a much-expanded property. It still has the half-mile of sand in front but now includes an 18-hole golf course and a tennis club on its 200 acres. Compare the above view to the one on this book's cover to trace the development over the years (0.)

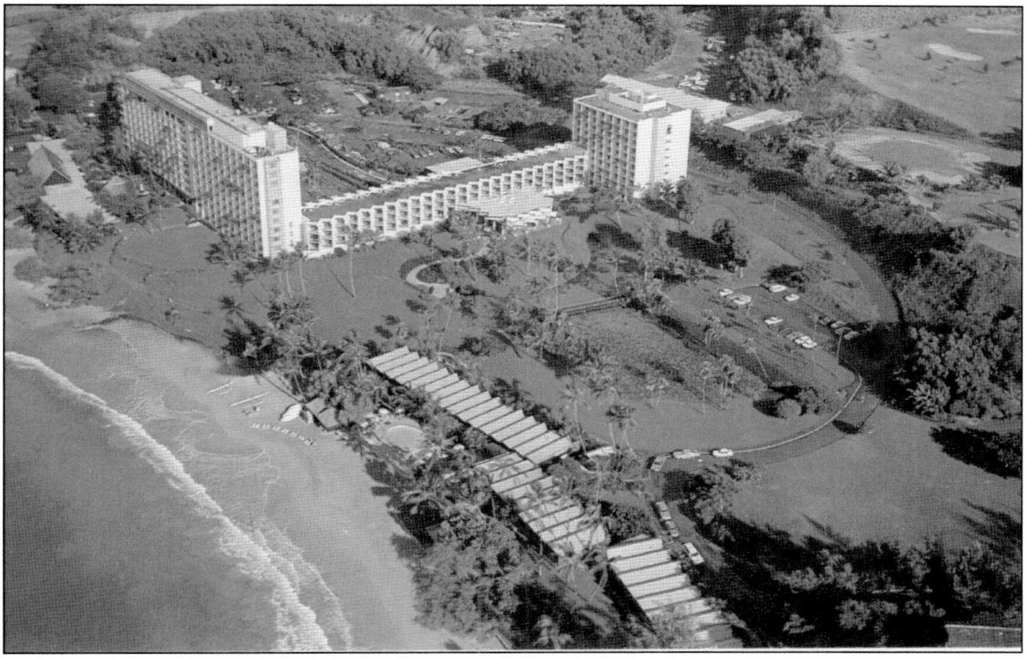

This last aerial of the Kauai Surf shows it as it was before it was bought by Chris Hemmeter and reopened as a very different Westin resort. It does not show the convention center that had been added. That facility held many local events such as Holoku Balls, but it was torn down by the new owners. (11.)

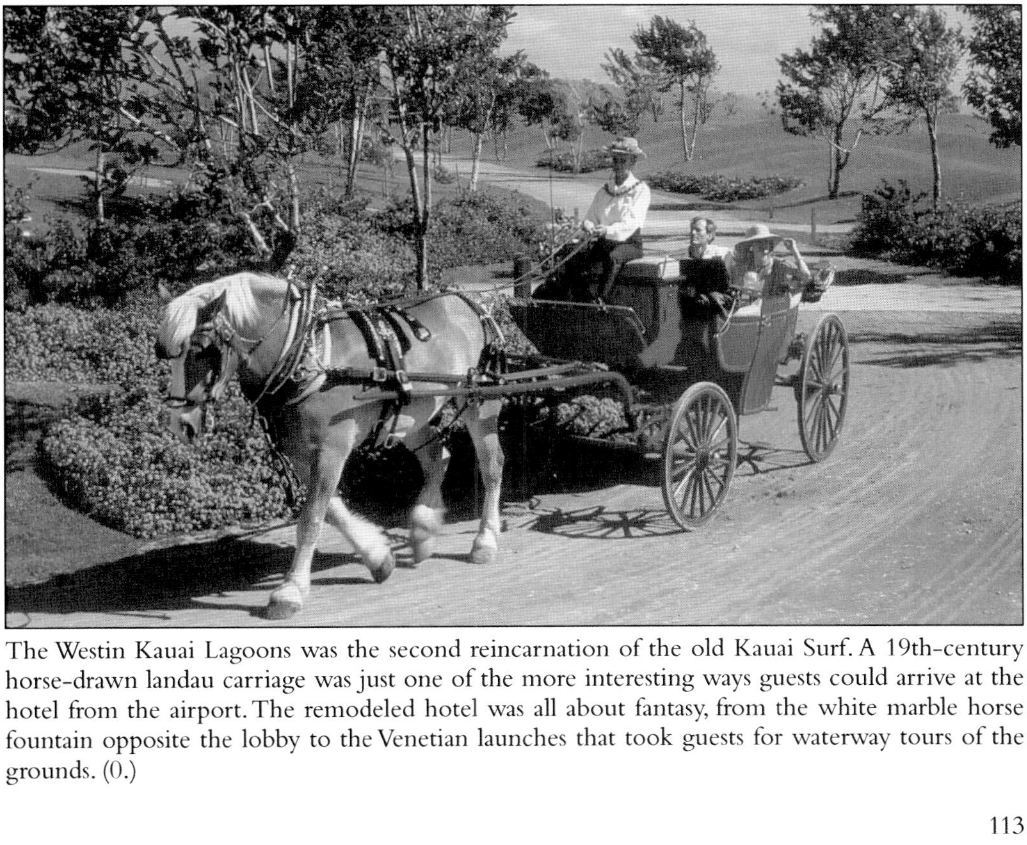

The Westin Kauai Lagoons was the second reincarnation of the old Kauai Surf. A 19th-century horse-drawn landau carriage was just one of the more interesting ways guests could arrive at the hotel from the airport. The remodeled hotel was all about fantasy, from the white marble horse fountain opposite the lobby to the Venetian launches that took guests for waterway tours of the grounds. (0.)

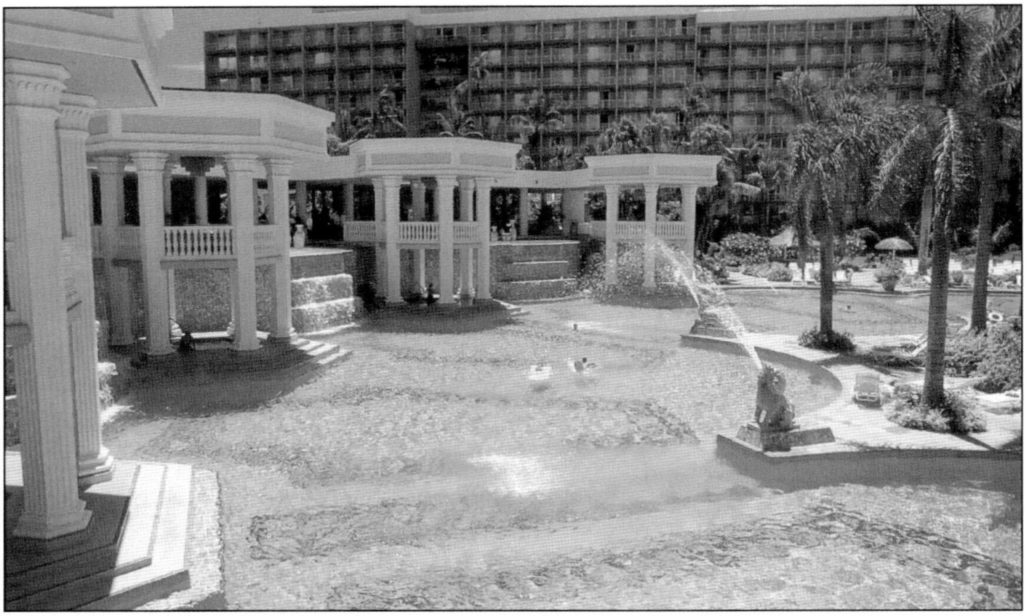

The Westin Kauai Lagoons at Kalapaki Beach opened with Hawaii's largest swimming pool, measuring 26,000 square feet. Roman columns surround multiple Jacuzzis. Each waterfall had a reflecting pool above, where tall urns on Lucite stands appeared to be floating on the surface of the water. The rooms in the background are in the newly added wing. (30.)

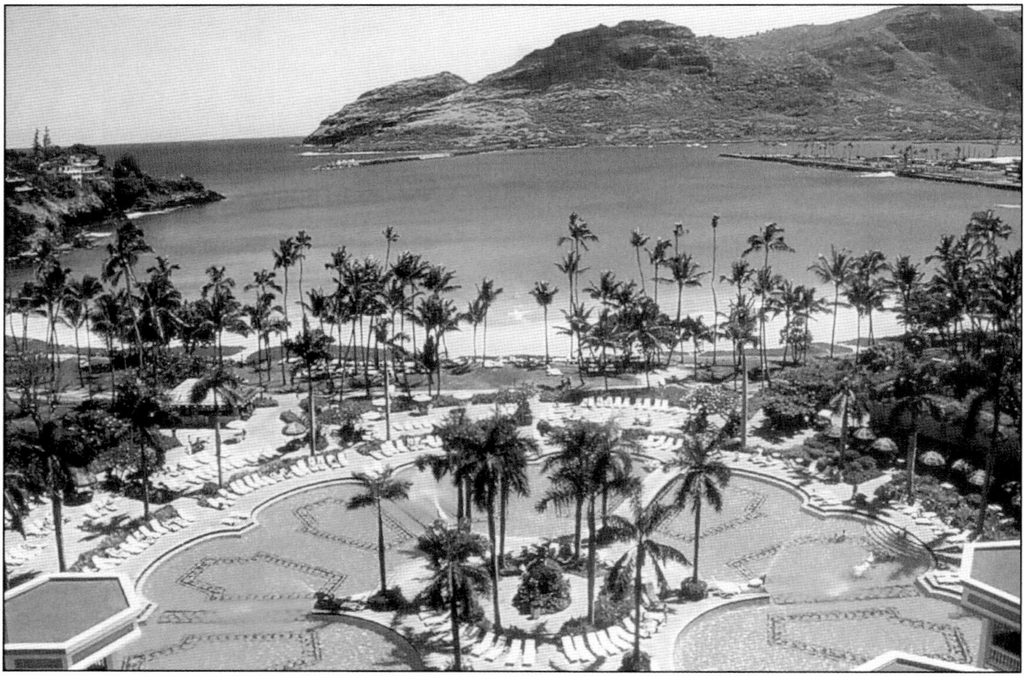

After the 1992 hurricane, the Marriott took over from the Westin. The largest pool in the Hawaiian Islands is now part of the Marriott. Under new management, the hotel underwent remodeling again. The new design kept the pool but filled in much of the white marble horse fountain and replaced it with plantings and a smaller pond. Planners returned the ducks and swans, although they were in a new location, and added koi. (0.)

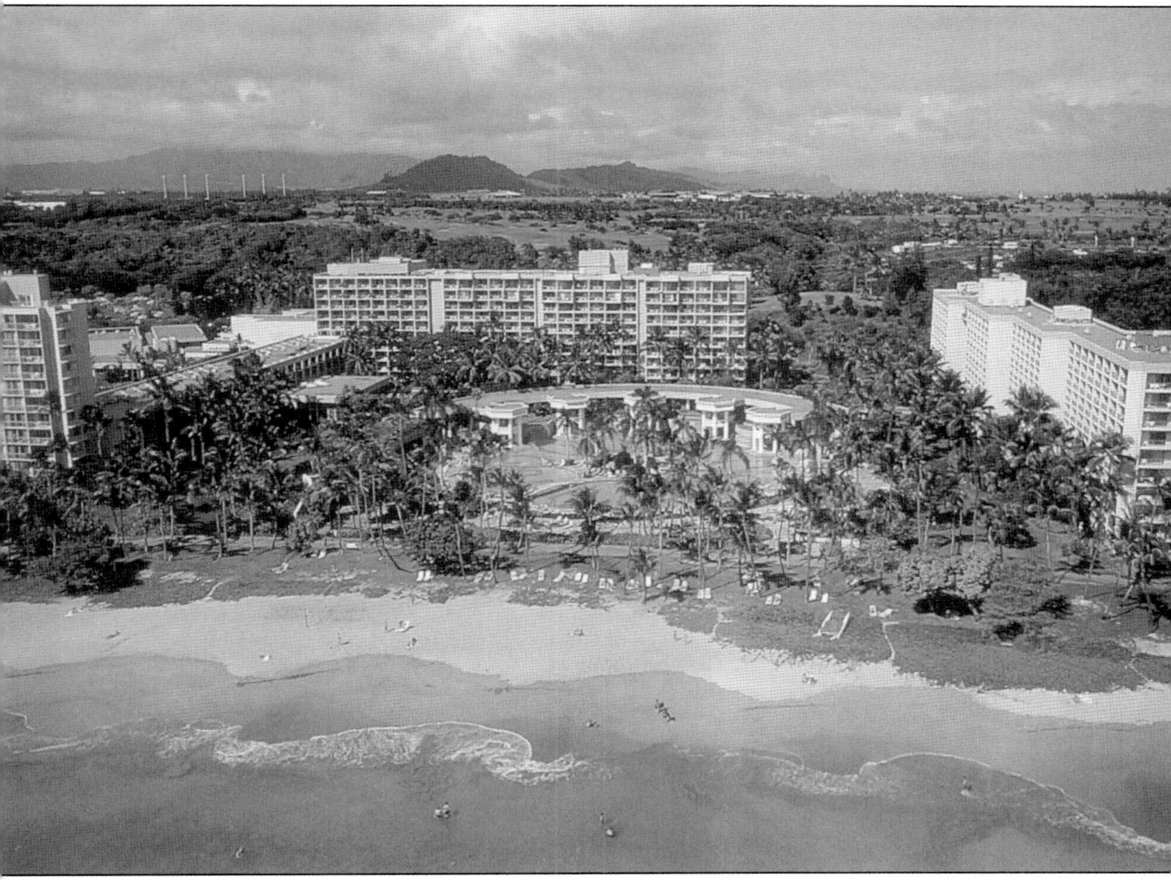

The Kauai Marriott on Kalapaki Beach took over the running of this property after 1992's Hurricane Iniki. This aerial shot looking into the property from high above Kalapaki Bay toward the hotel shows it with all its many additions. It is still the only hotel on Kauai with more than four stories. Fortunately, it cannot be seen from the town of Lihue that is inland and not at sea level. (30.)

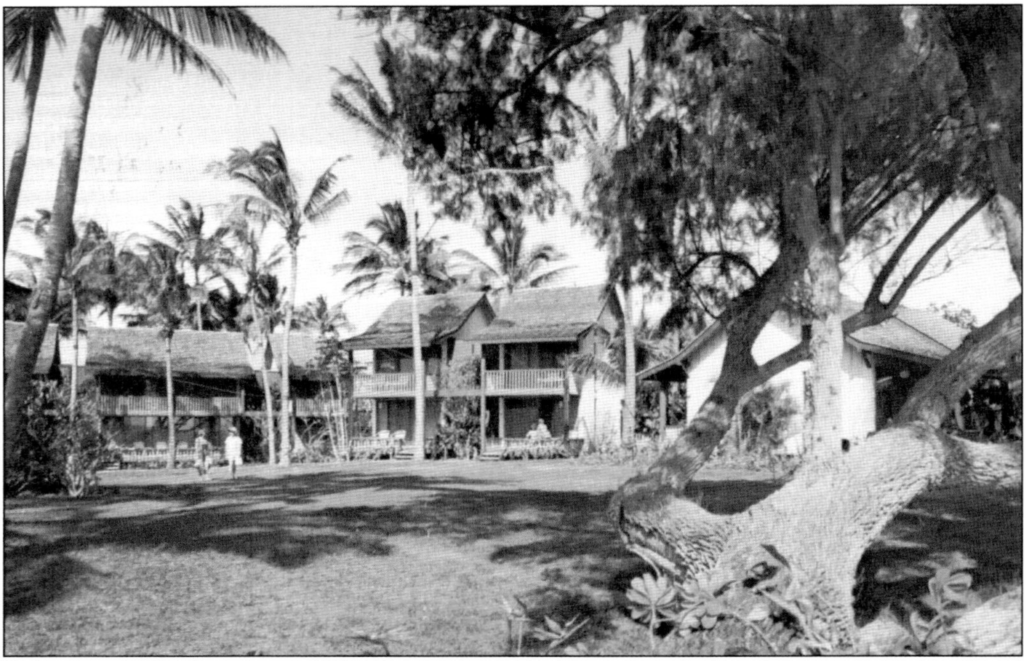

This postcard is of the original Waiohai at Poipu Beach that was begun by the Kimball family. The rooms had ocean views, and there were oceanfront cottages with plenty of space to relax or wander the grounds and beach. (31.)

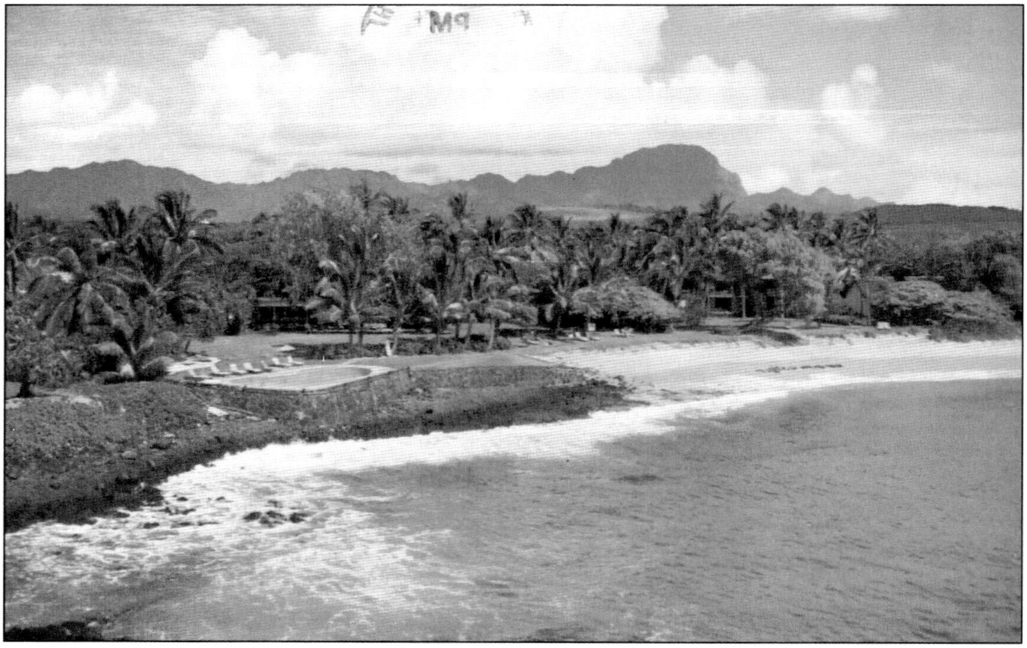

In the 1960s and 1970s, the Waiohai was a favorite place to stay for those who just wanted to relax and hear the ocean as they slept. This view from the Pacific shows its unique pool built right at the ocean break. (27.)

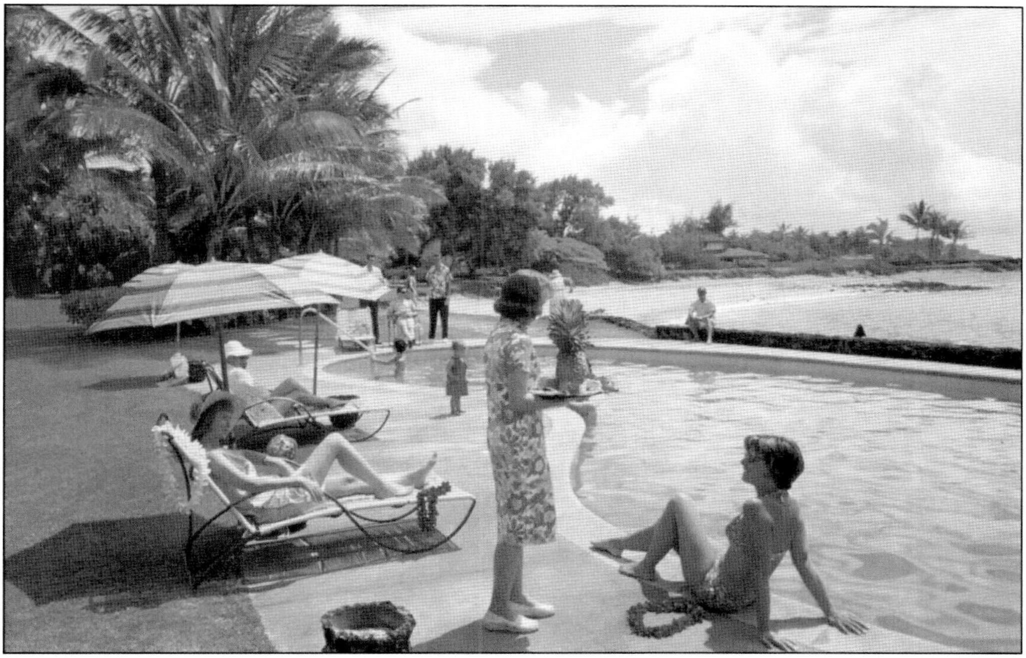

This view of the Waiohai is from the pool looking toward Poipu Beach. Its saltwater swimming pool with the view of Poipu Beach was one of the many features to recommend it. (27.)

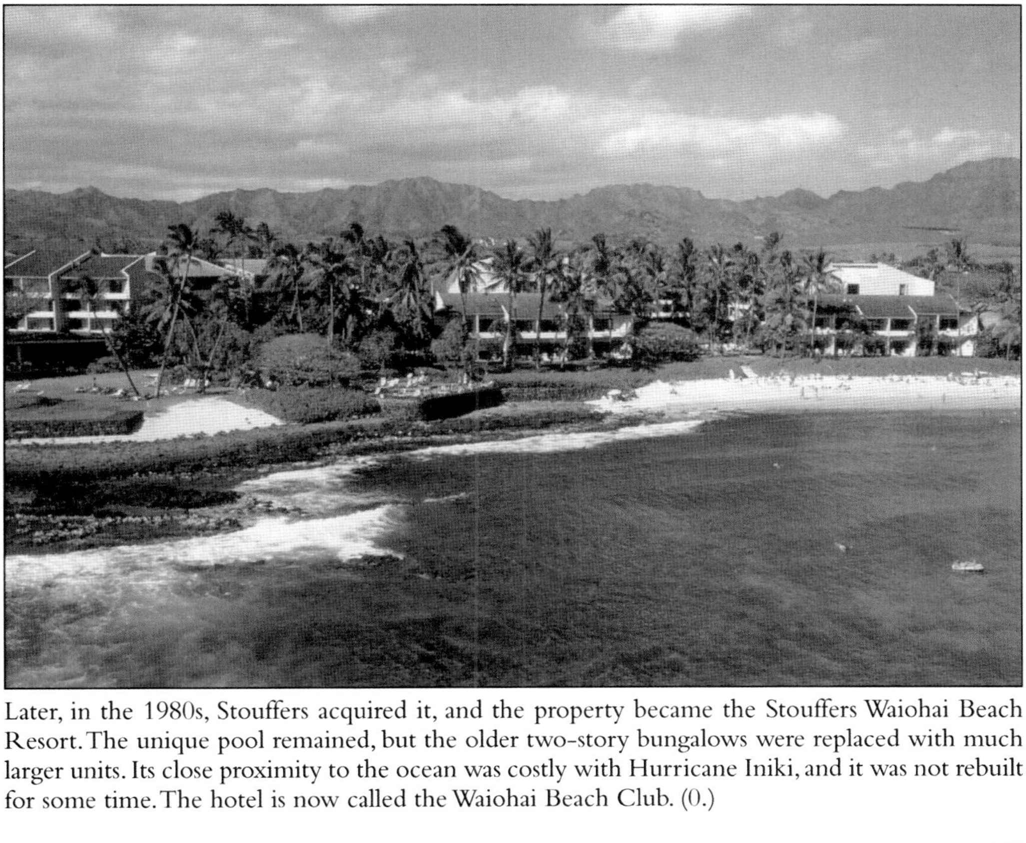

Later, in the 1980s, Stouffers acquired it, and the property became the Stouffers Waiohai Beach Resort. The unique pool remained, but the older two-story bungalows were replaced with much larger units. Its close proximity to the ocean was costly with Hurricane Iniki, and it was not rebuilt for some time. The hotel is now called the Waiohai Beach Club. (0.)

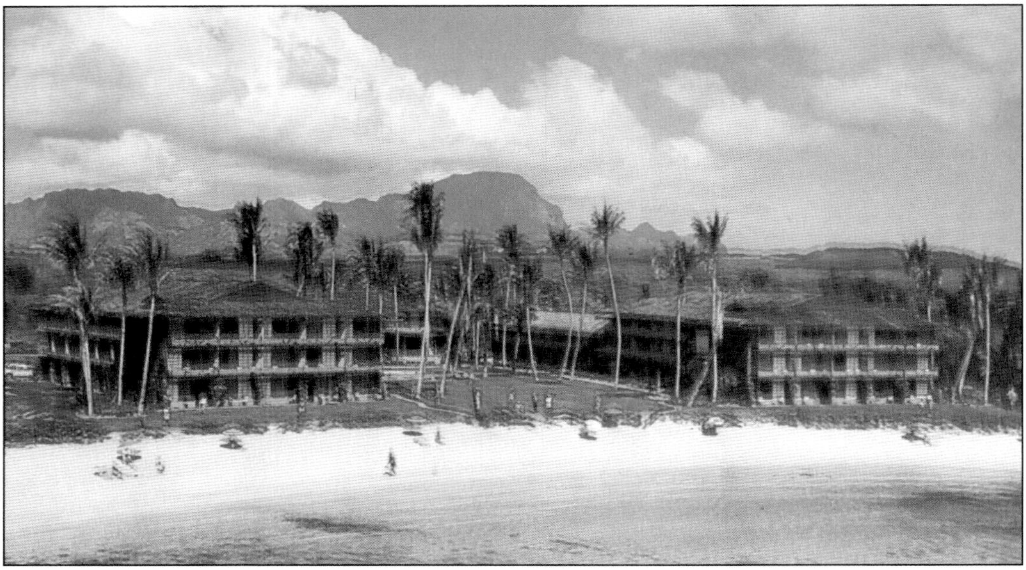

Poipu Beach Resort opened in 1968. The property belonged to the Knudsen Trust and was leased by Island Holidays. It had an unusually high return guest loyalty of 85 percent. When it closed due to Hurricane Iniki, returnees were three generations deep. Locals remember the $6.95 steak fry dinners that included mai tais and a show. But those mai tais should not be blamed for the dizziness experienced by viewing this image, which was originally printed out of registration. (27.)

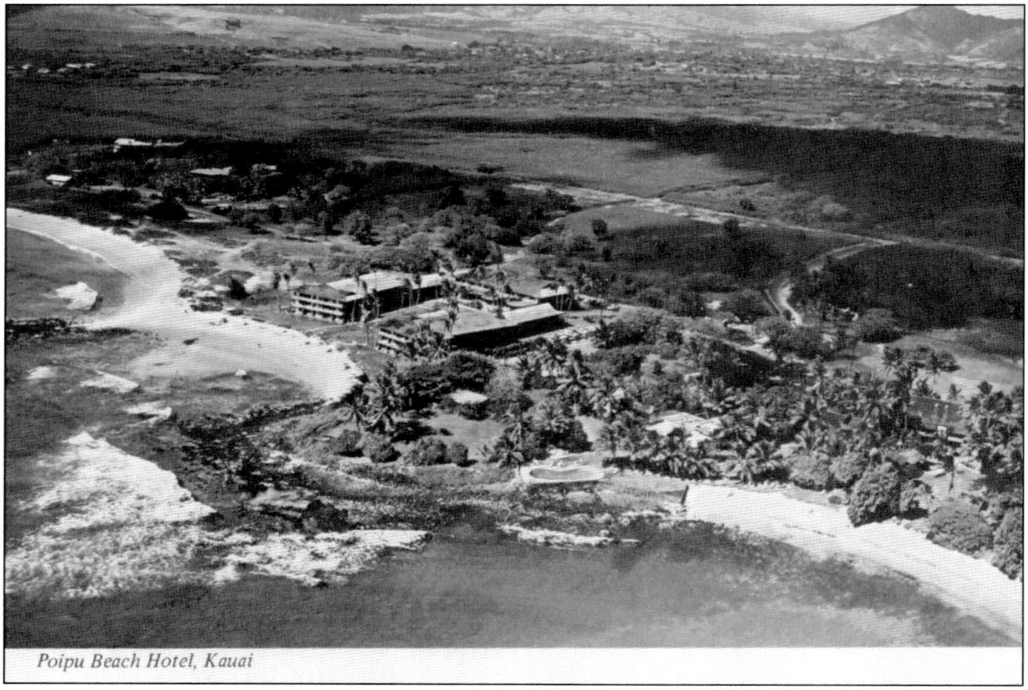

In this aerial of the Poipu Beach Hotel taken by W.J. Senda, the view also shows the Waiohai property next door. It is hidden by all the palms, but the image clearly shows its distinctive pool. The adjoining vacant property on the other side will be the Kiahuna, which at the time of the photograph has not been built yet. (11.)

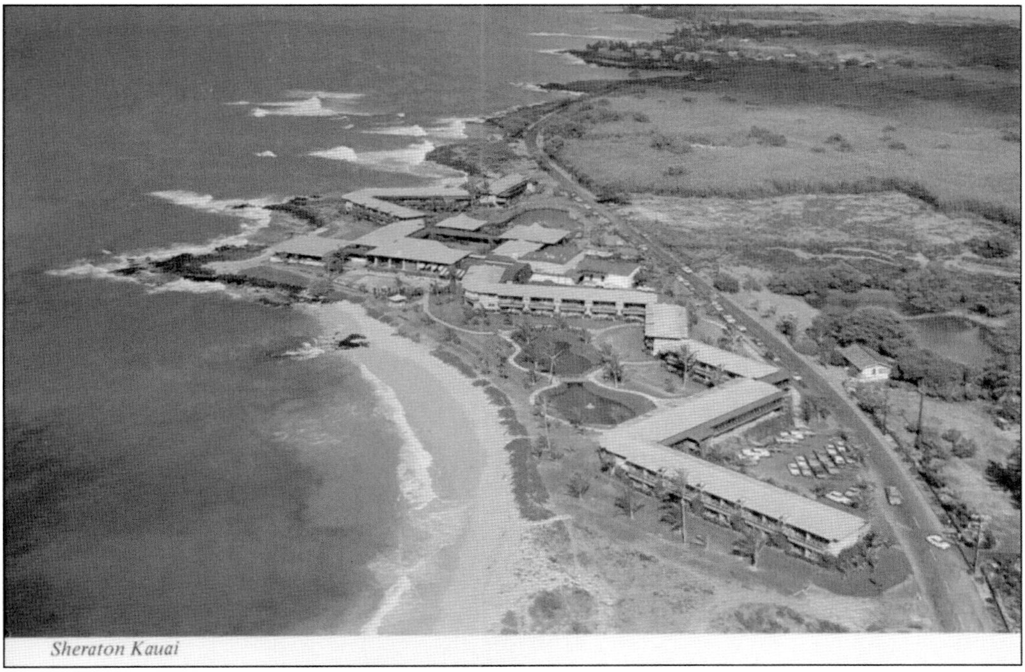

This postcard from the Senda family collection shows the hotel as it was in 1970, with the pool near the ocean and no part of the hotel on the *mauka* (toward the mountains) side of the road. The long strand of beach was washed away with Hurricane Iwa in 1982 and replaced. In the distance by Koloa landing, one can see the original Whaler's Cove. (11, A.)

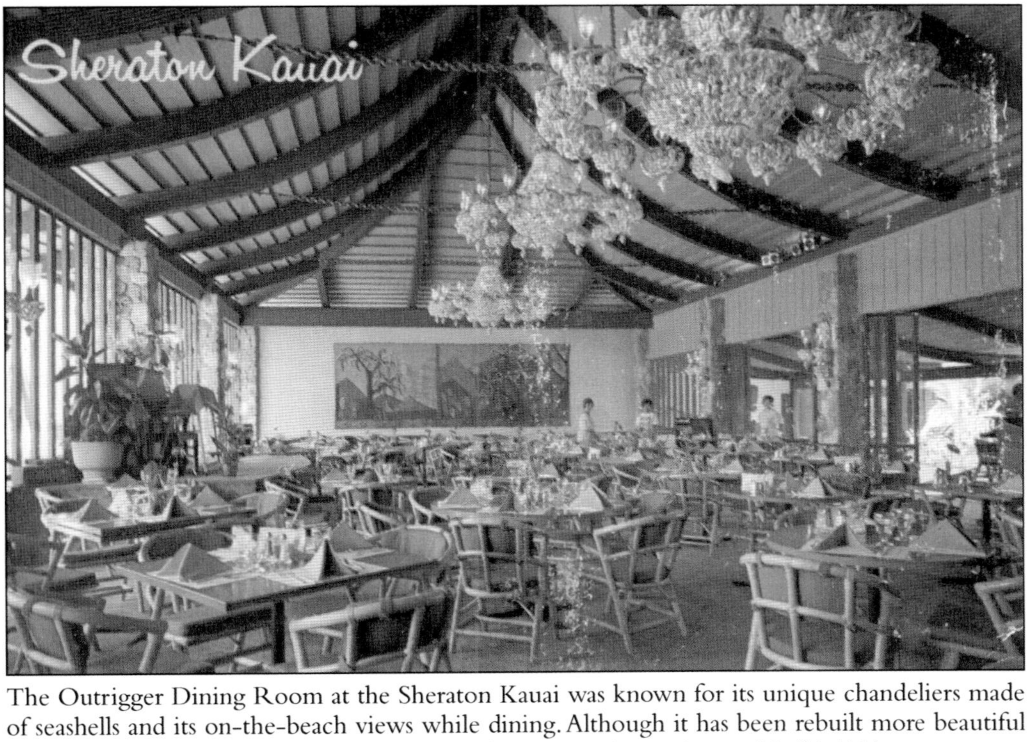

The Outrigger Dining Room at the Sheraton Kauai was known for its unique chandeliers made of seashells and its on-the-beach views while dining. Although it has been rebuilt more beautiful than ever, this restaurant was destroyed twice due to Hurricanes Iwa and Iniki. (11.)

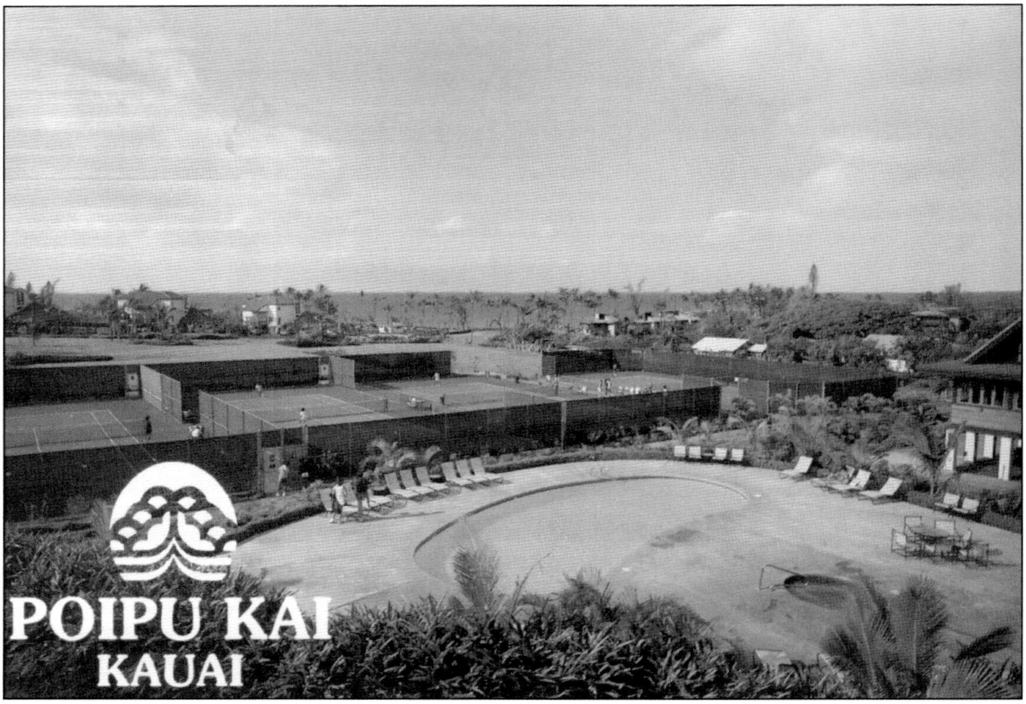

Poipu Kai was another one of the early condo resorts on Kauai. It was built about 1979. Originally Colony Resorts managed it. It is now called Aston Poipu Kai Condominium Resort and managed by several entities. (44, ZZ.)

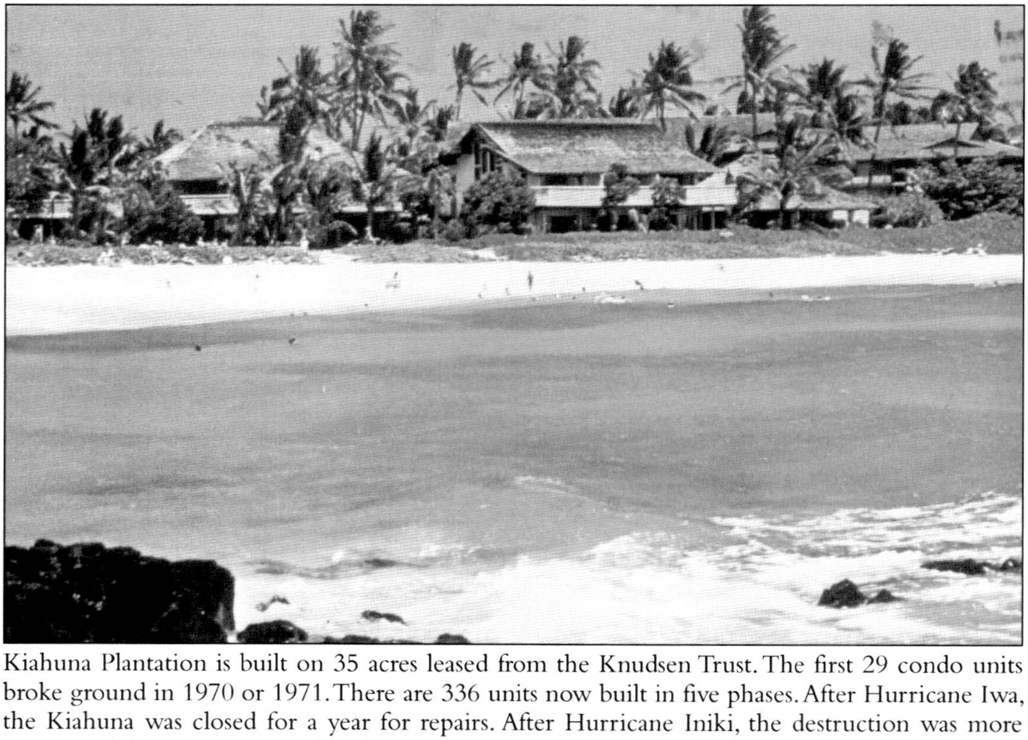

Kiahuna Plantation is built on 35 acres leased from the Knudsen Trust. The first 29 condo units broke ground in 1970 or 1971. There are 336 units now built in five phases. After Hurricane Iwa, the Kiahuna was closed for a year for repairs. After Hurricane Iniki, the destruction was more severe, and the property was closed for two years. (28.)

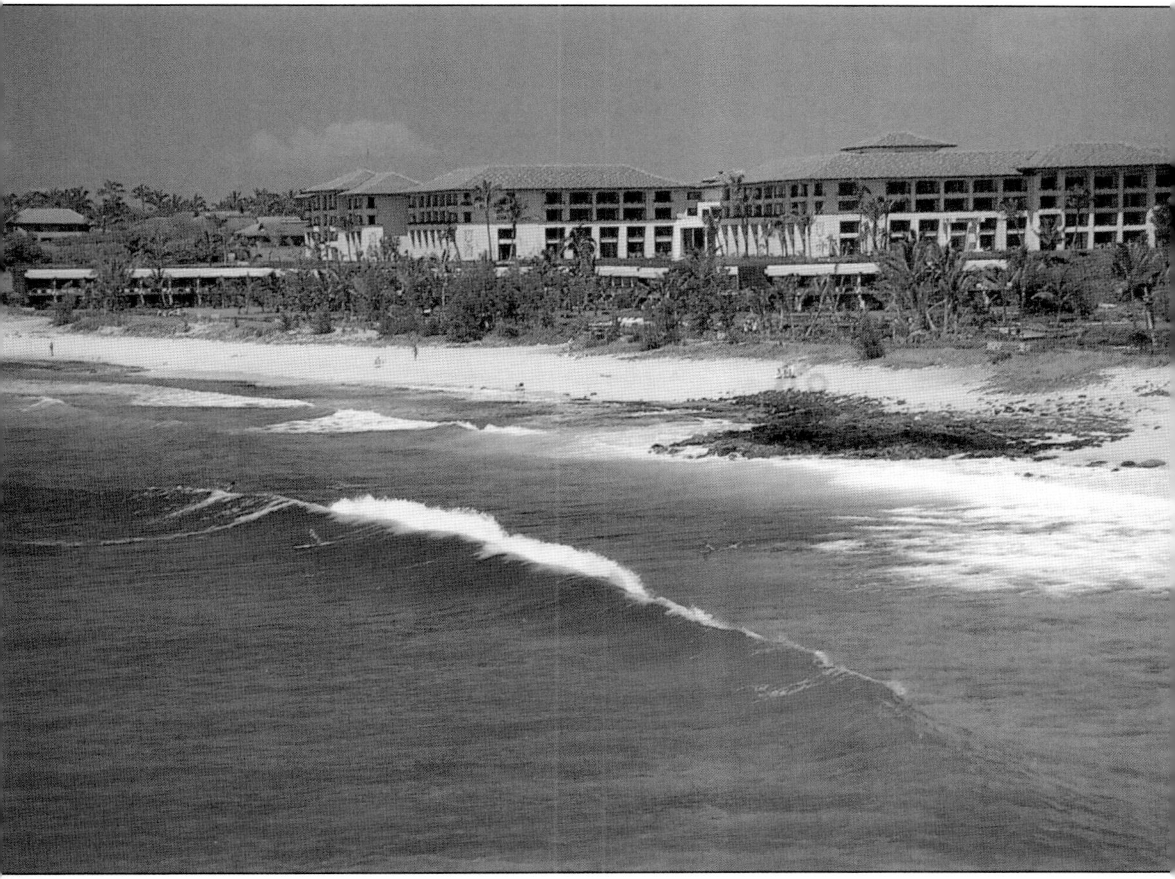

This Hyatt Regency view was before it became a Grand Hyatt on July 15, 2005. The hotel was built in 1992, opening just months before Hurricane Iniki hit Kauai with Category Five winds on September 11. Due to the brilliant idea to keep all the employees working who wished to keep a job, a housekeeper or waiter became a gardener or cleanup worker so the hotel could reopen in record time, seven months. (30.)

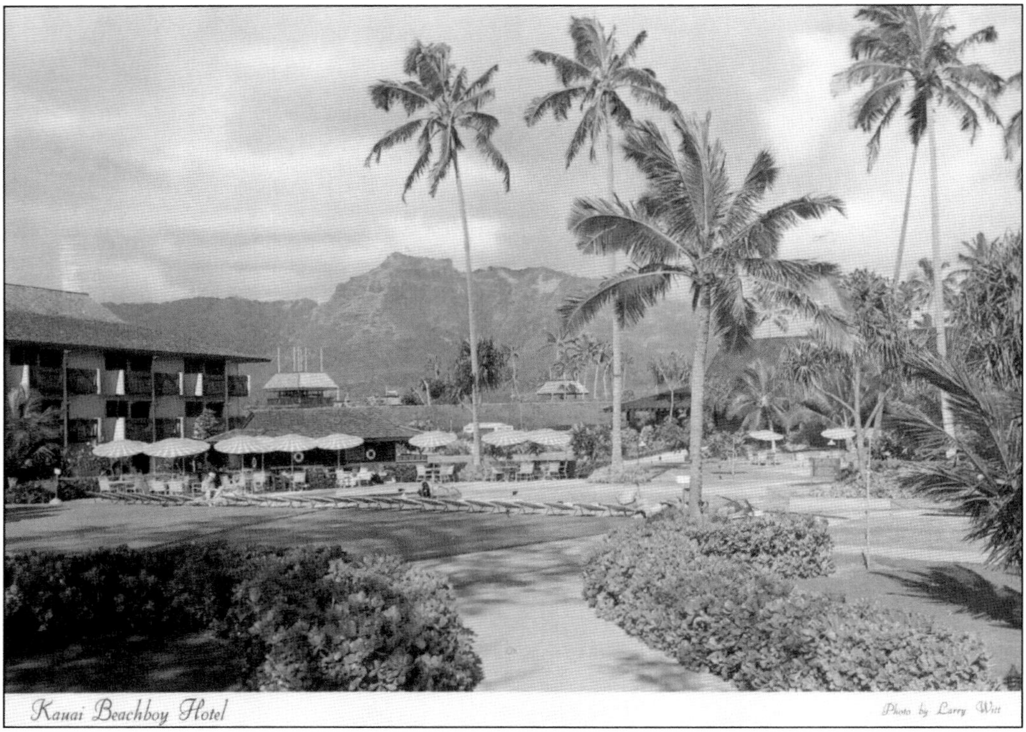

This postcard (above) of Kauai Beach Boy Hotel is looking toward Sleeping Giant. It is one of the hotels built within the Coconut Plantation Marketplace. The view below is taken looking toward the ocean. The writer of this card wrote back to Oxford, England, "This is our hotel, very comfortable and right on the beach. It is a great place to get away." (Above, 22, G; below, 15, S.)

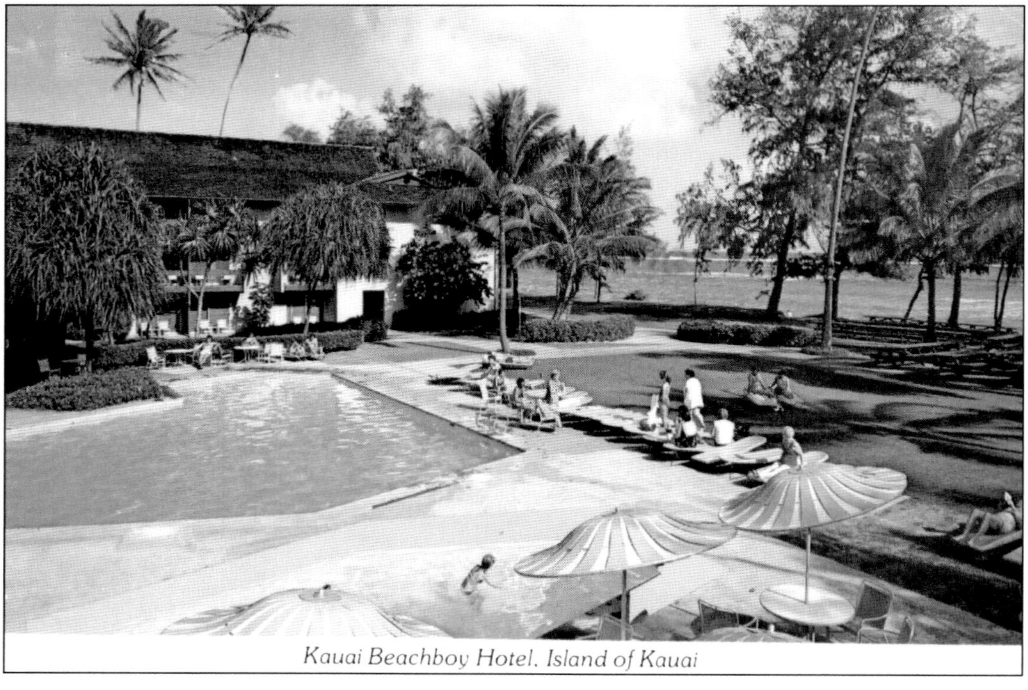

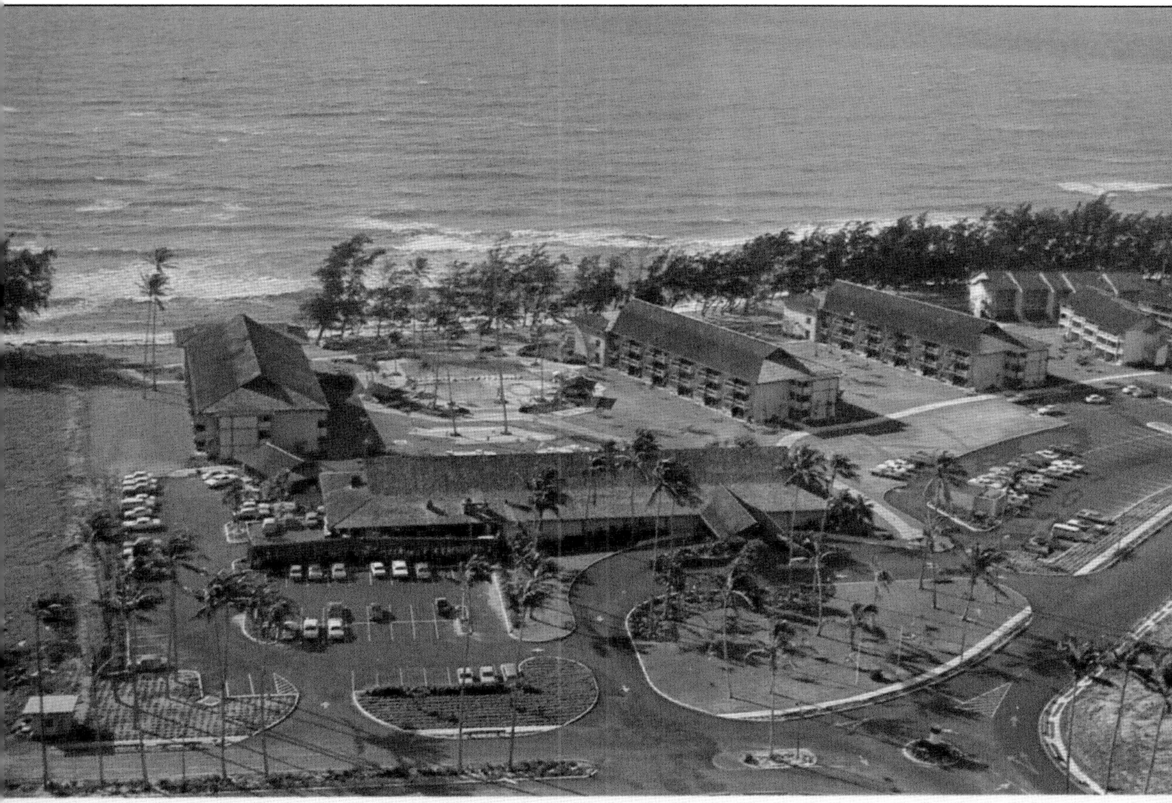

Kauai Beach Boy Hotel

When looking from the air, one can see that the Kauai Beach Boy Hotel was right on the ocean, with plenty of room to wander. No longer known as the Beach Boy, the property's newest name is as the Aston Aloha Beach Hotel. (11, A.)

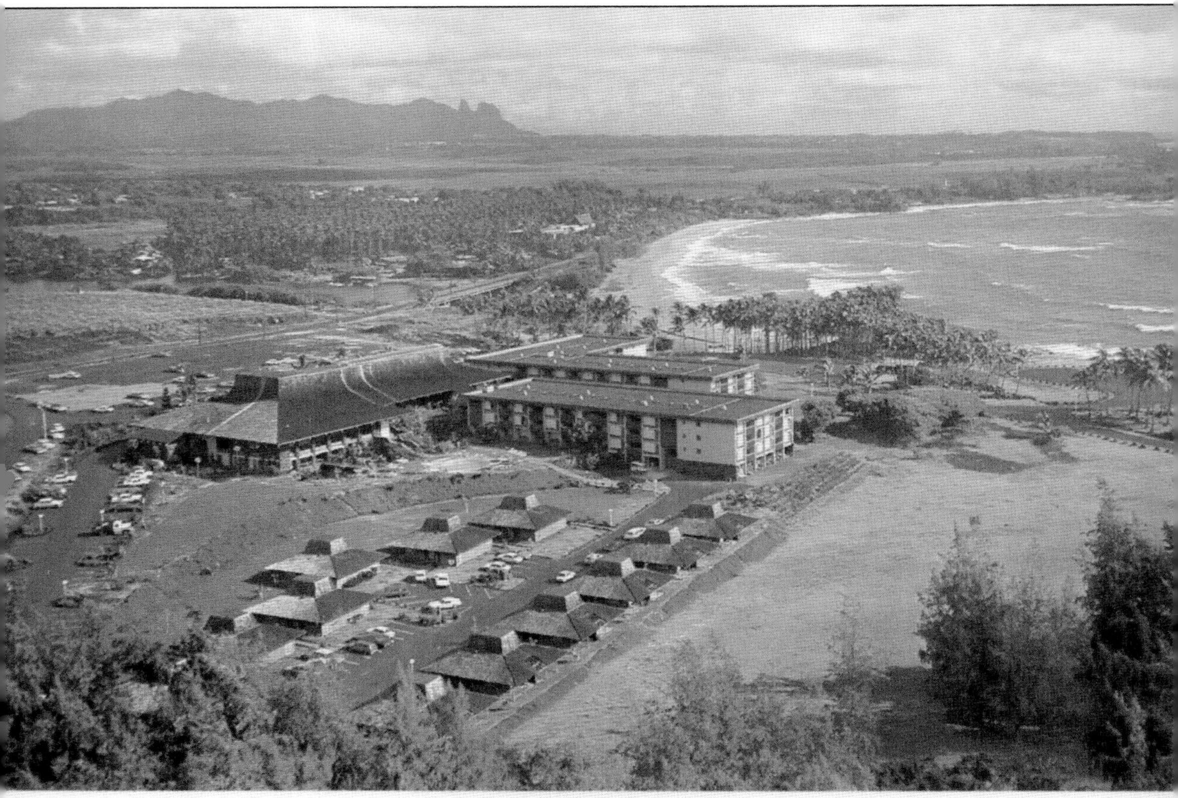

auai Resort Hotel

Kauai Resort Hotel was just across the river from the Coco Palms and on the *makai* (toward the ocean) side of the road. This resort stood on 8.5 acres of landscaped grounds at the mouth of the Wailua River. It is adjacent to both Lydgate Park and the Hikinaakala Heiau. In the distance are the distinctive Anahola Kalalea Mountains. The beach in the center of the photograph is Wailua. (11.)

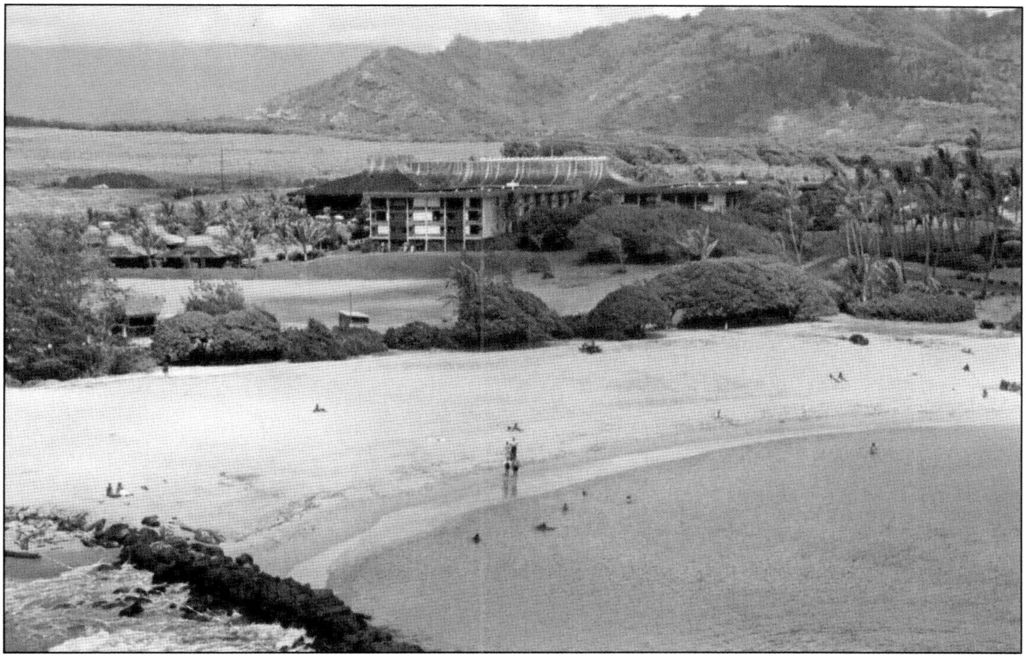

The view above is looking inland toward the Kauai Resort Hotel from Lydgate State Park, actually a county park. The rock breakwater creates a safe ocean pool for swimming for young and old. The postcard below shows the pool area of the resort. (Above, 18; below, 42.)

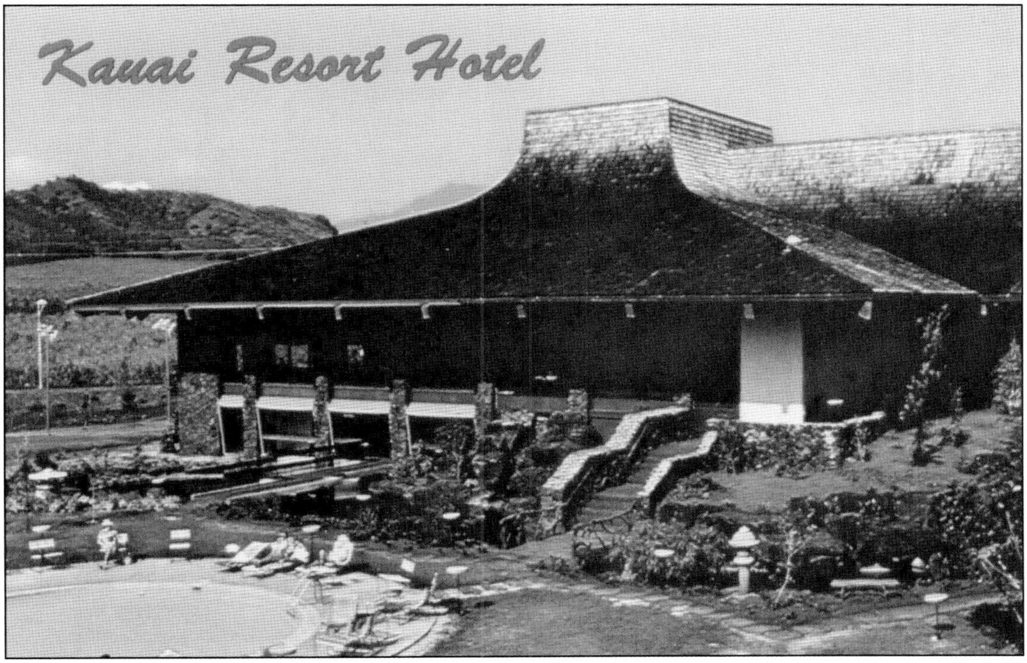

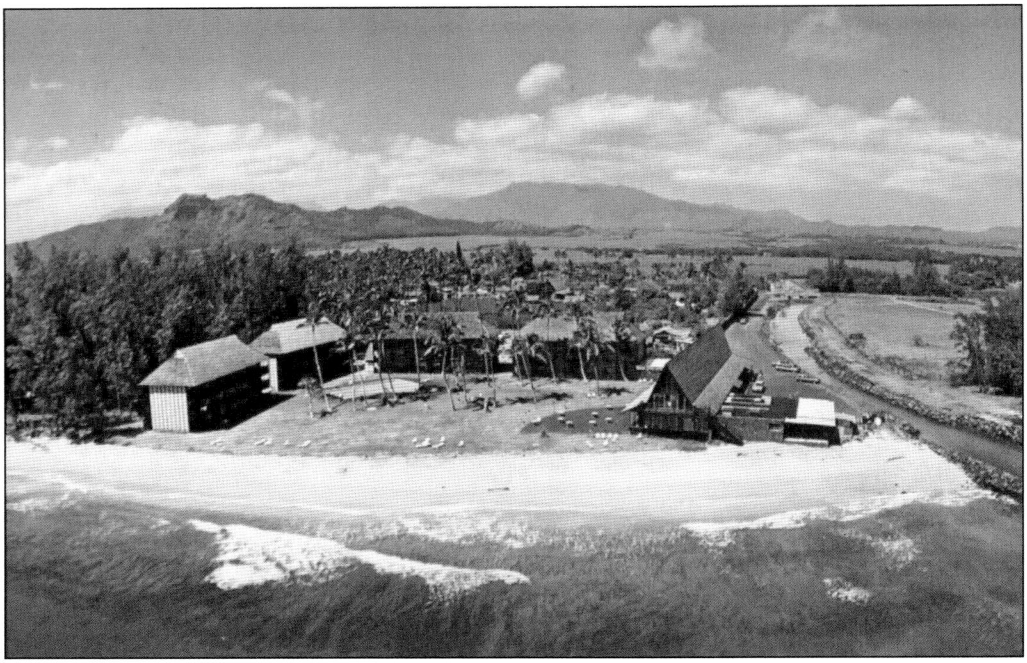

The Castaways was a hotel on Kauai's eastside. The steep-pitched roof belongs to a favorite restaurant, the Bull Shed. The hotel is now known as Mokihana of Kauai and became a timeshare about 1974. The Bull Shed is still there, but most of the sand is not. A seawall is the restaurant's only protection from ocean waves now. (O.)

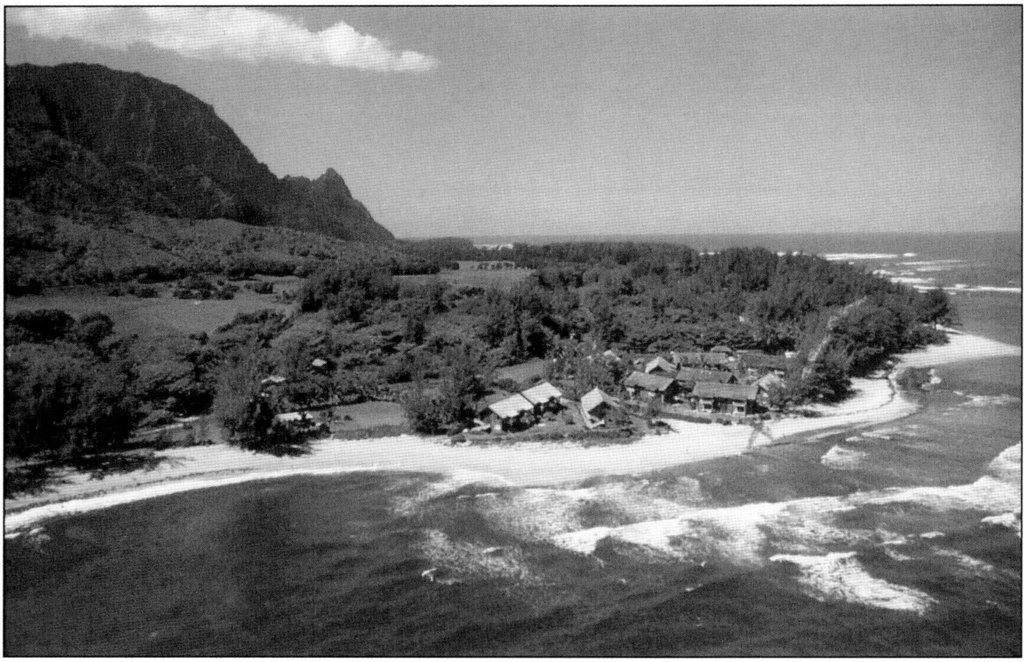

This postcard of the Hanalei Colony Resort calls attention to the fact that it is the only beachfront resort on the north shore. It can boast about quite a few things, including keeping the same name all these years. Built in 1969, the buildings are only two stories and remind one of less a stressful time. The rooms are free of modern electronic devices, so visitors can truly unplug. (O.)

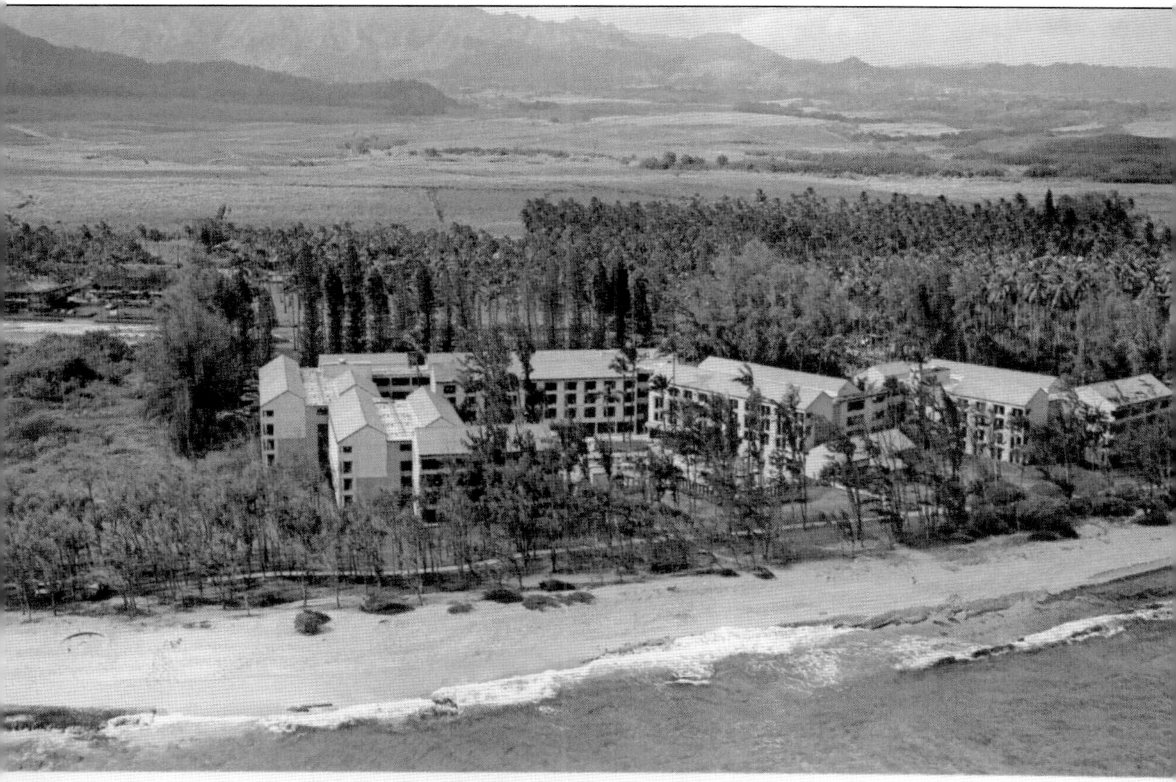

Holiday Inn On The Hawaiian Island of Kauai

This is the Holiday Inn on Kauai. Those who thought this was the Sheraton Coconut Beach would also be correct. Kauai residents never get used to the seemingly constant name changes of various hotel properties, and this hotel has had more than most. It most recently switched from the Aston Kauai Beach at Makaiwa to the Courtyard by Marriott Kauai at Coconut Beach. (15.)